KNOWLEDGE, POLICY AND POWER IN INTERNATIONAL DEVELOPMENT

A practical guide

Harry Jones, Nicola Jones, Louise Shaxson and David Walker

D1347604

First published in Great Britain in 2012 by

The Policy Press
University of Bristol
Fourth Floor
Beacon House
Queen's Road
Bristol BS8 1QU
UK

t: +44 (0)117 331 4054
f: +44 (0)117 331 4093
tpp-info@bristol.ac.uk
www.policypress.co.uk

North American office:

The Policy Press
c/o The University of Chicago Press
1427 East 60th Street
Chicago, IL 60637, USA
t: +1 773 702 7700
f: +1 773-702-9756
sales@press.uchicago.edu
www.press.uchicago.edu

© The Policy Press 2012

British Library Cataloguing in Publication Data
A catalogue record for this book is available from the British Library.

Library of Congress Cataloging-in-Publication Data
A catalog record for this book has been requested.

ISBN 978 1 44730 095 3 paperback
ISBN 978 1 44730 096 0 hardcover

Cover design by The Policy Press.
Front cover: image kindly supplied by Panos Pictures.
Printed and bound in Great Britain by TJ International, Padstow.
The Policy Press uses environmentally responsible print partners.

MIX
Paper from
responsible sources
FSC
www.fsc.org   FSC® C013056

Contents

—

List of boxes, figures and tables

Boxes

Figures

Tables

List of acronyms

AAAPG	Africa All Party Parliamentary Group
ACBF	African Capacity Building Foundation
AusAID	Australian Agency for International Development
BRAC	Building Resources Across Communities
BSE	Bovine spongiform encephalopathy
CCT	Conditional cash transfer
CHSRF	Canadian Health Services Research Foundation
CommGAP	Communication for Governance and Accountability Program
CPRC	Chronic Poverty Research Centre
CSO	Civil Society Organisation
DAC	Development Assistance Committee
DFID	Department for International Development
EBPDN	Evidence-based Policy in Development Network
EU	European Union
GCN	Government Communications Network
GDI	Gender-related Development Index
GDP	Gross domestic product
GEM	Gender Empowerment Measure
HDI	Human Development Index
ICT	Information and communication technology
IDA	International Development Association
IDRC	International Development Research Centre
IMF	International Monetary Fund
INCAF	International Network on Conflict and Fragility
IRPD	Institute for Research Planning and Development
KM4D	Knowledge Management for Development
LKN	Local knowledge node
MDG	Millennium Development Goal
MIMAP	Micro Impacts of Macroeconomic Adjustment Policies
MMR	Measles, mumps and rubella
MRC	Medical Research Council
MTEF	Medium-term expenditure framework
MTSS	Medium-term sector strategy
NCWCD	National Wildlife Commission for Conservation and Development
NGO	Non-governmental organisation
NIMBY	Not in my back yard
ODI	Overseas Development Institute
OECD	Organisation for Economic Co-operation and Development
OMB	Office of Management and Budget
PRA	Participatory rural appraisal
PRS	Poverty reduction strategy

PRSP	Poverty reduction strategy paper
RAPID	Research and Policy in Development
RCT	Randomised controlled trial
RIN	Research Information Network
SDI	Slum/Shack Dwellers International
Sida	Swedish International Development Cooperation Agency
SIGI	Social Institutions and Gender Index
SNV	Netherlands Development Organisation
SPARC	State Project for Accountability, Responsibility and Capacity
UK	United Kingdom
UN	United Nations
UNDP	United Nations Development Programme
UNOIOS	United Nations Office of Internal Oversight Services
US	United States
USAID	United States Agency for International Development
WIEGO	Women in the Informal Economy Globalizing and Organizing

Glossary

Autocracy: while more autocratic contexts can be largely contrasted with more democratic contexts (see below), autocracy can technically be defined as one context in which power of the executive and legislative is essentially combined and centralised. These autocratic contexts may also be defined as more authoritarian and totalitarian – the former characterised by a centralised ruling power base, the latter by an emphasis on an ideologically focused personalistic regime.

Beliefs: concepts we generally hold to be true, often in the absence of a broad or in-depth foundation in evidence. Beliefs are transient in that they can be reversed when confronted by contrary evidence, but can be strengthened should the evidence not be challenging enough. Beliefs are often paired with values, but the difference is subtle: we derive our values from our beliefs. Most importantly, beliefs and values govern the way we think and behave.

Boundary concept: a term that enables communication across borders by creating a shared vocabulary. It could be a term such as 'sustainability', 'resilience' or 'poverty' – which mean different things to different actors at different times.

Boundary object: a map, report, picture or other form of explicit knowledge. A boundary object is used as a tool to share understanding but do not lose its identity when discussed.

Boundary process: a formal process (such as strategy, budgeting or evaluation) within which knowledge is shared.

Boundary spanner: an organisation or an individual that operates across an interface, either by design or default. Also referred to in this book as knowledge intermediaries.

Complexity: the notion of complexity in development thinking has been built from a broad collection of ideas and principles borrowed from a variety of schools of thought and disciplines. In essence, complexity moves away from linear causality and predictability in thinking and practice, toward approaches that appreciate that progress is sensitive to the initial conditions and dependent on unpredictable feedback processes.

Democracy: the notion of a 'consolidated democracy' is contested, but such an entity is often viewed as a state that has stabilised and is highly unlikely to lapse into an authoritarian system given the presence of strong institutions and the rule of law. A consolidated democracy can be further defined as having what a more autocratic system does not; namely, relatively unrestricted political participation, clearly defined and transparent rules for changes in leadership, numerous checks and balances across state bodies and a variety of vibrant civil society actors.

Fragile state: this category of state typology, more than others, is highly contested. It can be defined as a context with exceptionally limited or low capacity to respond to shocks and/or stresses, but with correspondingly high susceptibility to crises, it is also often conflated as conflict/post-conflict context. We focus on both contexts for the purposes of this book.

Institutions: a collection of practices and ideas that are systematised into a self-perpetuating organisation or structure – either tangible (a government ministry, non-governmental organisation or think-tank) or intangible (a discourse, customary practices, belief system).

Interests: representations of avenues that individuals or groups can use to help achieve their goals. Interests encourage 'realist', calculated, strategic responses, whereas beliefs and values are rooted in more idealist, emotional motivations and moral obligations.

Intermediary: an individual or organisation that facilitates communication between otherwise more distant actors.

Knowledge: there is no single definition of knowledge. 'Content' knowledge can be descriptive, explanatory, normative or subjective: 'process' knowledge is concerned with where it is held, whether it is tacit or explicit, and with how collective meaning is developed. The term 'knowledge' is preferred in this book because the alternative term – 'evidence' – carries with it connotations of incorruptible truth that is unaffected by prejudices in its development and communication.

Knowledge brokering: the process of facilitating, by means of an intermediary, the linkages between the supply and demand of knowledge between different actors in order to promote maximum efficiency, innovative capability and impact of research.

Knowledge interaction: the process of intervening between the producer and user of knowledge to improve the supply and demand of knowledge and smooth the path between the two. Focusing on the different functions involved in knowledge interaction (as opposed to the different actors) can help us understand how knowledge to make best use use boundary spanners, concepts, objects or processes to foster engagement on policy issues.

Knowledge intermediary: an organisation or individual who acts at the interface between knowledge and policy. They may have a dedicated job description to perform this function, or may occasionally act as a knowledge intermediary in the course of their regular work programme.

Knowledge–policy interface: 'A critical point of intersection between life-worlds, social fields or levels of social organisation, where social discontinuities, based on discrepancies in values, interests, knowledge and power, are most likely to be located' (Long, 2001, p 243). The knowledge–policy interface is the arena in which information is filtered, brokered and transmuted through various lenses – whether political, social or economic – into a set of related decisions that eventually result in concrete plans or negotiated agreements.

Knowledge translation: more than simply communicating messages, knowledge translation is a two-way process enabling different actors (such as researchers and policy actors) to share understandings.

Norms: these can be considered the rules that define the sanctioning (or not) of a particular set of values and beliefs within a broader system of accepted behaviours. They can vary over time and space, thereby having variable implications for how knowledge and policy interact.

Policy: we define policy as a set of related decisions that give rise to specific proposals for action or negotiated agreements. 'Public policy can result in concrete plans …, specific proposals for action including regulation, economic instruments such as subsidies or taxes, or programmes of legislation with accompanying organizations and resources. But it does not only encompass these sorts of legislated actions. "Policy" may also result in voluntary negotiated standards … risk governance …, decisions about the allocation of public funds via research prioritization, [and] the provision of information to "win hearts and minds"…. Policy cannot be characterized by a single decision point. Instead, it is a series of decisions – one of which may be crucial in determining the ultimate direction of the policy – but all of which contribute to how it is planned and implemented' (Shaxson, 2009, p 2142).

Policy process: the definition of policy processes used in this book is broad, with an understanding that there is seldom a specific decision point in the policy process; rather, a series of decisions summarily contribute to change. Hence, our definition is that the policy process is one of 'translating political vision, through a variety of methods and decisions, into concrete plans or negotiated agreements'.

Policymaker: a person who 'makes the decision'. Our interest is not so much in defining this person, as much as highlighting the fuzziness of the word. In policy, there is very rarely (if ever) a single person making *the* decision, nor is there any definable point at which a policy is made. Thus the term 'policymaker' can cover both politicians and civil servants; when looking at specific policies, care needs to be taken to distinguish between the two.

Political context: the governmental, administrative, constitutional, electoral, doctrinal and ethical setting within which an agenda for change is developed. Analysing political context helps determine where there is likely to be political support for change, and why.

Power: we use Lukes' (1972) threefold conceptualisation of power – as overt, covert and hidden – and combine it with Foucault's notion of power as discourse, embedded in socially constructed values and ways of seeing the world. Power can influence the exercise of material resources in order to secure a desired change or position; can be used to negotiate institutions, norms and conventions, including the formal/informal 'rules of the game' or ways of doing things (see North, 1993); and can shape actors' preferences.

Acknowledgments

We wish to acknowledge the very thoughtful and constructive peer review comments provided by Fred Carden, Brian Head and Basil Jones; the valuable research assistance undertaken by Ben Clench, Laura Gisby, Ingie Hovland, Shreya Mitra, Madvee Muthu, Elizabeth Presler-Marshall and Kevin Waldie; the excellent editorial support provided by Roo Griffiths; and the insightful case studies provided by the DFID CSO Child and Youth Networks, Forest Action Nepal and Practical Action. Alex Bielak and Sarah Michaels contributed significantly to the thinking underpinning Chapter Five, as did participants at the Special Workshop on Knowledge Translation and Brokering in Montreal, Canada in October 2010 and the AusAID-DFID-UKCDS-funded workshop on research communication in London, December 2010. We would also like to thank the UK Department for International Development (DFID) for funding.

Acknowledgments

ONE

Navigating the knowledge–policy landscape

> Remember that all models are wrong: the practical question is how wrong do they have to be to not be useful. (Box and Draper, 1987, p 74)

Understanding the links between knowledge, policy and power in development

Knowledge is increasingly seen as a critical component of development. As early as 1998/99 the World Development Report emphasised the need for greater access to better quality knowledge in addressing development challenges, from infant mortality to agricultural growth. Indeed, the difference knowledge may make to poverty reduction is highlighted by the starkly different development trajectories (measured by per capita gross domestic product (GDP)) of South Korea and Ghana since the 1950s. While the former is now a fully fledged member of the Organisation for Economic Co-operation and Development (OECD) and itself a donor country, the other graduated to lower middle-income country status only in 2011 (see Figure 1.1).

Figure 1.1: The potential of knowledge in development

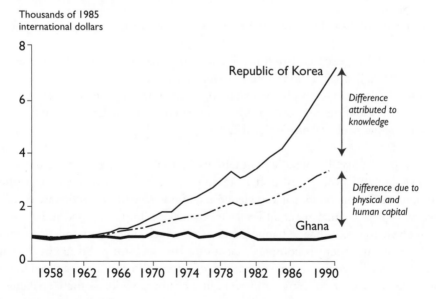

Source: World Bank (1999)

Over the past decade, however, there has been growing recognition by a broad array of development actors that there are no magic bullets to strengthen the knowledge–policy interface; instead, better systems and channels are urgently needed to harness existing and new knowledge sources so as to provide strategic, feasible and timely policy and programme solutions.[1] In particular, academic knowledge can play a useful role in shaping the thinking of policy actors and practitioners over time (Weiss, 1977), while policy research has the potential to have far-reaching impacts on programme design and budget allocations, with tangible impacts for those who are poor and marginalised. A case in point is the rigorous evaluation work carried out around Mexico's conditional cash transfer programme, Progresa/Oportunidades: findings have been utilised to secure greater investments in safety nets for poor people, not only at the national level, but also in similar programmes across Latin America, Asia and Africa. These now reach tens of millions of poor households (Behrman, 2007), and are continuing to expand on account, at least in part, of the robust knowledge base that is being generated on the strengths and weaknesses of many of the programmes (Fiszbein and Schady, 2008).[2]

Such cases of fruitful evidence-informed policy influencing are not the norm, however. Identifying what accounts for effective knowledge uptake in developing country contexts is a critical challenge if we are to ensure that the millions of pounds invested annually in knowledge generation contribute to more informed policy dialogues. The UK Department for International Development's (DFID's) Research Strategy Consultation Process in Africa in 2007, for example, highlighted a range of key concerns, including:

- a dearth of mechanisms to articulate and channel demand for knowledge/ research;
- problems of knowledge fragmentation, weak coordination and limited public access;
- the need for greater end-user involvement throughout the research process to counter supply- and often donor-driven research;
- a strong demand for problem-oriented, policy-relevant research; and
- capacity-building support to enable research users to better specify their knowledge needs (Romney et al, 2007).

Focusing on research uptake will not, by itself, strengthen the interface between knowledge and policy; research is an important but by no means the only component. Local contextual knowledge and knowledge from practice are equally necessary if policymakers at all levels are to make robust, reasoned judgements about how to make change happen. Choosing which types of knowledge to use and how to use them is complex because of the different political contexts in which policy is made and the wide variety of actors who could be involved in the policy process. Our collective understanding of how to address these challenges is growing, but remains in a fledgling state.

This book aims to address this gap by providing a practical guide to understanding how knowledge, policy and power interact to promote or prevent change. As the quote at the beginning of this chapter suggests, we acknowledge that, although some models provide useful analyses of some aspects of the interface between knowledge and policy, it is impossible to construct a single one-size-fits-all template for understanding such a complex set of relationships. Descriptions of the knowledge–policy landscape are also highly variable (depending on where and how you look at it and whom you talk to), and it can be difficult to navigate them unless time is taken to reflect systematically on specific dimensions. We therefore seek to provide readers with ways to identify and recognise problems that have hampered previous attempts to improve the knowledge–policy interface, such as persistent asymmetric relations between actors, crude assessments of political context, heavy-handed compression of incompatible types of knowledge and mistranslations of knowledge. Most importantly, the book aims to provide readers with academically rigorous yet practical guidance on how to develop strategies to negotiate the complexity of the knowledge–policy interface more effectively, so as to contribute to policy dialogues on key development goals. Box 1.1 sets out definitions of the key concepts we use in the book. Our focus is primarily on the dynamics of the knowledge–policy interface in international development, but we believe our general approach is also applicable to a broader array of policy arenas.

Box 1.1: Key definitions

Policy: we define policy as a set of related decisions that give rise to specific proposals for action or negotiated agreements. 'Public policy can result in concrete plans ..., specific proposals for action including regulation, economic instruments such as subsidies or taxes, or programmes of legislation with accompanying organizations and resources. But it does not only encompass these sorts of legislated actions. "Policy" may also result in voluntary negotiated standards ... risk governance ..., decisions about the allocation of public funds via research prioritization, [and] the provision of information to "win hearts and minds"....Policy cannot be characterized by a single decision point. Instead, it is a series of decisions – one of which may be crucial in determining the ultimate direction of the policy – but all of which contribute to how it is planned and implemented' (Shaxson, 2009, p 2142).

Policy process: the definition of policy processes used in this book is broad, with an understanding that there is seldom a specific decision point in the policy process; rather, a series of decisions summarily contribute to change. Hence, our definition is that the policy process is one of 'translating political vision, through a variety of methods and decisions, into concrete plans or negotiated agreements'.

Knowledge: Perkin and Court (2005, p 2) define knowledge as 'information that has been evaluated and organised so that it can be used purposefully', but there are historically different points of view about the content of knowledge, how knowledge is connected to truth and where it is held. Positivists such as Popper argue that knowledge functions primarily to describe the world, proposing theories that make predictions and testing them through experiments and direct experience. Kuhn argued against this, suggesting that worldviews or paradigms frame individual experience and shift as a result of collective value judgements as to which paradigm better fits wider values and belief systems. Further, Wittgenstein demonstrated that meaning and understanding are inseparable from language and 'doing', while Foucault observed that power infuses the processes of generating and using knowledge. Our conception of knowledge holds that the processes of evaluating and organising it are strongly influenced by power dynamics, values and belief systems. This means knowledge cannot be an external input to the policy process: instead, its production and use are interwoven in an ongoing and continually changing discourse, within the politics and power dynamics of policy making.

Power: we use Lukes' (1972) threefold conceptualisation of power – as overt, covert and hidden – as our starting point. Power can be about the exercise of material resources in order to secure a desired change or position; negotiating institutions, norms and conventions, including the formal/informal 'rules of the game' or ways of doing things (see North, 1993); or the ability to shape other actors' preferences (drawing on Foucault's notion of power as discourse and embedded in socially constructed values and ways of seeing the world).

Knowledge–policy interface: an interface can be considered the point of interaction between two systems of work, or more appropriately 'a critical point of intersection between life-worlds, social fields or levels of social organisation, where social discontinuities, based on discrepancies in values, interests, knowledge and power, are most likely to be located' (Long, 2001, p 243). Consequently, the knowledge–policy interface is best thought of as the arena in which information is filtered, brokered and transmuted through various lenses, whether these be political, social or economic, into a set of related decisions that eventually result in concrete plans or negotiated agreements.

The key contributions of this book

It is not the intention of this book to contribute yet another model to the canon of work on the knowledge–policy interface; a brief history of the evolution of thinking about the knowledge-to-policy process shows that each iteration contributes significant insights yet cannot explain the entirety of the process. For example, the 'linear' or 'mainstream' policy process model of the 1950s/1960s envisioned a regular cycle of agenda setting, formulation, implementation and evaluation, driven and informed by knowledge, irrespective of the issue at hand (Lasswell, 1951). From this emerged the evidence-based policy movement, which sought to develop frameworks to understand the drivers of and barriers to research 'uptake',[3] with the normative goal of increasing the influence of research on policy making. This has in turn given rise to a tendency for evidence-based policy studies, especially in the health sciences and economics, to prioritise some research techniques over others, setting experimental methods as the 'gold standard'.[4] However, although the linear model is often criticised for paying less attention to more qualitative and participatory sources, such as public service users' views and local knowledge (Tilley and Laycock, 2000; Rycroft-Malone et al, 2004), we argue that it made an important contribution by sowing the seeds of the current focus on ensuring the disciplinary quality of research-based and other forms of knowledge.

Critics of the evidence-based approach emphasised the political and epistemological dynamics of the production and use of particular sources of information (Luke, 2003; Marston and Watts, 2003) and shifted the focus from supposedly value-free *evidence* to the more complex and value-laden concept of *knowledge* (Sanderson, 2004), with the inherent and power-laden question: 'whose knowledge counts?' (Chambers, 2005). With this shift emerged a range of models that not only dealt more explicitly with questions of power, but also sought to encompass a broader array of non-state actors and networks and place greater emphasis on iterative processes and policy spaces. All of these offered insights into the importance of understanding the political context surrounding policymaking and the power relations among actors.

How these different models were applied in various sectors is beyond the scope of this book. However, it is worth noting that, from the 1990s onwards in the agricultural and health sectors,[5] work on the links between research, policy and practice emerged that emphasised the importance of appreciating the user's needs for knowledge (both in form and in content) and developing new structures to facilitate the flow of knowledge between the different groups of actors. This emphasis on knowledge interaction highlighted the need to forge partnerships between knowledge 'producers' and 'users' that recognise the 'co-construction' of policy knowledge (Lavis et al, 2006), including developing a shared understanding of what questions to ask, how to go about answering them and how best to interpret the responses.

Interest in the knowledge–policy interface continues to burgeon, as underscored by the increasing emphasis on the importance of strengthening the generation and application of rigorous evidence to policy decisions.[6] This interest can be seen in (for example) current reforms to the UK DFID's project approval processes, which require that funding applicants make an assessment of the strength of the evidence underpinning their work; these assessments in turn affect the requirements for subsequent evaluations.[7] It can also be seen in the academic arena in the emergence of journals such as *Evidence & Policy* (from The Policy Press) and the proliferation of articles about evidence-based policymaking in journals focused on health, the environment and agriculture (for example *Agricultural Systems, Environmental Science & Policy*). However, the main texts for scholars and practitioners have focused more specifically on research evidence (Nutley et al, 2007), evaluation evidence (Pawson, 2006) or evidence derived from citizen participation (Gaventa and Mayo, 2008), and have also concentrated primarily on OECD contexts.[8] More recently, work concerned with developing country contexts has emerged, but this has tended to look at particular sectors, for example natural resource management or health (Keeley and Scoones, 2003), rather than the broader development field that this publication tackles.[9]

Introducing concepts of power completes the picture, but in doing so it adds many levels of nuance to the analysis and makes it impossible to construct a one-size-fits-all model of the knowledge–policy interface. How, then, can we make sense of this complexity? Defining, selecting and promoting knowledge in policy is a highly variable process, concerned as much with matters of power and politics as with rational debate and problem solving. The complex nature of engagements between actors means that the knowledge–policy interface will depend on the nature and timing of interventions by the various actors, creating windows of opportunity or tipping points. However, this does not mean any analysis of the interface is driven solely by 'political will'.

Drawing the above analyses together leads us to argue that there are four critical dimensions for analysis: political context; the values, **beliefs** and credibility of the actors involved in policymaking; different types of knowledge; and the roles of knowledge intermediaries. Four broad corresponding questions can be identified that break the policy process down into manageable portions, while also making it possible to capture and discuss further dynamics:

- How does the prevailing political context condition the policymaking process, the behaviour of the different actors involved in it and the search for knowledge?
- Who is involved in policymaking and knowledge generation and use? How do these actors interact and what role does knowledge play in this process?
- What types of knowledge do different actors rely on and why? From where do they source this knowledge?
- What innovative ways of working that reflect an understanding of these dynamics could be used to mediate the knowledge–policy interface?

A final overarching question remains and is threaded through the entire book:
- How do power relations mediate all of these interactions?

While many of these points have been considered in isolation, they have not been brought together in a single package. By contrast, this book examines these factors synergistically, with the aim of helping development theorists and practitioners think pragmatically about the advice they can offer as they promote the better use of knowledge in policymaking. It does this by encouraging readers to think systematically about the context in which they work; the power dynamics of knowledge–policy processes; the constellation of actors involved; how knowledge is currently being used (or not); and ways it might be linked more effectively with policy processes. In short, this book seeks to provide a state-of-the art overview of current thinking about knowledge, policy and power in international development; present empirical case studies that provide concrete examples of how these issues play out in reality; and offer practical guidance on the implications of this knowledge base for a range of people:

- scholars and students of the policy process;
- policymakers in line ministries in the global North and South and their internal advisers (research programme managers, disciplinary specialists);
- external advisory bodies such as civil society organisations (CSOs), think-tanks and academic institutions;
- advocacy organisations and others looking to influence policymaking; and
- institutions with an oversight role (for example legislators, donor organisations, non-governmental organisations (NGOs)).

For readers interested in the theory of development (scholars, students), this book synthesises the literature in an innovative way, drawing conclusions that link the analytical literature clearly to practice and offer new entry points for analysis. For readers who play a role in shaping policy content (policymakers, NGOs, advisers, donors), this book tackles the problem of how best to navigate the many voices and conflicting perspectives on an issue and how to evaluate and apply different types of knowledge in particular policy and political contexts. Drawing on combined expertise from Whitehall and Southern contexts, it also gives guidance on how to work strategically with a range of actors across the spectrum of knowledge generation and use. While the tendency is for analysts to focus simply on improving the content of knowledge for a particular policy issue, this book shows that, by focusing more on the *processes* at the knowledge–policy interface, it is possible to improve its content as well. For readers who are less concerned with a specific policy issue and instead have a stake in improving the policymaking process (think-tanks, CSOs) or governance more generally, this book helps pinpoint problems and blockages preventing a robust interface between knowledge and policy and offers ways to tackle them.

Organisation of the book

Knowledge can play a number of roles in the policy process: it both anchors policy discussions in an understanding of the world and challenges policymakers to think more broadly about what could be achieved. But how these roles are fulfilled – and the way knowledge is ultimately used – depends on the four key factors identified above, each of which is outlined in a separate chapter of the book. These are:

- the **political context** (whether it be at a certain scale or a certain regime type) in which a policy process plays out;
- the relative strength and interplay of **actors' interests, values/beliefs** and **credibility**;
- the **types of knowledge** that are generated and sought; and
- the processes that mediate between sources of knowledge and policy decisions – what we term **knowledge interaction processes**.

Each chapter is divided into three main parts: an overview of existing thinking and trends in the literature; a presentation of a synthetic framework that we believe provides a useful and accessible approach to navigating the complexities of each chapter's theme; and a detailed discussion of practical implications and guidance as to how best to apply this framework to development work. All chapters answer key questions set out at their beginning, while making links to other themes presented in the book. In this way, the reader is able to better appreciate the varied and critical connections across the knowledge–policy interface as well as manage this complexity. In order to bring the more theoretical discussion alive, each chapter also contains empirical case studies from primary research at the knowledge–policy interface, in textboxes for easy reference. A final chapter presents conclusions from the book and offers recommendations for different audiences on how to strengthen the linkages between knowledge and policy so as to enhance initiatives aimed at promoting poverty reduction and social justice.

Chapter Two: Mapping political context

Despite being a one-party state with limited civil society participation, Viet Nam boasts vibrant dialogue between the country's research community and its policy actors. By contrast, Kenya, a parliamentary **democracy** with an active civil society, faces limited uptake of knowledge in the policy process (see Jones et al, 2011). How can we explain these differences and what implications do they have for practice? The subtext of this chapter is that the answer – 'it all depends on political will' – is a simplistic escape clause. Understanding the flow of knowledge in policy requires a clear understanding of its political economy. The nature of the political system (including the level of democratic competition between branches and levels of government and between the state and civil society); the type and extent of incentive structures to utilise knowledge; and the capacity of political institutions to absorb change can all determine whether – and to what extent – knowledge is used to inform policymaking.

This chapter draws together insights from existing analytic and comparative political economy models (Polity IV, DFID Drivers of Change, the UN Development Programme (UNDP) Democratic Governance Framework, among others) to develop and apply an accessible framework that allows readers to think systematically about both the constraints and the opportunities for knowledge–policy interactions that different political contexts present, from established democracies to autocracies and fragile states. It aims to overcome any simplistic preconceptions that readers may have about state type and knowledge uptake in the policy arena, illustrating these complexities with a case study on the changing role of knowledge in the policy process in successive Nepalese political regimes.

By the end of this chapter, readers will have a good understanding of the political context factors shaping the policy process in their sector and/or country of interest and should be able to answer the following questions:

- What context-specific pressures are development actors under that may affect how they seek out, generate and/or apply knowledge in different political settings?
- How do opportunities for knowledge production and knowledge use vary between different political contexts?

Chapter Three: Engaging actors

The Millennium Development Goal (MDG) agenda, which sets a range of poverty reduction targets to be achieved between 2000 and 2015 across the globe, has been one of the most widely subscribed development initiatives in history. However, the compromises that were reached in order to arrive at just eight goals were many and complex, which speaks volumes about the power dynamics that exist between different knowledge and policy actors on the international development stage. In this vein, Chapter Three provides an overview of the range of actors involved in the production, translation and use of policy-relevant knowledge, looking at what role they play and what factors shape their behaviour.

While most analyses of the knowledge–policy interface have focused largely on bureaucrats and academic researchers, this book uses a much wider lens. Under policy actors we include legislators, political parties, the private sector and civil servants; under knowledge actors we consider think-tanks, academic institutions and consultants; under intermediaries we include the media, knowledge gateways and portals and communication organisations, among others. In order to think systematically about the role of each of these, we apply a framework that considers the way that interests shape an actor's involvement in the production and use of knowledge; how actors' prevailing beliefs and values influence, and are influenced by, knowledge; and how actors' abilities to make credible knowledge claims, either individually or as part of broader networks, shape their role in the knowledge–policy interface. The chapter draws on a case study of two CSO networks on child and youth rights and their efforts to shape donor policy commitments through a range of knowledge interaction strategies.

By the end of the chapter, the reader will be able to answer the following questions:

- Who is involved in policymaking and knowledge-generation processes in international development?
- How do the interests, values, beliefs and credibility of policy, knowledge and intermediary actors shape the knowledge–policy interface?

Answering these questions will help readers analyse the diverse interests and influences at work surrounding the particular knowledge–policy interface in which they are engaged, make appropriate decisions for choosing partners and entering into strategic alliances as well as understand where to make allowances for other stakeholders.

Chapter Four: Integrating different types of knowledge

Over the past decade, there has been increasing interest in, and funding for, results-based science in the international aid arena, with knowledge generated from medical-style experimental randomised controlled trials, which some see as the 'gold standard'. Such evaluations have their role and value, but, given the complexities of development interventions, this type of methodology risks narrowing down the range of questions asked about development to the extent that we may not be able to maintain a nuanced understanding of the process of policymaking or the ultimate impacts of aid.

This chapter argues that there are many types of knowledge, from evaluations to experiential learning, from academic journal articles to oral histories, each of which has a different contribution to make to policy and practice. It first presents strong conceptual and practical reasons for taking a broad view of what knowledge is used in policy, before describing how the processes of production, use and influence of knowledge vary between the different types. For research-based knowledge, practical (that is, project- and programme-derived) knowledge and participatory knowledge, this chapter shows what their value is for policy; what determines if and when insights from these knowledge sources are used; and what shapes the influence they have on policy and practice.

By the end of the chapter, the reader will be able to answer the following questions:

- What sources of knowledge do different actors at the knowledge–policy interface rely on and why?
- How do power relations between actors serve as a filter for privileging some sources of knowledge over others?

Answering these questions will help readers understand the relative value of different types of knowledge and how to deal with competing knowledge claims to a policy issue.

Chapter Five: Facilitating knowledge interaction

Climate change presents developing countries with the pressing challenge of how to mainstream adaptation into policy processes effectively. Adaptation requires a wide variety of actors to draw on scientific knowledge on natural hazards and changing environmental conditions. However, lessons on aid effectiveness show this cannot be achieved by high-level political actors operating in a technocratic policy-making mode or by relying on one-way knowledge transfer alone (Jones et al, 2008). What is crucial is to set up a variety of interaction processes at a number of levels, so scientific knowledge can be combined with local understandings and emerging good practices.

This chapter begins with an overview of the emerging literature on knowledge interaction, which highlights the complexities of promoting dialogue across different types of knowledge and policy actors. It draws attention to the strong demand for intermediary activities to support these dialogues and presents an innovative framework drawing on work by Michaels (2009) that sets out a spectrum of knowledge interaction functions. This framework considers not just mechanisms that promote knowledge uptake, but also the individual, institutional and systems features needed to increase social learning and innovation and transform development policy and practice. The potential as well as the challenges involved in applying this functions approach are illustrated by discussing the experiences of Practical Action, an international knowledge-focused intermediary organisation that aims to improve the flow of technologies both upstream and downstream. However, a key learning point is that it is not necessary to be badged as a dedicated 'knowledge intermediary' in order to act as one, and that in some cases it may be more appropriate to alter structures and incentives in existing organisations so individuals and teams can perform whatever intermediary functions are needed at any particular time or place.

By the end of the chapter, readers will be able to answer the following questions:

- How do we decide how best to behave as a knowledge intermediary?
- How do organisational and system factors shape knowledge interaction processes and when, where and how can policymakers make best use of knowledge in order to tackle complex problems?

Readers will be able to assess the full range of knowledge intermediary functions and the implications for their own organisation wherever they are on the knowledge intermediary–policy spectrum. They will also understand the types of organisational and system changes they and like-minded organisations will need to support in order to shape knowledge–policy interactions.

Chapter Six: Conclusions and policy implications

The concluding chapter of the book ties together the key arguments and discusses emerging implications for development policy and practice. It organises this discussion around different knowledge and policy actor audiences: knowledge producers, knowledge users, intermediaries and donors.

In short, then, making sense of the complexities of the knowledge–development policy interface can seem daunting, but this book seeks to provide the reader with an accessible framework and a set of analytical tools with which to systematically map and understand the dynamics of the flow of knowledge into development policy. By synthesising a broad range of literatures and empirical case studies, the book offers a fresh perspective on the interplay between knowledge, policy and power. It enables readers to enhance their ability to identify and negotiate strategic entry and veto points in the policy process and ultimately to contribute to transformative development policy and programmatic change.

Notes

[1] See, for example, Dunning (2000); Purani and Nair (2006); World Bank (2007); Menkhoff et al (2010).

[2] Note that views are mixed on the impacts of cash transfers. While they have been found to mitigate transient poverty arising from economic shocks and to promote service uptake, their impact on wellbeing outcomes has been less robust than advocates originally anticipated (Fiszbein et al, 2011).

[3] Cracknell (2001); Landry et al (2003); Brehaut and Juzwishin (2005); Young (2005); Ammons and Rivenbark (2008); Moynihan et al (2008).

[4] The topic of evidence-based policy emerged rapidly in the 1990s within the health sciences in the Anglo-Saxon world, quickly coming to favour randomised controlled trial approaches based on clinically rigorous sampling procedures and the seeking out of already established and translatable lessons (Victora et al, 2004; Jones, 2009a). In this regard, the influential work of organisations such as the Cochrane Collaboration (healthcare) and the Campbell Collaboration (broader social policy, most notably criminal justice) has been key to the endorsement of quantitative and experimental techniques as the model to be followed in evidence-based policy initiatives.

[5] Kaimowitz (1990); Lomas (1997); Röling (1988).

6 Datta (2009) points out that, the week after the 2008 election of Barack Obama, a directive was issued within the US Agency of International Development to strengthen the evaluation culture after eight years of results-based budgeting approaches at the expense of transparency and learning.

[7] See, for example, DFID (2009a).

[8] Standard guidance in, for example, the UK Treasury's Magenta Book and Green Book (summarised in Sutcliffe and Court, 2006) deals with different types of evidence but does not take account of the power dynamics involved in the use of knowledge in policy. Nor does it account for recent developments in thinking about policy – notably the application of complexity theory to governance and policymaking. While a great deal of thought is being put into what complexity means for policy processes (see Hallsworth, 2011), this has not yet made it through into the guidance that policymakers are bound to follow.

[9] Exceptions include Carden (2009) and Court et al (2005). In the case of Carden, the work focuses exclusively on examples from the International Development Research Centre's projects and is thus more an evaluation of one donor's practice. As Court and colleagues were affiliated with the Overseas Development Institute, as are the authors of this volume, we build on – and go beyond – the insights in their work.

TWO

Mapping political context

Political economy approaches have gained considerable currency in development circles in recent years. Somewhat surprisingly, however, given the recognised importance of the 'knowledge economy' in shaping development trajectories, this approach has paid little attention to the intersection of knowledge, policy and power. A key objective of this chapter, therefore, is to review the more useful conceptualisations of political context as mapped in various state-function typology and process frameworks. This in turn underpins a model to map varied political contexts and implications for the knowledge–policy interface that, we argue, can be applied to development realities and practice. The ultimate aim is to promote a more coherent response to the gaps and strengths in political context that affect how knowledge is used in policymaking. Such an approach is especially important given that much of the thinking and scholarship on the knowledge–policy interface has focused on developed country contexts;[1] relatively limited attention has been paid to the mediating variables of political context that are often very different in the developing world.

By the end of this chapter, readers will be able to answer the following questions:

- How do I begin to disaggregate 'political context' into more manageable components that are both analytically robust and useful for looking at the knowledge–policy interface?
- How can I analyse the knowledge–policy dynamics of political context factors, including:
  - » the separation of state powers between the legislature and the executive;
  - » electoral processes and other types of formal political participation;
  - » the informal types of political relationship that take place outside of mainstream policy processes;
  - » the type and magnitude of supranational or external forces at play; and
  - » the capacity of political institutions to absorb change?

The chapter first focuses on approaches to understanding political contexts, looking at various frameworks that have been used in the past before settling on a hybrid approach combining insights from both state typology and state function frameworks, which, we argue, are key to understanding how political context affects the production, translation and use of knowledge. A third section digs deeper to analyse our hybrid framework's implications for theory and practice at the knowledge–policy interface.

Defining political context

Since the early 1990s, there has been a 'political turn' in the study of international development and its associated disciplines, spurred on by the promotion of the good governance agenda, interest in social capital (Hickey, 2005) and the broader rise of new institutional economics (Dutraive, 2009). This (political) turn has implications for defining political context. On the one hand, it points to an intensified focus on the political processes at the heart of state functioning, which have historically been sidelined in favour of disciplines determined to explain or simplify development paths in terms of technocratic logic, often rooted in simplified principles of neoclassical economics (Tornquist, 1999). However, this sea change has also encouraged a proliferation of conceptual approaches that have attempted to understand and depict political contexts, accompanied by a wide array of new languages, tools and methodologies.

Within such research, there have been attempts to develop typologies of statehood and create corresponding indices, with the aim, for instance, of measuring degrees of democracy based on comprehensive but sometimes problematic arrays of attributes (such as the Freedom House and Polity IV datasets) (Munck and Verkuilen, 2002).[2] And although these have been useful for those seeking to understand both political personalities and processes, terms such as 'incentive', 'institution', 'agent' and 'structure' have often flowed across documents and meeting rooms with little concern for their original meaning or intent[3] (see Box 2.1).

Box 2.1: Core concepts in the Drivers of Change Framework

Agents refer to both internal and external actor interests in a situation; *structures* are the long-term context characteristics, such as the natural resource base or environmental conditions.

Institutions are the rules that shape human interaction and political-economic competition. They may be formal or informal – the former are institutions that are legally codified and include entities such as the legislature and the judiciary, while the latter are institutions that are typically socially codified and value-based. As such, formal institutions set the rules of the game, while informal institutions set the shape of the games within the rules (North, 1990). Different groups in society (particularly political elites) face various *interests and incentives* that affect the generation of particular policy outcomes that may encourage or hinder development.

Values and ideas, including political ideologies, religion and cultural beliefs, can have a significant effect on political behaviour and public policy formation and implementation.

To compound matters, the term 'political will' often arises in discussions about critical decision makers in policy processes. This is the notion that policy decisions are ultimately dependent on, and driven by, abstract or isolated political decrees; whether or not it is an intentional get-out clause, its effect is to simplify the range of influences at play in policy decisions while simultaneously short-circuiting all further analytical possibilities. Indeed, political will has been called 'the slipperiest concept in the policy lexicon … the *sine qua non* of policy success which is never defined except by its absence' (Hammergren, 1998, p 19). Indeed, one of the flagships of the increased emphasis on political context analysis in development practice, the Drivers of Change approach, has itself often included an undefined notion of 'political will' in its methodology, which has contributed to inconsistent quality in its application and outputs (Leftwich, 2006).[4] As such, it is important to recognise that 'political will' emerges from a context, and that failure to unpack the underlying dynamics encourages a simplistic view of the policy process as a linear, unidirectional flow of momentum.

The point of highlighting both the numerous advances and the distractions that have accompanied the 'political turn' in international development is to stress the importance of developing a common language and a succinct framework in political economy analysis that helps us understand how political decisions across diverse contexts affect, and are affected by, knowledge and power relations.

Unpacking political context mapping frameworks

There are arguably two sets of approaches that can be used in describing the political context: those that focus on state function and those that focus on state typology, that is, those that examine the individual characteristics within states (the relationship between the legislature and the executive, for example) and those that focus on whether the broad functions collectively combine to create a type of state (autocratic, fragile, post-conflict, democratic, for example). While it would be possible to identify pointers about knowledge-policy implications from comparing these frameworks, it would likely prove resource intensive and insufficiently systematic. Hence, we argue that in order to achieve a comprehensive and operational understanding of the knowledge-policy implications, it is key to develop a framework that works across a variety of state typology and state function approaches. For instance, while an understanding of the difference between the World Bank's 'deteriorating' countries' (World Bank, 2005a), the Organisation for Economic Co-operation and Development's (OECD's) 'governance environments' (OECD, 2007) and the Department for International Development's (DFID's) 'weak but willing' countries (Torres and Anderson, 2004) may help in identifying possible implications and restrictions on the use and production of knowledge, it is important to develop a framework that works across a variety of state typologies and state functions. To being with, we outline some key state typology and state function frameworks, with examples of each as Table 2.1 summarises.

Table 2.1: Key aspects of comparative political economy frameworks

Framework	Components of the political system
State function	
DFID Drivers of Change	Focus on the interaction between structural features, formal and informal institutions and individual agents Highly open and flexible methodology, with intrinsic value based on facilitating conceptual discussion
DFID Politics of Development	Increased explicit emphasis on the political dynamics of change and comparability Importation of additional political science concepts and formal framework without detailed methodology
UNDP Democratic Governance Framework	Similar to Drivers of Change, inspects types of institutions, principles of governance and consolidation of democracy No formal checklist, but narrative description of relevant dimensions
World Bank Worldwide Governance Indicators	Database-oriented project, drawing on perceptions of governance aggregated from dozens of further datasets. Categories usefully include 'Voice and Accountability', 'Regulatory Quality' and 'Rule of Law' Has been critiqued for being imprecise and offering limited causal prescriptions useful for policymakers
State typology	
Freedom House	Focus on civil and political rights using extensive catalogue of sub-criteria and indicators Minimal disaggregation across the checklist reduces usefulness for broader political economy analysis
Polity IV	Focus on distribution of power between state and society Emphasis on comparative political economy with extensive and explicit coding rules Coding is complex, but large empirical scope
International Network on Conflict and Fragility	Focus on definitions of fragility Directed towards supporting networking and decision making
Strategic Governance and Corruption Analysis (Government of the Netherlands)	Political context mapping, with additional emphasis on informal, societal and intangible factors Detailed methodology focused on policy planning applicability rather than political science rigour

State typology frameworks focus on categories of states that summarise core governance patterns. The **Freedom House** set has a particular methodology based on political rights, civil liberties and electoral democracy, eventually distilled into a typology of states that are categorised as 'free', 'partly free' and 'not free'.[5] Within each is a familiar range of sub-questions based on principles of the electoral process, individual autonomy, corruption, military influence, representation for minority groups and so on. In a similar vein, although without the dominant focus on civil liberties and rights, the **Polity IV framework** presents a state typology focused on the distribution of power between state and society and divides countries into those deemed democratic, autocratic and anocratic.[6] These frameworks are not without their detractors: some argue that the Freedom House dataset has a neoconservative ideological bias, whereas the lack of theoretical justification for weighted scoring systems in the Polity IV framework has opened it up to considerable interpretation (Munck and Verkuilen, 2002; Giannone, 2010). In addition, neither distinguishes explicitly between stable and fragile states. For this purpose, the **OECD Development Assistance Committee's International Network on Conflict and Fragility** is more useful (OECD, 2007). This uses the following four criteria to differentiate fragile states: post-conflict/crisis or political transition situation; deteriorating governance environment; gradual improvement; and prolonged crisis or impasse. This fourfold schema is more or less echoed in both DFID's fragile state typology system and that proposed by the World Bank. A final framework is that developed by the **Government of the Netherlands** (Unsworth and Conflict Research Unit, 2007), which analyses governance and corruption, although its focus on practical applicability may come at the expense of theoretical rigour, as it prioritises often messy, real-life concerns.

While a typology that separates out authoritarianism versus democracy versus state fragility may be a useful initial framework for analysis, understanding **state functions** is equally important (Saez and Gallagher, 2009), given the widely divergent realities of countries fitting these labels.[7]

The **Drivers of Change** approach, espoused by DFID since the early 2000s,[8] is a useful starting point, given its broad conceptual durability (Leftwich, 2006; Edelmann, 2009). In essence, the framework relies on a distinction between agents, structures and institutions (formal 'rules of the game' and informal 'games within the rules') to understand how reforms are produced, propagated or blocked in a national-level environment. On the basis of this thinking, DFID considered a further model in the mid-2000s: the **Politics of Development** framework.[9] This suggests the importance of the wider historical and cultural setting; the legitimacy of the political process; the immediate pressures from interest groups and district representatives; and the politics of the implementation stage (Leftwich, 2006).

The United Nations Development Programme's (UNDP's) **What, How and Why of Democratic Governance** framework, developed through its Public Administration Network (Cheema and Maguire, 2002), considers the 'what' to be the institutions, processes and practices that make up its core structure, consisting of components such as parliament, the judiciary, political parties and so on; the 'how' to be factors contributing to the effectiveness of these structures, such as degrees of access, participation, accountability, responsiveness and so on; and the 'why' to be internal and external factors that consolidate (or limit) the democratic system.

Similarly, the World Bank's **Worldwide Governance Indicators** utilise a broad range of analytical categories, many of which are well aligned with the thinking above, that are highly popular both within the Bank and among researchers, donors and investors (Arndt and Oman, 2006). These are voice and accountability; political stability and absence of violence/terrorism; government effectiveness; regulatory quality; rule of law; and control of corruption – which themselves comprise several hundred sub-categories.[10]

Mapping knowledge–policy linkages across political contexts

There are a number of critical differences between the frameworks above, and it is clear that, in order to reach a framework for analysing the knowledge–policy interface, which existing approaches largely ignore, we need to develop our own. To do this, we have synthesised important aspects from across these approaches to develop a hybrid that is both academically relevant and sufficiently practical for a time-constrained bureaucrat or development project manager to engage with the knowledge–policy interface. Our framework identifies three characteristics of state typology and five characteristics of state function that are of key concern to the generation, flow and uptake of knowledge in the policy process. These are summarised in Table 2.2 and analysed in more detail in the rest of this section.

In terms of state typology, we separate out **more consolidated democracies**[11] from **more autocratic governance** and **more fragile or post-conflict states**.[12] This is a broad-brush approach, but we acknowledge that the lines between the categories are blurred and that there is no particular reason to suppose that each category implies a particular type of state function. Indeed, it is important to set the two notions (category and function) against each other in analysing the knowledge–policy interface, as in Table 2.2.

When analysing state functions, we draw out five key characteristics. First, it is clear that the **type of power restraint among government institutions** is a common and critical variable. This aspect incorporates the separation of powers between state legislatures, executives and judiciary bodies and draws on the potential differential impacts of these relationships on the use and production of knowledge. For instance, experiments examining the relationship between information use and decision making (built on rigorous control-group methodologies) have demonstrated that while increased accountability and transparency measures do not necessarily adjust the potential for reform, they do show notable increases in the amount of evidence debated and used to elaborate on potential avenues for policy exploration (Huber and Seiser, 2001, cited in Court and Cotterell, 2006).

Within this, we further separate out the often-overlooked issue of decentralisation, as this can also be considered a form of restraint on power. Indeed, whether or not formal structures contribute to greater uptake and use

Table 2.2: A summary framework for understanding the political economy of the knowledge–policy interface in different political contexts

State function	Sub-components	More consolidated democracies	More autocratic governance	More fragile or post-conflict contexts
			Implications for knowledge production and use*	
Restraints on power (separation of powers)	Triangulation of authority between legislative, executive and judicial bodies	Parliamentary systems are not necessarily more impartial in use of knowledge than presidential systems, given greater separation of powers in latter	Policies for initial reform are easier (strong leadership, unchecked executive), but consolidating reform requires input from legislature and citizenry, making knowledge–policy links more networked and potentially more complex	Although low capacity means knowledge incentive structures may be weak (Chapter Four), potential for incorporating knowledge into policy is less constrained by path-dependent policies, bureaucratic inertia and institutional resistance
Decentralisation	De-concentration Delegation Transfer of functions Devolution	Decentralised knowledge is broad-based and resource-intensive in development phases	Critical to determine location of 'autocratic predicament' line (balancing decentralisation for accountability with desire for security) to understand where knowledge is most likely to have an effect	With decentralisation there needs to be an increased emphasis on networking and coordination among increased number of actors
Regulation and competitiveness of political participation	Regulations as to when, whether and how participation occurs Degree to which alternative preferences can be delivered	Likely to be high demand for and supply of knowledge – suggesting possibility of multiple entry points and increased need to locate high-impact policy windows and maximise the effort put into knowledge dissemination and interpretation	Lack of community involvement may have significant negative effects on programme effectiveness because of lack of new knowledge sources Entry points are critical factor in understanding where knowledge may have an effect on policy, as veto/closure points are likely to outweigh them	Weak lateral accountability and civil society mistrust may require greater emphasis on research-based knowledge rather than citizen knowledge or knowledge from practice

State function	Sub-components	Implications for knowledge production and use*		
		More consolidated democracies	More autocratic governance	More fragile or post-conflict contexts
Informal politics	Non-codified or parallel procedures Personality politics Patronage or public good	Requires examination of deeper social institutions (such as gender inequality) and structures to improve knowledge–policy interface, as informal politics are broader-based than formal political structures and processes	Priority focus is impact of personality and politics of elite 'selectorate' in determining flow and uptake of knowledge	Political accountability often takes form of generosity at cost of public purse – a priority for improving knowledge–policy interface will be creating and maintaining demand for (and legitimising) different types of knowledge
External forces	Geostrategic dynamics Trade Aid and donor support Conflicts International standards	Knowledge generation and access is relatively open – key is to balance transfer and translation of broad-based inputs and outputs	A protective culture exists in terms of knowledge access and collection; the key is to create models of knowledge generation and access	Minimal state structures raise the prominence of international pressures, think-tanks, donors and NGOs – although care needs to be taken to ensure that weak structures do not succumb to outside ideological influence
Capacity to absorb change	Degree of stability of institutions and processes Responsiveness to internal and external policy formulation and implementation	Influence–network approaches: multiple demands for knowledge for different purposes that may end up in conflict with each other	Command–hierarchy approaches: centralised demand for knowledge, although often through semi-independent bodies	Low capacity and instability means knowledge incentive structures (Chapter Four) will be weak, lessening demand for knowledge and encouraging greater reliance on external organisations to provide it (with the caveats as outlined under 'External forces')

Note: * In the interests of brevity, only selected implications are presented here. The purpose of the table is to provide a broad overview of the issues at play when considering knowledge–policy dimensions across different political contexts.

of knowledge in policy processes is likely to depend to some extent on the type of decentralisation being undertaken in that context.[13] We can distinguish four forms of decentralisation for these purposes: de-concentration, delegation, transfer of functions and devolution.[14] In practice, these forms exhibit a broad range of relative power relationships between central and local elites (Hossain, 2005), each of which may vary depending on the quality and complexity of communication and accountability structures (Chisinga, 2007). India's federalised states, for instance, can be a complex terrain in which to negotiate the promotion of transfer of knowledge (Hickey and Braunholtz-Speight, 2007). The many *panchayat raj* (local assembly) institutions vary markedly in structure and in their interest in supporting the chronically poor. Campaigns for the 'right to information' for those beyond the literate and urban elites have had mixed impacts, as they have had to negotiate a long implementation path from bureaucrat, to contractor, to village leader and the community at large (Hickey and Braunholtz-Speight, 2007).

Second, it is clear that the **regulation and competitiveness of political participation,** including elections and other accountability and transparency mechanisms, are regular features of the frameworks discussed – the so-called 'rules of the game'. However, fluid as these concepts are, they need to be allocated specific definitions for our framework, to ensure an instrument that is relatively accessible, consistent and clear. It is therefore useful to consider two separate sub-components. The first relates to how far non-elites have access to institutions that regulate when, whether and how political participation can occur – how far groups, networks or coalitions can participate in politics on a stable basis with 'no significant groups, issues, or types of conventional political action … regularly excluded from the political process' (Marshall and Jaggers, 2011, p 26) . The second relates to the degree to which alternative preferences for policies can be expressed competitively, identifiable through the regular transfer of groups and coalitions out of power. In essence, this is a distinction between 'mere participation' and 'being heard and witnessing corresponding action',[15] each of which is important but has separate implications for the production, use and transfer of knowledge. This means analysing electoral accountability and conduct, as demand for and manipulation of knowledge to inform policy can increase dramatically during election periods.

The third aspect of the framework concerns the role of **informal politics**. The *de facto* distribution of power within a state, and therefore some of the central influences on the knowledge–policy interface, is determined by formal as well as informal institutions. In many countries, this concerns different systems of patronage, that is, hierarchies of patron–client relationships. Informal institutions can have complex effects; sometimes, they may work to include groups that otherwise have limited access to policy processes, and at other times, they may lead to capture of the policy agenda by certain powerful groups while others are excluded – the 'games within the rules'.

This aspect identifies the role of personalities and identity (rather than party) politics as critical in absorbing, rejecting or shaping knowledge–policy linkages.

Indeed, there is an insufficient understanding of the 'primacy of the personal' (Chambers, 1995) in studies of international development, and of the fact that any individual in society is naturally open to experience or closed to progressive ideas – each of which may have particular consequences for the flow of knowledge in the development of policies, given sufficient centralisation of power (McCrae, 1996). How these personal attributes play out is more closely examined in Chapter Three.

The fourth broad category involves **external factors**. This does not feature heavily in many frameworks, primarily because they are often focused on the political economy of particular administrations or sectors rather than with more regional or global inertia and change. In considering the knowledge–policy interface, however, the external factors determining the flow and interaction of knowledge between Northern and Southern contexts become a critical concern, and one that needs to be better highlighted. For example, Chapter Four contrasts the often highly technical language in particular organisational or donor contexts with the language used in bottom-up campaign messages and participatory methodologies.

External forces can include geostrategic dynamics, trade, aid, conflicts and international standards. There are prominent examples, for instance, of how conditional aid has an impact on political context, such as in the 'third wave of democratisation'. It has been argued that the growth and influence of the European Union, the 'domino effect' (regional contingency) as well as changes in official outlook from bodies such as the Vatican, have all been cited as significant influences on the notable expansion in numbers of democratic states from the mid-1970s to the early 1990s (Huntingdon, 1991). Moreover, a substantial amount of research on development issues is funded by international donors; according to a recent survey, in 2001-05 an average of 33 donors were operating per partner country (IDA, 2007). The implications of these factors for the knowledge–policy interface are addressed in Chapter Three, but issues relevant to the political context are discussed later on in this chapter.

The final variable in our hybrid framework concerns the **capacity of a political system to absorb change,** which refers to the stability of institutions and processes in different contexts. Drawing on DFID's Capability, Accountability, Responsiveness framework, this can also be considered the 'ability to get things done' – that is, to formulate and implement policies effectively (Moore and Teskey, 2006). To extend previous metaphors further, while it is necessary to examine both 'the rules of the game' and 'the games within the rules', it is also key to consider whether games can actually take place at all, and how this affects the ebb and flow of knowledge in different contexts.

It is in this instance where the state typology terms 'fragile', 'deteriorating', 'unstable', 'weak', 'post-conflict', 'fledging' and 'transitional' come into use, as such polities are often in a condition of more considerable change, tending towards either stability or conflict. The 2009 global report on conflict, for instance, indicates that 50% of such states[16] are likely to undergo a major regime change within a five-year timeframe, and more than 70% are likely to do the same within a decade (Marshall and Cole, 2009).

In thinking about the relative importance of the capacity to absorb change within a knowledge–policy interface model, it is useful to begin with Ian Bremmer's 'J-curve' (Figure 2.1), which describes the connection between a country's openness and its relative capacity to absorb change and remain stable (Bremmer, 2006). The J-curve shows how closed, authoritarian, undemocratic or 'not free' (on the Freedom House index) states can remain stable through the suppression of civil society dialogue/insurrection or reduced accountability. On the right-hand side of the curve, more democratic or 'free' polities achieve a greater degree of stability by opening up the public sphere and ensuring accountable political systems. In the 'well' of the curve are those polities that are relatively unstable, characterised by their incapacity to absorb change without disruption to their 'normal' political processes.

Figure 2.1: Bremmer's J-curve

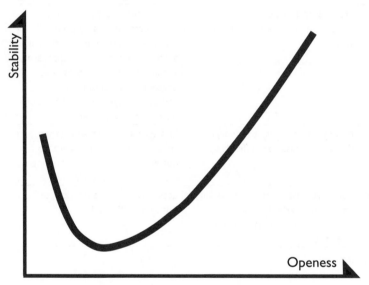

Source: Bremner (2006)

The types of structures in place can also influence a state's (in)capacity to manage change, as Table 2.3 shows. There is a distinction between 'command–hierarchy' structures and 'influence–network' structures, the former being more common in authoritarian regimes and the latter in more democratic systems (Moore and Teskey, 2006).

Together with the J-curve, Table 2.3 provides a useful framework for discussing the potential impact of varying state capacities on the generation, use and transmission of knowledge for policy processes.

Table 2.3: Two approaches to analysing state capacity

Factor	State approaches to managing change	
	The command–hierarchy approach	**The influence–network approach**
Underlying image of how actors within different state organisations and society do or should relate to one another	Emphasis on hierarchical relations and on clear boundaries between different formal organisations. State does/should stand 'above' and 'outside' society	Emphasis on the value of dense, possibly egalitarian networks of relations that cross organisational boundaries. State and societal actors are interdependent
Typical ideal modes of state/ public action	Framing and implementing (clear) policy in a coherent and unified way	Using influence and contacts to determine what is politically possible, to coordinate different actors within the state apparatus, within society and across the 'state–society boundary', maximising synergy. Public action may appear fragmented
Important resources required by the state	Money and capacity to manage (state) organisations effectively	Linkages and trust with other actors, including 'centrality' to important networks, convening capacity, political skills
Implicit approach to 'accountability'	Formal, transparent accountability, based on clear roles and responsibilities; often process-oriented	Less formal, more political and outcome-oriented

Source: Moore and Teskey (2006)

Implications for knowledge–policy interactions and managing power relations

Based on our framework of political context characteristics, we now explore each component in more detail, using indicative examples of these from real-life cases that illustrate their relevance to the knowledge–policy interface. It is important to note, however, that we do not address the question of how knowledge affects policy implementation (the outcomes of policy) in different political contexts. This is in part because of our focus on the decision-making process (and the politics involved in this), and in part because isolating and determining the impact of knowledge on policy is highly issue-specific (see Chapter Four and Ramalingam and Jones, 2008). Our analysis also does not deal with issues such as geography, resource endowment or historical specificity (including path dependency) as explicit categories. In analysing political context the political institutions are considered the primary nexus through which such structural factors take effect (Rodrik et al, 2004; Dutraive, 2009).

Mechanisms to restrain the power of government institutions

Questions this section will help you answer:
- Are there checks and balances in the political system that encourage policy scrutiny? To what extent can the executive and the legislature challenge the quantity and quality of knowledge used in policy making?
- In what circumstances does a focus on a particular government branch make more sense in order to promote the integration of particular forms of knowledge into policy?
- What are the formal arrangements that exist to promote such knowledge uptake (for example via select committees or parliamentary processes such as passing legislation)?
- At what level is power really held in terms of how knowledge is used to advance policy?
- How do different types of decentralisation affect connections between knowledge and policy making?

In terms of systemic restraints on the power of the executive branch, consolidated democracies have both advantages and challenges relevant to the knowledge–policy interface. For instance, the prospects for enhancing and maintaining an ideal of 'neutral competence' or impartial judgement in the review of knowledge for a particular policy are clearer for presidential than for parliamentary systems – where the executive and the legislature are less divided (Weimar, 2005). The experience in the US, where executive agencies have encountered greater difficulty than legislative ones in maintaining policy neutrality, suggests that efforts to promote the impartial demand and use of knowledge would do better to focus on supporting legislative agencies (Weimar, 2005). The Office of Management and Budget in the US executive, for example, has been shown to be less 'neutrally competent' at developing and storing budgetary information than the Congressional Budget Office in the legislature (Weimar, 2005).

The lack of separation of these agencies in parliamentary systems, however, as historically demonstrated in the UK's 'Whitehall' civil service, can mean civil service managers have a virtual monopoly on providing advice to ministers. In such circumstances, the potential for neutrally conceived policies is more likely to be enhanced by developing independent or semi-independent agencies such as think-tanks and universities, rather than through work with legislative bodies (Weimar, 2005).

Many countries in the South have inherited or emulated these models, suggesting that consolidating democracies have similar lessons to learn (and dangers to be aware of) in relation to restraints on the executive. Latin America, Eastern Europe and parts of Asia have experienced a series of democratic 'waves', with implications for an expanded and more complex separation of powers interacting with the knowledge–policy interface – although many hurdles can and do arise in the form of weak horizontal accountability and the return of authoritarian rule (O'Donnell, 1996). Similar trends have been noted in a number of African regimes,[17] including increased demand-side competition in relation to policy research requests. This has occurred as a result of the expansion and solidification of legislative bodies, which has added to demands that previously came only from executive bodies (AAPPG, 2008). These expansions have also created a number of opportunities for different actors to determine the credibility of research-based and other forms of evidence. For instance, different legislatures (rubber stamp, emerging, informed, transformative) will have different entry points and ways of working (see Chapter Three, Box 3.6).

By contrast, executive bodies in less democratic contexts are able to function relatively freely, within a range of unlimited to slightly moderate restraints. In the former case, either there is no legislative assembly or, where one exists, it has no ability to amend or suspend Acts decreed by the executive. In slightly more moderate political contexts, the ruling party is able to table legislation, block certain Acts and refer concerns to an independent judiciary. Following Venezuela's 2005 elections, for instance, which the opposition party boycotted, a consequently stronger executive seized the opportunity to promote a range of ideologically specific market policies – as well as to cement its own authority (Corrales and Penfold-Becerra, 2007). By contrast, when President Chávez's two thirds majority control over the legislature was lost in 2010, there were sweeping repercussions, including the requirement for cross-government negotiations on the selection of Supreme Court justices and electoral authority bodies (*The Economist*, 2010).

Among the central implications of this dimension is, first, that for some autocracies policies relating to initial reform are typically easier to promote, given their reliance on strong leadership and an unchecked executive; consolidating reform in the long term often requires input from the legislature and the citizenry (Williamson, 1994; Haggard and Kaufmann, 1995, both cited in Court and Cotterrell, 2006). Second, where demands for evidence from an executive branch are largely unchallenged, requests can be based solely on a need for macroeconomic advice rather than on a need for advice relating to social or democratic issues, which may be more pertinent to the progressive achievement of human rights (Court and Cotterrell, 2006). Indeed, the increasing use of think-tanks for the provision of policy evidence in China demonstrates the country's thriving demand for information to support reform processes (Zhu and Xue, 2007). However, the sourcing of such knowledge has been limited to semi-independent institutes, which are constrained in the degree to which they can comment on longer-term measures that will enhance democratic functions (Stone, 2005). Finally, an unrestrained executive branch in an autocracy can effectively close down discussions, as described in Box 2.2.

Box 2.2: Knowledge flows in autocratic polities

Even given significant structural restraints, new knowledge can sometimes influence policy processes in autocratic polities, although such change is often subject to reversals as this example from Iran illustrates. The Iranian Institute for Research Planning and Development (IRPD), for instance, a government think-tank, conducted a joint policy research project with UNDP between 1996 and 2000 to influence the process in which Iran's Third Development Plan (2000-04) was implemented. Three determining characteristics set the scene: there was consistency of vision between IRPD and the government planning department; IRPD had a reserve of experienced Iranian researchers; and there was a pre-established research relationship between the parties (Alamuti, 2002). IRPD's close government affiliation enabled it to put forward an evidence-based study recommending a separation of the functions of the executive and a decentralisation of executive ministries.

Even so, when the President became more interested in a socialist agenda, he was able to remove key personnel from the programme on account of the unrestrained powers vested in the executive, thereby destabilising the fledgling knowledge–policy linkages forged between IRPD and the government planning team (Alamuti, 2002). A key implication therefore in relation to promoting demand or supply of knowledge in this context is the structural risk evident throughout the programming stages; despite a number of favourable linkages between IRPD and the government, the process remained consistently vulnerable owing to the presence of a relatively unrestrained executive.

While there is very limited established research on the range of impacts fragile state structures have on research–policy interactions, it is commonly assumed that weak lateral accountability limits the room for research to influence an agenda that is likely to be focused on short-term goals. Indeed, in unstable, deteriorating or post-conflict contexts, executive power is often bolstered through acts of martial law or winner-take-all elections. The case study in Box 2.4 continues the focus on Nepal discussed earlier in order to begin to outline the practical challenges facing navigation of the knowledge–policy interface in fragile state contexts.

Moreover, for contexts in flux, government uprisings or seizures of the executive can provide both windows of opportunity to promote knowledge-based policies and outright closure. Such eventualities imply that actors and networks would benefit from an ongoing awareness of emerging opportunities, while considering the implied risks of increasing political tensions. The Young Lives project in Ethiopia, a longitudinal policy research initiative involved in linking evidence on child poverty to national poverty reduction strategy development, encountered these issues in 2005 when controversial electoral results led to reduced political space for civil society-generated evidence and inputs into poverty policy dialogues.

This sudden change in the political landscape highlighted the importance of embedding flexibility within policy knowledge exchange strategies, including options for drawing on alternative policy interlocutors in response to evolving windows of opportunity (Jones and Sumner, 2011).

Decentralisation

In theory at least, the implications of decentralisation for promoting the supply and demand of knowledge in democratic contexts can be positive; sub-national elections create demand from a broader constituency, as do increased restraints on executive power. Restraints on excessive political power are also theoretically strengthened by empowering citizens to use different types of knowledge, counterbalancing the often research-driven agenda of central government (see Chapter Four, Figure 4.2).

In practice, of course, there are numerous questions of legitimacy and capacity complicating this ideal relationship. For instance, the Micro Impacts of Macroeconomic Adjustment Policies programme in the Philippines aimed to institutionalise poverty-monitoring tools throughout the country, but national institutes did not have the authority to dictate to the provinces (Carden, 2009). Similarly, an attempt to strengthen the research–policy interface in a context of decentralised government in Ghana concluded that, although government–civil society relations at the district level had improved (in that civil society had become more assertive in challenging local government), decentralised government structures were insufficient for the networks to have an impact on policy and to challenge entrenched views (deGrassi, 2007). Consequently, civil society independence and capacity can affect the cross-traffic of knowledge, despite the presence of decentralised structures. Box 2.3 illustrates some of these complexities drawing on the example of the forestry sector in Nepal.

Box 2.3: Decentralisation and knowledge–policy linkages in Nepal

Looking at how research is used to inform policy decision making at different historical junctures highlights the importance of informing any knowledge–policy interaction initiative with a keen understanding of the balance of power between the central government and decentralised authorities. This is vividly illustrated by the example of the Nepalese forestry sector, which has inspired considerable interest over the decades among government, civil society and international agency actors alike.

Under the Rana regime, which began in the mid-19th century, orders from the top became policy without the input of evidence. Feudal rulers made personal decisions to clear forest lands to sustain the regime and maximise personal benefit and that of their families and allies. This said, up until the first half of the 20th century rulers did accept forestry science provided by colonial India that was consistent with their interests, such as that related to the supply of timber to India and commercial forestry.

After the Rana rulers were overthrown in 1951, there was a seismic shift in forest policy, with a new emphasis on nationalisation and decentralisation. These **populist motivations were based on insufficient scientific analysis** and policy-focused social science, with an emphasis on 'fine and fence' bureaucracy and top-down managerial approaches, despite being framed ostensibly as decentralisation.

External forces in the form of transnational environmentalism in the 1970s and 1980s began to highlight a growing crisis in Nepal. International expert knowledge began to influence government policy in the sector for the first time while the *panchayat* decentralisation programme, ostensibly designed to increase the prominence of grassroots voices, was not fully supported by mechanisms to facilitate participatory knowledge amplification and uptake. This hollow 'ideological decentralisation' therefore counteracted the increased external emphasis on evidence and expert knowledge, with little growth on the grassroots knowledge supply side.

In the late 20th century, polycentric power centres became more prominent, each of which began to question the use of science for its historical association with particular social and identity groups. While in theory decentralisation could have heralded greater space to articulate grassroots views and promote more meaningful policy decisions, in practice this shift resulted in a chaotic policy environment under the post-2006 transitional state. Compounding this, institutions and officials have changed frequently, leading to unclear policy direction for local government units working on forest management.

Source: Paudel et al (2010)

In contrast with democratic polities, autocratic countries are more likely to retain a hold on power through centralisation of resources, decision-making and knowledge. This fear of decentralisation is based on the truism that delegating authority allows for the development of alternative patronage systems, which can evolve to threaten central elites or provide an impetus for political secession (Landry, 2008). Not surprisingly it can have significant lasting effects in terms of building the role of participatory knowledge in policy processes. Post-communist countries, for instance, despite being largely democratic on paper, demonstrate reduced scores on the Civil Society Index as a result of historically partial (Bulgaria, Croatia, Romania, Ukraine) or totally absent (Georgia, Macedonia) political decentralisation.[18]

In some cases, however, autocratic polities are also able to decentralise through de-concentration or delegation in order to get closer to treading the 'autocratic predicament' line, that is, balancing the need to decentralise in order to improve growth and accountability with the desire to maintain security (Landry, 2008). In so doing, countries such as Viet Nam and China provide tight regulatory control that simultaneously facilitates knowledge–policy linkages – provided that the knowledge is not 'alternative' or threatening to a broader policy agenda (see Chapter Four). The *doi moi* reforms in Viet Nam, for example, are seen to have instigated an increased acceptance of a relatively autonomous civil society in the 1990s. These shifts are increasingly institutionalised in sets of decrees, such as the Grassroots Democracy Decree 79, which enables pro-poor participation in commune development activities (Sabharwal and Thien Huong, 2005). This said, *bona fide* decision making remains highly dependent on research or operational knowledge drawn from within a small range of international and semi-independent think-tanks (Sabharwal and Thien Huong, 2005).

In less stable states, the type of decentralisation exhibited is likely to be based largely on the *transfer of functions*, that is, the shift of authority from state power to private, non-governmental organisation (NGO) or other external agents owing to the weaknesses of institutional capacities. This can lead to a significant fragmentation of knowledge and knowledge production activities with negative consequences for more integrated evidence-informed policy decision making (Landry, 2008).

Regulation and competitiveness of political participation

Questions this section will help you answer:
- Do different mechanisms to regulate political participation (such as elections, rule by birthright or choice by a 'selectorate') mean different ways of working in the knowledge–policy interface?
- Is decision making a highly technocratic process, or are other voices actively encouraged to participate? Who and why?
- How well are opposition parties and independent civil society groups able to source and use new knowledge? Where do they get it from and is it of good quality?
- What are the opportunities for public debate, either in the media or in other fora?

It might be taken for granted that, in consolidated democracies with highly regulated and competitive participation processes, there will be advantages for knowledge–policy linkages. However, when considering the particular roles of knowledge in policy making, the picture becomes more complicated. Regulation of knowledge production and use tends to vary depending on the nature of the issue, who is seen to be credible (see Chapter Three), and the different types of knowledge (see Chapter Four). For example, case study evidence suggests that, when research from scientific laboratories has been involved in policy processes, this has tended to remove the process from democratic political space and instead lead to more opaque and technocratic decision making (Irwin, 2001; Buhler et al, 2002). Political institutions tend to treat different types of knowledge differently, and 'expert' knowledge, especially scientific knowledge, may be accepted without public examination and debate. Meanwhile, knowledge brought by underrepresented groups may be viewed with more suspicion – possibly as a result of being sourced and presented in an alternative fashion – even in well-established democracies. There are, of course, examples of where regulation of knowledge use in democratic policy processes has been exemplary – such as the UN's promotion of Democratic Governance Assessments. These were seen to contribute towards both consolidating democracy and fostering a culture of evidence-based policy making in a range of contexts. The bottom–up approach used by the Mongolian government (see also Malawi and Zambia) to inform governance indicators sought input from local-level media and marginalised groups. This initiative assisted in the establishment of a legitimate evidence base for the National Action Plan to Consolidate Democracy while also setting a precedent for accountability (UNDP, 2008).

Examining 'competitive participation' in relation to the practical production and use of alternative knowledge in policymaking in democracies reveals other particular advantages and constraints. For instance, the relatively high demand for knowledge in such contexts, whether it is used or not, can have broader long-term enlightenment functions that also serve to legitimise administrations (Weiss, 1979, cited in Pollitt, 2005). However, a study of the ways in which performance information is used by executive, legislative and citizen end users in consolidated democracies reveals that ministers, legislators and citizens rarely read or consider the performance measurement information that is increasingly available to them, in part because of information overload, but also perhaps because of different concepts of knowledge (see Chapter Four) (Weiss, 1979, cited in Pollitt, 2005).

Furthermore, attitudes towards knowledge use can be driven by broader and more strategically overt influences. The UK government's reaction to the outbreak of bovine spongiform encephalopathy in the 1990s demonstrated that, despite an apparent demand for an evidence-based policy response, genuine alternative approaches were actively constrained where they were considered to contradict government interests regarding agricultural support and limited state intervention (Millstone and van Zwanenberg, 2007). Similarly, government–civil society relations were seriously strained over the debate regarding evidence promoting intervention in Iraq in 2003 (Glees, 2005). This occurred primarily as a consequence of an initial poor assessment of the intelligence, but also as a result of the later politicisation of this intelligence. Both issues could have been brokered more delicately by the Joint Intelligence Committee (Glees, 2005), with lasting structural and credibility implications for the evidence-based policy arena.[19]

On the other hand, autocracies regularly demonstrate high levels of regulation and constrained competition in participatory processes as a defining characteristic. These features naturally have significant implications for the legitimacy and applicability of the knowledge sought and absorbed in centralised development plans. The case of the National Wildlife Commission for Conservation and Development (NCWCD) in Saudi Arabia shows that the participation of semi-independent research bodies in policymaking can influence policy processes in terms of the provision of operational and scientific knowledge, despite community participation being constrained. Even in the case of limited involvement of local institutions and promotion of participatory biodiversity management structures, the project was relatively successful. This owed largely to the drive resulting from an international multidisciplinary conference and the framing of the approach in terms of traditional values based on the management of scarce natural resources sanctioned by Islamic law.[20] The point to take away is that, despite limited meaningful civil society participation, knowledge can be legitimised in alternative ways depending on prevailing values in a political system.

More autocratic contexts also pose particular challenges for promoting knowledge-based approaches, given that the real locus of decision making is often opaque with the real sources of power often covert or hidden. Initiatives in these contexts should therefore recognise that a thorough political economy analysis is required – one that places significant emphasis on informal networks. For instance, in the late 1990s and early 2000s, DFID undertook a multi-country project to create and improve links between researchers and policymakers regarding social and participatory development approaches (Fisher and Holland, 2003). The project included an undertaking in Uzbekistan to provide social knowledge alternatives routed outside central planning approaches, while also providing new poverty analysis methodologies. Although modest and dependent on unique policy entry points (the President's interest in social democracy), the intervention was considered successful in invigorating 'consumer' demand for knowledge. In this case it did not make sense to promote direct confrontational policy reform, regardless of the availability and type of evidence. Instead, the selection of unorthodox entry points for knowledge, which also satisfied a middle-ground demand for topics that are more or less agreed by government, brought results. However, this is not to say that evidence does not count. In the same context, a project focusing on the reduction of domestic violence used a combination of entry-point strategies as well as new participatory research to achieve significant policy change. This example elucidates the point that, while identifying entry points is critical in autocratic contexts, robust and participatory evidence can still add much-needed legitimacy to a policy message.[21] In the same vein, in China, for example, while competitive participation continues to be restricted, channels are increasingly being introduced that deregulate the role of participatory knowledge in policy processes. Deliberative fora such as public consultations, surveys and expert meetings are now more a part of the Chinese *ruan quanli* (soft power) governance approach (Leonard, 2008). The point here is to appreciate the policy entry points as much as evidence availability, but not to write off meaningful civil society participation despite a more autocratic political context.

In fragile or post-conflict contexts, the issue of regulation and competitiveness is again complex. In states that are increasingly more open (moving up the right-hand arm of the J-curve), coalition platforms may function as 'blank slates' – less constrained by path-dependent policies, bureaucratic inertia and institutional resistance. Additionally, movement towards a more democratic system is likely to provide well-regulated participatory functions that also offer great potential for an airing of alternative policies while movement towards a more autocratic system offers an increase in degrees of regulation only. For fragile contexts caught in 'the well' of the curve, however, the defining feature is likely to be whether or not actors and networks are willing and able to participate at the knowledge–policy interface at all. In Bosnia-Herzegovina, for example, civil society organisation (CSO) actors rarely cooperate with the government, despite its growing interests in evidence-based policymaking (Struyk et al, 2007). CSO capacities are highly underdeveloped and awareness among public officials of the importance of including CSO input in policies is almost non-existent (Struyk et al, 2007).

Electoral processes

Here, it is important to go beyond the question of participation *per se* towards 'being heard' – where electoral accountability and conduct determine the timing and types of demands for knowledge. Autonomous think-tanks in the South, for example, have started to develop in parallel with democratisation processes. In Korea and Taiwan, for instance, where democratic processes have become increasingly consolidated, think-tanks have a record of being supported by national universities and international researchers (the latter often on a *pro bono* basis). Thus, both independent and party-affiliated think-tanks have emerged to strengthen the knowledge-base of parties and civil society activists when the policymaking process is increasing in complexity (Datta et al, 2010).

However, the implications of this relationship are not always positive. While increased inter-party competition in India, for example, alongside the development of a partisan political culture, has strengthened the demand for policy research, it has also meant that links with research institutions tend not to be systematic. Politicians have therefore sought advice from researchers predominantly for election preparation purposes, rather than maintaining an awareness of critical knowledge demands on an ongoing basis (Datta et al, 2010). Exceptions include organisations like PRS Legislative Research Agency in New Delhi, which provides research briefs to parliament in a more independent manner.[22]

Within more democratic contexts there are a number of differences between parliamentary democracy and presidential systems that are potentially relevant to how knowledge is demanded – such as differences in rates of change of leadership or regime transitions and the corresponding roles ascribed to key players in these transitions. Understanding these dimensions may be critical to obtaining a fuller picture of the power dynamics at play in the demand and supply of knowledge during the electoral process. First, parliamentary systems tend to be less stable, owing to a greater rotation of leadership. Second, presidential systems involve a greater degree of reshuffling or breakdown during tenure changes, compared with smoother leadership transitions noted in parliamentary systems. Therefore, the provision of evidence during a crisis in a parliamentary system would be handled differently from the provision of evidence during a crisis in a presidential system (Carden, 2009). For instance, the presidential system in Mexico allows a significant cadre of technocratic actors that exist outside of the civil service to participate in government policymaking (in contrast to a parliamentary system such as the UK where the technocratic function of the state is undertaken by the civil service). This diverse platform of expert knowledge in Mexico is networked through the National Science and Technology Council (NSTC) with a mandate outside legislative government functions to provide broad evidence-based input to policy matters and maintain the stability of the system (Camp, 2007). Those designing a policy intervention during a government crisis in this context would therefore do well to look first at entry points into the NSTC. In a context where parliamentary procedures hold sway, persons and specialist teams in the legislature would need to be examined.

By contrast, more autocratic contexts involve a wider variety of 'electoral processes' such as succession by birthright, or forced or annexed seizure. Each of these will have different implications for the power relations at play in the knowledge–policy interface. Little systematic theoretical or empirical work has been done in this area to date, however. The usual assumption is to consider such systems 'closed' and consequently to list a series of negative factors affecting the use of knowledge. However, electoral moments in autocracies can reveal a variety of entry-points for evidence-based policy influencing. The difference between an informal designation process (Viet Nam) and a dual system where birthright and elected leaders share control (Morocco), for instance, is manifest in the degree of regulation and openness. In the former case, leaders are chosen within ruling elites without any degree of competition from alternative views or platforms. In the latter, there is more regulation of the executive as a result of co-dependence between a monarch with notable executive powers and a head of government with both executive and legislative powers. Yet in Viet Nam, the well-documented appetite for evidence-based policy has grown since the *doi moi* reforms in 1986, and has since been driven forward through the internal appointment of an economic and social 'moderniser' as general secretary (Nachiappan et al, 2010). Similarly, the promotion of debate and reform in the scientific research and tertiary education system in Morocco was enriched in the changeover from King Hassan II to King Mohammed VI in 1999 (Khrouz et al, 2003, cited in Rached and Craissati, 2003). This comparison demonstrates the usefulness of systematically clarifying the varying processes and horizons of 'electoral' processes in autocracies in order to appreciate the power relations and entry/veto points that influence the bridging of research into policy and vice versa.

In more fragile states, the instigation of a transition government provides particular opportunities to promote channels that enhance the supply and demand of knowledge in policy processes. However, the perception of knowledge partiality at such moments can also be detrimental to security (see Box 4.4). For example, during recent elections, the Zimbabwe Electoral Commission announced that funding for an election poll was unavailable and that, even if donor funding were to come forward, it would be treated with suspicion (*New African*, 2010). This suggests that an awareness of both the benefits and the risks of a particular knowledge promotion strategy are required – particularly in fragile contexts.

To this end, actors undertaking such strategies would do well to undertake an intensive situational analysis and adopt a 'do no harm' approach when attempting to invigorate knowledge–policy linkages. In the case of Zimbabwe, DFID's knowledge support strategy has largely consisted of technical assistance and policy support in the redesigning of ministries, with an eye toward donor re-engagement eventually based on the Hague governance principles, which are designed to guide international interactions with Zimbabwe.[23]

Informal politics

Questions this section will help you answer:
- Are relationships based on personal links a key feature of the political system? Are they based on wider social structures or on personal patronage?
- How do informal relations permeate government structures – such as the legislature or the executive? What are the implications?
- How are different types of knowledge used in informal politics?
- What are the implications for whose knowledge is recognised as a legitimate basis for policymaking?

The capture of the policy agenda by certain powerful groups while others are excluded is a feature of representative democracy that is difficult to change, even in established democratic legislative bodies, such as the British House of Commons (Rodgers, 1993). Indeed, the role the 'old boy' network plays in politics has been well documented in Britain, Japan and the US.[24] For instance, 'gender' can be considered a type of informal category that has an effect on whose knowledge is taken into account in decision making. The formal system of representative democracy has been defined and accepted as 'male space' for centuries, both in Europe and in most other societies around the world (Rodgers, 1993). While the politics of gender representation is likely to be a cross-cutting issue in other types of polities, the point is to note the intransigence of social systems despite significant restraints on power and political participation.

It is also important to examine the interaction of informal politics at the knowledge–policy interface in relation to different layers of governance. Devas (1999) presents a framework of variables related to personal actor interests at the levels of municipality, development authority and public utilities/state municipal service.[25] Taking the well-known example of municipal-level participatory budgeting processes in Brazil, the author points out that, while participatory knowledge has played a strong role in feeding into local policy decision-making processes in a number of cities, public involvement in final decision making has still been minimal, with consultation opportunities limited to a minority portion of the budget (5%) (Souza, 2001; Devas, 2002). In addition, local councillors in

Belo Horizonte had to be 'bribed' with personal allocation powers to accept the budgeting system. Although the Porto Alegre system is considered less clientelist, it also is dependent on the personal interests of particular mayors and officials.

However, this is not to say that citizen participatory knowledge – or other knowledge types for that matter – has no grip over informal processes. The presence of 'vote banks' in India, for instance, although often considered inimical to democratic processes, can often allow for a mechanism that can at times work in favour of poor people.[26] Indeed, such systems can deliver at least *some* public goods and explain why voter turnout in poorer areas is often higher than in middle-class areas (Devas, 2000). These processes do also interact with further informal processes at the development authority or state municipal service level. For instance, development authorities in Bangalore can (and do) redevelop land unaccountably under 'eminent domain' bylaws, the success of which depends on the level of direct 'vote bank' democracy between slum dwellers and councillors (Benjamin, 2000). In essence, a type of vote bargaining with local or ward councillors operates at the interface of formal and informal politics and can be considered part and parcel of a 'porous democracy' (Benjamin and Bhuvaneswari, 2001). In this sense, where questions of extreme poverty and inequalities are concerned, it may be productive to expand definitions of democratic policymaking and more fully interrogate the multilayered dimensions of 'informal politics'.

In more autocratic polities, the particular role that informal politics plays in absorbing, rejecting or shaping knowledge–policy linkages is understudied. We might infer that high regulation, constrained competition and limited legislative powers can open the space for informal clientelist influences; but the defining characteristic for autocracies is that, owing to higher forms of regulation, the nexus of informal power is based near the top of the political hierarchy. Informal networks, *guanxi wang*, in China suggest that informal politics plays a significant role in bureaucratic processes. This is illustrated for example by the passage of a 'secret revolution' at the Chinese 13th Party Congress so as to retain the helmsmanship of Secretary Zhao Ziyang. This means that promoting the demand or focusing the supply of particular forms of knowledge at these levels and autocratic processes may enhance the extent to which policymakers take up and use evidence. Democratic contexts, by contrast, may require an examination of deeper social institutions and structures, as informal political power interests tend to be more diffuse.

Informal politics in fragile contexts are less structured and constrained by formal accountability mechanisms or personalistic regimes. More than elsewhere, accountability takes the form of redistribution or generosity at the cost of the public purse (Chabal and Doloz, 1999), otherwise known as 'pork-barrel politics'. There is a common assumption that such patrimonial or neo-patrimonial systems (officials using public goods and resources to secure support of clients) provide a negative incentive for developmental functions. There are, however, also contemporary arguments that discuss the benefits of 'going with the grain' of such governance systems, as well as the importance of several social networks that link power-holders at the top of the political process to those at the bottom (Evans and Rauch, 1999; Kelsall, 2008).

For instance, formal political institutions and processes in Pakistan are on the whole populated by the socioeconomic elite. However, Pakistan has a fairly representative *informal* culture, which accommodates a wide range of competing interests. While disadvantaged people are often not in a position to alter their status significantly, they have considerable ability to manipulate events to ensure high-level members of state institutions address their interests. This can be done because of the social mechanisms of patron–client ties, which may be in the form of kin relations, political party affiliations, *quam* associations or religious brotherhoods (Lyon, 2004). Understanding and catering for these deeply embedded state–civil society relationships, informal as they are, is critical in designing and implementing appropriate policy processes. Knowing that much of the flow of knowledge to policy is justified on this basis helps actors understand and access entry points to raise a given agenda. This said, there are two important implications for the development of a knowledge–policy interface strategy: first, the identification of critical informal power arrangements in such contexts is likely to demand supplementary resources in the form of additional power-mapping activities; and second, accessing such networks and influencing may itself be a time- and resource-intensive exercise – albeit one that needs to have its usefulness balanced with ethical challenges of perpetuating unequal access and control of knowledge.

External forces

> **Questions this section will help you answer:**
> - To what extent is the issue under discussion affected by international agreements, either multilateral or bilateral?
> - How do these agreements influence what is and is not considered for policy development? To what extent do national ideologies contrast with international agreements, and with what effect?
> - If external forces are influential, does this mean having to rely on external organisations to provide and analyse the evidence? What are the implications for local evidence providers?

As humanitarianism and long-term development practice moves on into the 21st century, transnational approaches and influences are becoming more vibrant and complex (Keck and Sikkink, 1998). The Paris Declaration and the International Aid Transparency initiative, for example, are both symptomatic of a larger conflagration of non-national knowledge and policy processes. In this mix, Southern actors are increasingly amplifying, widening and consolidating their voices. Nyamugasira (1998) notes that non-governmental actors in the South are taking over the 'hardware' of development (mechanical or structural developments, maintenance functions) while encouraging their Northern counterparts to take over the 'software' (campaigning, advocacy, development and maintenance of knowledge interactions and flows), an action the latter engage in to fulfil and maintain legitimacy in their work (van Rooy, 1994, cited in Chapman, 1999; Bryer and Magrath, 1999). Indeed, policy discussions are increasingly between equals and are adjusted beyond simple funding relationships (Batliwala, 2002).

In a similar vein, in terms of knowledge generation processes, while donor support[27] for indigenous research capacity building is low overall, donors such as the Swedish International Development Cooperation Agency, the International Development Research Centre and DFID are increasingly including Southern research capacity building as part of their portfolio (Fisher and Holland, 2003; Jones and Young, 2007). However, donors are often unrealistic in assuming that lack of information is the most important or immediate constraint to policy improvement. This is not necessarily the case; absorbing and combining international knowledge with local specific knowledge often presents more of a challenge than knowledge generation and access to knowledge – but has potentially significant payoffs. For instance, the complex transnational cases of Women in the Informal Economy Globalizing and Organizing and Slum/Shack Dwellers International reveal that not only can grassroots movements mobilise internationally, but they can also change policies while keeping a locus of power through supportive federations of national NGOs.

Related to the above is the contested issue of the 'piper calling the tune'. Many authors are vocal on this topic: research and research communication funding is seen as inhibiting legitimacy, autonomy, efficiency and downward accountability by donors who expect considerable attention and respect to be paid upward to them (Edwards and Hulme, 1992, 1995). Hudson (2002) problematises this argument, however, by outlining that funding received from one department in a major funding agency may go into advocacy work that attempts to restructure another – a case of 'the larger the building, the more cracks'. Indeed, Anderson (2000), in his extensive survey of Oxfam International, finds no significant correlation between government funding and its effect on constraining advocacy expenditures. Other authors declare it is more the *content* of donor funding than its relative *proportion* that is important in transnational advocacy work (Minear, 1987). Furthermore, whether it be a bilateral agency or an international NGO, respective country offices often retain considerable veto power in terms of responding to upstream or 'top-down' agendas.

Similarly, external forces – in the form of universal precedents – may influence the knowledge–policy agenda by adjusting understandings (rather than volumes) of 'knowledge' – provided the political context is such that it allows for the expression of popular alternatives. The Bolivian water privatisation project, for instance, promoted by the International Monetary Fund but later overturned by mass civil society 'Cochabamba' protests, was driven partially by a reconceptualisation of the agenda as one based not on 'anti-privatisation' as such but on the universal right to water access. This was made possible because of minimal and unclear national legislation on water access and rights that could confront extra-national discourses developed from international rights principles (Nelson, 2003).

In more autocratic contexts, however, donors promoting improved linkages between knowledge and policy may face challenges of legitimacy and coordination.

This is not to suggest that all 'autocratic contexts' face similar challenges – some face hurdles in funding magnitude as well as content; others struggle mostly with content issues; many face both to varying degrees. In the Middle East and North Africa, for instance, a protective culture exists in terms of data access and collection, and there is still a lack of effective models for evidence-based policymaking. Contradicting official government positions can lead to lack of access to funding, limited promotions and lost career opportunities. Indeed, many independent social research organisations are seen as adversaries rather than collaborators with the government (Rached and Craissati, 2003). By contrast, in Viet Nam, donor-funded initiatives act to support research capacity in various policy fields, although funding is limited to a select number of research organisations, including regional universities and research bodies based in ministries. While support tends to remain *ad hoc* and there is a lack of comprehensive civil society engagement that determines policy processes or content, donors do work to support improved research in 'new areas', such as gender (Sabharwal and Thien Huong, 2005).

The key point to draw on here is that the roles of external forces often go way beyond the basic supply of funding to create a knowledge base. Fruitful transnational advocacy initiatives have drawn their legitimacy from the organisation of networks and federations, as well as the filtering of knowledge through universal principles. Indeed, magnitude of funding is not necessarily a critical factor in determining the development or use of knowledge in policy discussions: it is just as much the content attached to the funding that has critical implications.

In considering fragile or security-focused states, note that minimal state structures bring international pressures, think-tanks, donors and NGOs to the fore, each with their own impact on the supply and demand of knowledge. In Bosnia-Herzegovina, for instance, the most important facilitating factor in the promotion of evidence-based policymaking has been the country's participation in plans to join the European Union (Struyk et al, 2007). It is suggested that 'negotiations pressure' may be having similar positive effects on the use of evidence-based policymaking elsewhere in the Western Balkans (Struyk et al, 2007). International think-tanks have become an increasingly important actor in post-conflict environments, with their aim of influencing the course of international politics related to interventions and peace building. They shape international views of post-conflict societies in which they operate and critique policy options adopted by the international community. Their impact is thus 'ideational' rather than direct (de Guevara, 2007).

Finally, it is interesting to consider not only the obvious role of donors in such contexts, such as influencing the policymaking agenda and promoting capacity building for knowledge-based methods, but also the different types of NGOs present and their relative legitimacy. Building Resources Across Communities (BRAC, formerly the Bangladesh Rural Advancement Committee), for instance, has worked on a variety of direct programmes in Afghanistan, but has also taken steps to respond to the lack of knowledge supply services in the country by constructing a scaled-up research unit. This supports BRAC and others in their enquiries and was generated through BRAC's very particular entry points – trading links, religious ties, a similar conflict history and reduced strategic interests (Mushtaque et al, 2006).

Capacity to absorb change

Questions this section will help you answer:
- During moments of significant regime change, are policymaking processes transparent? Is it relatively easy to see who is taking decisions and at what points in the process knowledge is likely to be needed/demanded?
- What support is given to policy processes in terms of bridging the gap between what knowledge is needed and what is available?
- What key issues need to be taken into account to identify windows of opportunity, where improving access to knowledge will lead to better policymaking?
- Do policymakers have the resources and political security to interact widely with a variety of organisations that provide knowledge? If not, whom do they rely on and what are the implications of this in terms of the breadth and depth of knowledge they are able to access?
- Are there channels that facilitate interaction between CSOs and policymakers and are they in keeping with CSO capacity levels?

During moments of political change, a state's capacity to absorb change and manage the knowledge–policy interface will vary between more consolidated democracies and more autocratic contexts (see Table 3.3). For instance, this chapter has already discussed one important implication for consolidating African democracies, that is, increased demand-side competition in relation to policy research requests, in part because of the expansion and solidification of legislative bodies that request evidence to inform their executives. If we apply a capacity lens to this example (comparing influence–network approaches and command–hierarchy approaches – Table 3.3), we can note that this growth in demand has also been supported through the enhanced utilisation and growth in the capacities of research organisations, such as the African Capacity Building Foundation, which is currently supporting policy research units within government legislative wings in order to advance the quality of policy debates and outcomes (Datta and Jones, 2011). This suggests that, although capacity constraint issues may still be important, the critical issue for donors operating in democracies is likely to be negotiating the balance of actors operating in the knowledge–policy interface through an 'influence–network' strategy. In other words, donors looking to build capacity to absorb change in more democratic contexts would do better to focus on 'convening capacity', political skills, linkages and trust – rather than emphasising hierarchical relations and/or taking the lead in framing policy.

Contrastingly, the very structure of more autocratic contexts in times of rapid change implies there may be centralised demand for knowledge among policymakers, albeit often directed towards semi-independent bodies. A further issue is the reduced capacity of policymakers to interact with research and grassroots communities owing to a lack of technical skills and resources. In highly regulated structures, then, building capacity at the knowledge–policy interface through command–hierarchy approaches is best done by working with the grain of typical modes of state or public action (Table 3.3). This may entail thinking through the dynamics of the knowledge–policy interface where policy is framed and implemented in a top-down and unified way, or where the critical resources are not convening capacity or linkages but rather the ability to manage hierarchical organisations effectively, with accountability mechanisms that may be more formal than in more democratic contexts.

Ultimately, capacity to absorb change will vary according to where on the J-curve a political context is situated, as well as whether it is to the left or right of the base of the curve (the left tends towards a more restrictive or closed political context, while the right tends towards openness and participation). If it is to the left, knowledge policy strategies would do best to align with command–hierarchy approaches; if to the right, influence–network approaches. For command–hierarchy approaches, capacity-building efforts are best focused on organisational effectiveness of state bodies and upward/downward types of accountability. For influence–network approaches, resources to develop state capacity are best invested in lateral accountability and convening/participatory measures. For an institution looking to develop a policy process or to advise on the use and development of information, these differences are critical, as they will determine which actors to consult, which knowledge translation processes to follow and which types of knowledge are most relevant to the political context.

A time dimension also needs to be considered here. Newly formed democratic polities are likely to have weaker institutions and a less organised civil society. A comparative analysis of CIVICUS Civil Society Indexes across post-communist Europe shows continued strong civil inertia and disillusionment owing to forced participation in communist regimes. This lack of formal civil mobilisation has left the political space available for informal mechanisms to play a significant role in the exchange of evidence-based policy processes (Fioramonti and Heinrich, 2007). Consequently, to achieve their goals, knowledge production and use strategies need to be aware of the lasting effects of political regimes and/or trajectories.

Unlike stable democracies or autocracies, fragile or post-conflict states (situated in the 'well' or base of the J-curve) are characterised by their *incapacity* to absorb change – which has particular implications for the role of knowledge in policy processes (see Box 2.4).

Box 2.4: Challenges facing evidence-informed policy change in a fragile state context: lessons from Nepal

Recent examples of forest management policy discussion in Nepal reveal that, despite opportunities for research-based policymaking since the peace agreement in 2006, policy processes tend to be guided more by the contingencies of transitional politics, which privilege political muscle over knowledge power.

For instance, as part of work on the 12th Three-year Development Plan, the National Planning Commission asked the Ministry of Forests and Soil Conservation to prepare an approach paper. Both agencies failed to provide clear direction, however, and the paper ended up involving just a few officials inside the ministry. Similarly, permits for hotels to operate in Chitwan National Park became a contentious policy issue in 2009, with the ministry favouring extension and local communities citing negative environmental impacts. Under pressure from the hoteliers and powerful business organisations, the government ultimately went for extension. Later that year, the government declared three new protected areas a few days before the Copenhagen Summit to draw global attention to its commitment to mitigating climate change. The declaration was purely political. Strong civil society opposition, also not based on evidence, finally led the Prime Minister to cancel one of the three.

Five key patterns emerge from these cases underscoring the challenges facing evidence-informed decision making in a fragile state context:

- Limited space for public reasoning: patronage networks and multiple politico-cultural groups result in a contested notion of 'public' and 'national' and lack of common ground for negotiation.
- Weak accountability: policymakers do not have to produce a convincing rationale for their decisions, and in fact may structurally avoid research and evidence.
- Limited civil society use of evidence: CSOs capitalise on unstable politics in favour of their own interests, without referring to any evidence.
- High donor influence: donors see political transition as a way to mobilise resources to influence policymakers on 'democratic' policies, rather than being guided by rigorous evidence.
- A discourse of urgency: researchers compete to produce relevant evidence in sufficient time to influence a specific decision. In the process, they risk compromising the robustness of their findings.

Source: Paudel et al (2010)

Conclusion

This chapter has provided a succinct framework readers can use to answer some of the core theoretical and practical questions about knowledge–policy linkages in different contexts. By systematically considering the basic constituents of political contexts, we have provided an approach to identify the broad range of potential impacts they may have on knowledge–policy dynamics. Each context is composed of formal political structures, including restraints on power (executive, legislative); elections; and degrees of regulated and competitive political participation that create incentives for decision makers attempting to retain power. However, each context also demonstrates different types of informal relations; varying degrees of external influences (donors, international conventions, international NGOs); and, to a lesser degree, specific forms of decentralisation, which once again filter the incentives for knowledge use and production. The framework in Table 2.2 synthesises these characteristics and implications and will be a useful starting point for both analysis and practice.

Four key points emerge from this chapter. First and foremost, it should be clear that using 'lack of political will' to explain away an inert or unsuccessful policymaking opportunity is a tired and redundant rationalisation of complex yet understandable processes. Readers should now be comfortable in asserting that the 'political will' of any actor depends on the multiple push and pull factors playing on their individual choice horizons, and should be able to begin to disentangle them.

Second, consolidated democracies, autocracies and fragile state contexts all have particular characteristics that influence the links between knowledge and policy. For example, in considering the effect of external forces, readers can analyse how political context determines the extent of the protective culture around access to knowledge and its accumulation, how administrations respond to the transfer of knowledge from outside sources and how they react to international pressure and ideational influencing. Being familiar with these dimensions will not tell you precisely what to do to connect the dots between knowledge and policy for a particular project, but it will help answer the 'why' questions: Why develop this particular strategy for improving the knowledge–policy interface? Why intervene now?

Third, within these different political contexts are a number of sub-variables that will naturally vary from state to state. Restraints on power in more democratically consolidated contexts will vary by presidential or parliamentary system; in more autocratic contexts, the roles of 'selectorates', military designations and hostile disenfranchised legislatures come to the fore, while in fragile or security-affected states, the issue may be a total lack of restraint on domestic political power dynamics. Again, understanding these currents and investigating them in relation to a specific project will help readers nuance their overarching strategy for linking knowledge to policy.

Finally, while this initial framework helps develop a more systematic analysis of the knowledge–policy interface within certain political contexts, some important decisions still remain in hands of the analyst or practitioner. These concern issues of sequencing and prioritisation of opportunities for intervention (relating these to their potential impact given the strengths and weaknesses of the different institutions) and of the type of monitoring and evaluation procedures that need to be set in place to ensure that progress is thoughtfully assessed. Naturally, each of these issues is highly context-specific, and each needs to be addressed by an actor or network while being set within a broad and innovative framework that captures the risks and complexity of policy programming. There is a range of toolkits that break down these individual issues,[28] but they can overlap confusingly. The rest of this book helps the reader develop an appropriate sequence for analysis by focusing on the parts played by different actors, the types of knowledge needed to make effective policy and the roles of knowledge intermediaries.

Notes

[1] See, for example, Jasanoff (2005); Nutley et al (2007); Pielke (2007); Head (2010).

[2] The Freedom House dataset demonstrates degrees of civil and political rights, whereas the Polity IV dataset examines a broader array of characteristics based on how they relate to particular regime types.

[3] Furthermore, broader research on political contexts has tended to privilege certain levels of analysis, such as the local, national or regional, while omitting the global (Hickey, 2005).

[4] The DoC is one of many major analytical frameworks, see Table 2.1 and Grindle and Thomas (1990).

[5] www.freedomhouse.org

[6] www.systemicpeace.org/polity/polity4.htm

[7] Overemphasis on such basic typology approaches also has the potential to conflate absence of state functions with anarchy while promoting simplistic views of nation-statism (Hagmann and Hoehne, 2008).

[8] In capturing good practice and addressing ongoing challenges, DFID published a How To Note on political economy analysis that provided additional thought, specifically on the myriad processes behind political decisions.

[9] This was designed in part by Leftwich (2006).

[10] The 'voice and accountability' component, for instance, incorporates aspects such as the Press Freedom Index, military presence in politics and domestic/international travel restrictions, among many other dimensions and indices.

[11] The notion of a 'consolidated democracy' is contested, but such an entity is often viewed as a state that has stabilised and is highly unlikely to lapse into an authoritarian system given the presence of strong institutions and the rule of law, making it 'the only game in town' (Linz and Stepan, 1996). A consolidated democracy can be further defined as what a more autocratic system is not: namely, relatively unrestricted political participation, clearly defined and transparent rules

for changes in leadership, numerous checks and balances across state bodies and a variety of vibrant civil society actors.

[12] This definition draws on the Polity IV framework but recognises the emphasis on freedom of association in the Freedom House analysis, as well as the special cases that are found where the political context is particularly fragile.

[13] For instance, a convincing study has shown that federal democracies are likely to disburse 31% more income than unitary 'authoritarian regimes' – with corresponding implications for differential transfers and demands for knowledge (Landry, 2008).

[14] 'De-concentration' involves a transfer of responsibilities to government 'field staff', such as local officials, while power is still located in the central government. Delegation refers to a transfer of responsibilities to semi-autonomous organisations in 'the field' that are still closely linked to the central state bureaucracy. Transfer of functions refers to situations where communal functions are transferred to private or non-governmental institutions. Devolution refers to the transfer of tasks and resources as well as decision-making power from central to lower-level authorities that are democratically elected (Cheema and Rondinelli, 1983).

[15] This distinction is based on that presented in the Polity IV framework.

[16] Marshall and Cole (2009) utilise their own definition of 'anocracies' here, but suffice it to say that this refers to states in fragile or unstable positions.

[17] Consolidating democracies in Africa (based on Polity IV and Freedom House criteria) are Benin, Botswana, Cape Verde, Ghana, Lesotho, Mali, Mauritius, Namibia, São Tomé and Príncipe, Senegal and South Africa (Siegle, 2007).

[18] www.civicus.org/csi

[19] Instead, both events undermined public confidence in the credibility of evidence-based policymaking. In the former case, this resulted in tangible effects, such as the increased isolation of the Spongiform Encephalopathy Advisory Committee from offering alternatives in subsequent debates (Millstone and van Zwanenberg, 2007).

[20] The NCWCD undertook a biodiversity management programme from 1986 to 2002 (Faizi, 2002).

[21] A successful programme to reduce domestic violence in Uzbekistan, for example, focused evidence not so much on shifting the discourse regarding the 'traditional Uzbek family' but rather on perceptions of human rights among men in the armed forces military schools, eventually scaling this approach up into a national education programme (Ismoilov, 2004).

[22] PRS Legislative Research provides briefs while parliament is in session and prepares briefs on likely topics when it is not. It is maintained by external funding sources, so is independent from the 40 political parties in parliament.

[23] DFID's work in Zimbabwe, parliamentary notes (www.publications.parliament.uk). The Hague Principles focus on Internationally agreed criteria for engagement with Zimbabwe, and include full and equal access to humanitarian assistance, commitment to macro-economic stabilisation, and commitments to timely and observed elections – among other criteria.

[24] See, respectively, J. Scott (1982); Schaede (1995); Gamba and Kleiner (2001).

[25] The original framework has 12 categories, including aspects relating to the power capabilities of rich/middle-income households and low-income households, as well as traditional authorities' practices (for example chieftainships).

[26] A 'vote bank' is a portion of the citizenry that votes consistently and predictably in favour of a particular party or candidate.

[27] The role of international NGOs also constitutes a significant presence in such networks (see Chapter Three for details on the role implications of these actors themselves).

[28] Start and Hovland (2004); Hovland (2005); Nash et al (2006); Ramalingam (2006); Sutcliffe and Court (2006); Walker and Jones (2010).

THREE

Engaging actors

The growing literature on the links between knowledge, policy and power reflects a diversity of approaches to understanding the role of different actors.[1] Having shown how political context affects the relationships between knowledge and policy, this chapter delves deeper to outline the relationships between people (as individuals or in organisations) and their knowledge. It looks at the various factors influencing how different actors seek out, filter, interpret and ultimately use knowledge in policy and the implications this has for how they engage with the policymaking process. Its purpose is to help readers develop a strategy to analyse and engage with the wide variety of actors who operate at the knowledge–policy interface.

> **By the end of this chapter, readers will be able to answer the following questions:**
> - What shapes how different actors behave at the knowledge–policy interface?
>   » Do actors always act in their own self-interest, or are there other issues to consider?
>   » What role do values and beliefs play in how knowledge is used in policy?
>   » Different actors have different degrees of credibility when it comes to knowledge for policy – what influences this, and what influence does this have?
> - What effects do these factors have on the openness and transparency with which different actors share knowledge?
> - What are the implications for less powerful or more fragmented voices?

This chapter first synthesises prevailing conceptions of actors' behaviour in the policy arena, then develops a simple tripartite framework that distinguishes between actors' interests, their values and beliefs, and their credibility. Examining the roots of each of the three dimensions enables us to analyse the implications for how knowledge is used in policy, and to develop practical pointers to strengthen the quality of interaction between different actors at the knowledge–policy interface.

Understanding different actors' behaviour at the knowledge–policy interface

Early work on the knowledge–policy interface drew on a 'knowledge-driven' model of the policy process and considered the role of relatively few actors (Neilson, 2001a). Empirical and theoretical work viewed policymakers as 'problem solvers', drawing on knowledge to guide and improve policy. While

Weiss (1979) took a more nuanced view of research–policy links with her notion of enlightenment, in practice bureaucrats and staff in executive agencies were generally cast as neutral facilitators of evidence-based policymaking, working through applied reason and logic irrespective of influence from political context, intermediary knowledge brokers or the type of knowledge being used. They were seen as providing objective, apolitical inputs into different stages of decision making, which were instrumental to meeting the pre-set goals of policy.

Subsequent work challenged the narrow and linear focus of this model and correspondingly widened the field of actors considered (Court et al, 2005). Policymaking was recognised as a process of pragmatic decisions taken in uncertainty, with bureaucrats unable to assess every option or systematically weigh every source of information. This body of work recognised that it was now impossible to take the uptake of knowledge for granted because it occurred in a patchy and opportunistic manner, subject to the influence of organised strategies. Policy processes were seen as more plural and conditional, with a variety of actors influencing the outcomes and the knowledge used. This analysis encouraged a wider view of the possible producers of knowledge and intermediaries, including, for example, civil society organisations (CSOs), grassroots movements, political parties, the private sector, donors, consultants and extension agents.

However, this second paradigm failed to address the politics and power underlying the process. It still presumed that knowledge itself was relatively neutral; little attention was paid to knowledge content, and assumptions were made about the overriding usefulness of incorporating knowledge into policy. For example, work on innovation systems argued the importance of both the supply and the demand of knowledge and the need for intermediaries and regulatory framework conditions (Rath and Barnett, 2006), but retained an assumption that innovation and the uptake of knowledge would generally be 'good' – that promoting such innovation would lead to social and economic benefits (Jones et al, 2009a). What this missed was the fact that actors take part in policy processes for a wide variety of reasons – and probably quite rarely in order to 'link knowledge and policy' (at least not primarily).

A third generation of approaches has taken an increasingly political perspective on the process, seeing knowledge production and use as entwined with, and inseparable from, power structures and dynamics. Knowledge often serves to add legitimacy to political action after the decision, and what counts as 'legitimate knowledge' is itself determined politically (Autes, 2007). This means that when analysing the role of actors at the knowledge–policy interface, the politics of interaction are important determinants of how knowledge is used. The concept of 'discourse' is particularly relevant here. Foucault defined discourse as 'systems of thoughts composed of ideas, attitudes, courses of action, beliefs and practices that systematically construct the subjects and the worlds of which they speak' (Lessa, 2006, p 285), highlighting the interconnectedness of knowledge and power in policymaking. Discursive structures (for example concepts, metaphors, linguistic codes, rules of logic) are often taken for granted, but they contain cognitive and normative elements that determine what actors can understand and articulate, and hence which ideas they are likely to adopt (Campbell, 2002). For instance, referring to a group that rejects formal authority as 'terrorists' rather than 'freedom fighters' can shape such a group's access to resources and legitimacy. The structures themselves are created, adapted and given meaning by the interactive processes of communication and policy formulation that serve to generate and disseminate these ideas (Schmidt and Radaelli, 2004). Understanding discourse enriches our understanding of the ways actors affect, and are affected by, wider structures as they deal with knowledge in the policy process.

Analysing actors' behaviour: the interests, values and credibility framework

Synthesising across these approaches, we propose a tripartite framework that enables a rich and practical analysis of the role of actors at the knowledge–policy interface. First, acknowledging that actors are political means that we need to understand their **interests** – what motivates them to engage with the process of policymaking around a particular issue. Second, the knowledge that actors deem as fit for policymaking is shaped by what they believe to be important about an issue, which is in turn influenced by why they value it. This means that we need to analyse how actors' **values and beliefs** affect what they consider to be valid knowledge. Finally, whether or not particular sources of knowledge are used in policymaking depends on power dynamics between actors and the extent to which they are considered to have the more powerful argument or reasoning. In other words, understanding an actor's **credibility** will give important clues as to their role at the knowledge–policy interface.

In this section we discuss each factor in turn, examining how it affects the way knowledge is used, communicated and brokered, and produced and codified. Table 3.1 summarises the main aspects of the framework, which are discussed in more detail in the rest of the chapter.

Actors' interests

Broadly speaking, there are four different approaches to studying the effects of actors' interests on their behaviour. The first focuses on the role of the individual and includes approaches such as rational choice theory, which emphasises actors' unchanging preferences and how they shape their micro-level decision making (Niskanen, 1973). This school of thought assumes that the driving force for policy and action is the rational pursuit of self-interest and explores how actors use the power (economic, political, socio-cultural) at their disposal to maximise these interests (Hunter, 1997). Tools for 'stakeholder analysis', drawing on schools of thought such as political economy analysis and game theory, have been used for decades by donors such as the World Bank (Booth and Golooba-Mutebi, 2009). These traditionally focus on the interests and influence of key actors and

Table 3.1: Analysing actors' behaviour at the knowledge–policy interface: the interests, values, beliefs and credibility framework

Dimension	Implications for actors' behaviour at the knowledge– policy interface		
	Using knowledge	**Brokering and communicating knowledge**	**Producing and codifying knowledge**
Interests	Powerful actors can use knowledge as 'ammunition' to reinforce the interests of those with the most to win or lose. They often do this to remain in power, justify their cause after the fact or ensure that issues simply do not make it through the policy process (formally or informally). Strong actor interests often give rise to risk aversion in policymaking and can dampen the use of professional expertise and independent intermediaries in policymaking.	Knowledge sharing can be increased if the cost of doing so is outweighed by the benefits of greater influence, but not if the knowledge is held by decision-making elites (which can result in decisions being 'closed'). The extent of actors' interests in media organisations can affect how messages are transmitted to citizens and in turn citizen involvement in policymaking. CSOs can play an important role in bringing a range of voices to the table, but have their own interests that affect how they engage.	Actor interests can be a strong driver of the contours of knowledge production – research priorities, data generation and evidence from citizens and practice tend to reflect interests of powerful actors such as donors, national governments and the private sector. Career incentives are particularly important in shaping research, which often aligns poorly with policy agendas.
Values and beliefs	Values and beliefs are reflected in policies via political goals and choices, which in turn define what knowledge is sought and used (in extreme cases strongly held values may insulate against the search for new knowledge). Values help shape interests and the 'rules of the game', and may sometimes lead to actors using knowledge to act against their individual or group interests.	Actors will often frame arguments around values and beliefs to build key constituencies or mobilise action on an issue, particularly using the concept of 'unfairness'. How knowledge is communicated will reflect what is deemed to be unfair and to whom. Coalitions and networks tend to form around shared values and belief systems that are often strong enough to overcome the competitive self-interest of individual groups. Actors that frame issues for the public (for example think-tanks) can play an important role in broadening the knowledge communicated in policy.	While there is a widespread belief that generating knowledge is an intrinsically valuable activity, actors with strongly held beliefs can work to avoid having those beliefs questioned by arguing against contradictory knowledge.

Dimension	Implications for actors' behaviour at the knowledge– policy interface		
	Using knowledge	**Brokering and communicating knowledge**	**Producing and codifying knowledge**
Credibility	How decision makers define who is a credible 'expert' will have a strong effect on what knowledge is used in policymaking on any issue. Credibility is stronger if an actor is part of a like-minded group (formal or informal), although styles of decision-making processes (open or closed) will affect who is consulted and on what. Close relationships can develop between credible institutions and the political process; if these become institutionalised, they can hinder the use of alternative sources of knowledge.	How credibility is defined will influence what knowledge is communicated and how it is received, particularly when new policy issues arise for which there is no established roster of 'experts'. Knowledge networks can play a powerful role in bolstering the credibility of their individual members. Actors defined as credible can play a powerful role in deciding what knowledge is communicated, particularly where an issue is complex or has a highly technical language that limits the involvement of others.	How different actors generate knowledge will affect whether they are viewed as credible and whether the knowledge is seen as legitimate in policymaking. An emphasis on methodological rigour may privilege scientific knowledge over lived experience and result in policy being research-driven rather than reflecting citizen wants and needs.

have been used to understand the opportunities and constraints in promoting or implementing particular reforms, among other purposes.

The second approach – pluralism – places a stronger focus on the role of the group and is concerned with how individuals' participation in a particular group – for example a consumer society – shapes their interests. Pluralists examine how multiple and diverse groups in society negotiate the allocation of resources and the formulation of rules and regulations to advance their interests (Mouffe, 1992). They see this process not as a zero-sum game but rather as a process of reaching a democratic equilibrium.

The third approach stems from Marxist theory, which argues that actors have predefined objective interests based on their class. Although individual actors may be unaware of this, ultimately broader socioeconomic structures determine their collective interests. For instance, while women may be socialised to accept and even perpetuate patriarchal social structures and practices, their 'class' interest – what Molyneux (1985) dubs their 'strategic gender interests' – is to transform gender relations to become more egalitarian (ibid).

The final approach is concerned primarily with the role of institutions and how these filter and channel actors' interests (see Box 3.1, as well as Chapter Two). As Steinmo and colleagues (1992, p 9) argue, 'unless something is known about the context, broad assumptions about "self-interested behaviour" are empty'. In other words, how actors form their preferences depends on the particular problem they face rather than being fixed forever, and this shapes not just their strategies but also their goals:

> The institutions that are at the center of historical institutional analyses – from party systems to ... business associations – can shape and constrain [actors'] political strategies in important ways, but are themselves also the outcome (conscious or unintended) of deliberate political strategies, of political conflict, and of choice. (Steinmo et al, 1992, p 10)

Related work in this field approaches structure and agency as complementary, interacting forces (see Giddens, 1984). While structure orders and allows for social practices, actors performing these practices draw on and reproduce (or change) structures (see Chapter Two, Box 2.1). For example, Grindle (2002) shows how social sector reforms in Latin America secured 'against the odds' were born from the interaction of structure and agency: well-organised and highly strategic groups of actors took advantage of opportunities presented by particular moments in decision-making processes in order to find the 'room for manoeuvre' for their preferred changes.

Box 3.1: What are institutions?

The term 'institution' encompasses formal organisations as well as customs and patterns of behaviour and action. By defining who is able to participate in different decision-making processes, shape actors' strategies and influence what actors believe possible and desirable, these rules structure the policy process and the political behaviour of bureaucrats, elected officials and interest groups (Steinmo et al, 1992; Steinmo, 2001). There is also a historical dimension, as historical legacies and established policies and programmes generate political constraints and opportunities, and previously enacted policies impact on future courses of action generating 'path dependency' (Collier and Collier, 1991; Beland, 2005). Formal and informal institutions thus affect which ideas and whose knowledge is used in the policy process, and through what channels, and the degree of openness of various actors to certain sorts of ideas. Factors such as the political rules of conduct (consensual, competitive or conflictual), political governance structures (unitary, federal or consociational) and governance processes (pluralist, corporatist or statist) all set the parameters of what people talk about as well as who talks to whom in the policymaking process (Schmidt and Radaelli, 2004).

Here we take a synthetic view and argue that we need to consider how macro, meso and micro factors shape diverse actors' interests and their incentives at the knowledge–policy interface. As we explain in more detail below, we also consider how these interests are influenced by actors' beliefs and values as well as their credibility at the knowledge–policy interface. These bodies of work have different foci, especially in terms of the relative balance between macro- and micro-level incentives (for a breakdown of the role of institutions in different political contexts, see Chapter Two). However, all approaches are applicable to a range of state and non-state actors, including branches of government, donors, the private sector, civil society, political parties and academia.

Actors' interests: using knowledge

We can begin to understand how policy goals are shaped by analysing which actors are affected by an issue and how knowledge is drawn on as 'ammunition' to reinforce the interests of those with the most to win or lose, with the highest capacity to fight their corner, or with special access to the corridors of power (Weiss, 1977). In these knowledge contests the winners 'create reality' according to their interests and their presentation of the underlying content, principles and reasoning for a policy. It is possible to assess the relative influence of different actors on a particular policy process or decision by analysing their interests going into a negotiation and mapping the final decision in relation to that starting point (Dür, 2008). Actors with strong vested interests often operate with a 'pragmatic and flexible epistemology', using whatever knowledge best justifies their cause after the fact; powerful actors may be able to keep certain issues off the agenda altogether, or block proposed changes that run counter to their interests (for example as per Lukes' (1974) understanding of hidden power).

Understanding actors' interests also helps us to better understand their knowledge use patterns:

- Elected officials are likely to be particularly concerned with the factors keeping them in power or protecting a renewal of their mandate. This means they may take few risks in the policies they propose (to avoid public criticism), or they may be disinclined to advocate for policies that take a long time to bear fruit (in relation to the length of their mandate).
- For politicians, the extent to which proposed policies provide definite, short-term concrete benefits to their constituents or patronage networks is important. However, they may also specify goals broadly in order to allow room for discretion and manoeuvre in the future.
- Recruitment processes for civil servants will shape how they use knowledge: if hiring processes are highly politicised, professional expertise will become less relevant. Instead, civil servants will be encouraged to draw on knowledge sources aligned with the interests of the ruling powers (Olowu, 1999, cited in Hyden et al, 2003).
- The role of interests in the policy process may also help explain instances of ambiguous policy guidance; limited policy coherence in multi-sectoral issues such as natural resource management or environmental preservation may not be so much a matter of weak integration of multiple knowledge sources as a reflection of competing actors' interests in the absence of clear rules for managing trade-offs (Molle, 2008).

As well as determining what knowledge is used, interests shape which intermediaries are involved more actively in policy debates. CSOs are presumed to serve as a bridge between the interests of particular societal groups and the policy process, but policymakers are likely to use their discretion to encourage the participation of CSOs predisposed to support their favoured policy. This means that CSOs whose mission is aligned with favoured political agendas may find it easier to engage in certain policy debates (Stone, 2004, see Box 3.2).

Actors' interests: brokering and communicating knowledge

Tactics as to how to broker knowledge in line with one's interests and how to broker it within the policy process are important. Actors involved at the knowledge–policy interface are more likely to share their knowledge, communicate perspectives and open up decision processes where they can see that the benefits of their influence outweigh the costs of engagement and the potential for their message to be corrupted or used against them. For example, the link between science and policy can be strengthened where researchers are given explicit incentives for openly communicating the results of their work (RIN, 2009); they are much less likely to speak out on an issue or against a particular actor if this may harm their career.

This means that knowledge can be a valuable resource, helping actors build alliances with others, making them aware either of how a current problem affects them or of how a proposed policy/action supports or damages their interests. However, certain actors may want to suppress information on an issue or keep communication in informal channels and among a small group, particularly if their position is unlikely to resonate with the interests of a broader population. This may have the effect of restricting access to a decision-making elite, resulting in the space for policymaking being 'closed' to other stakeholders or effectively 'hidden' from view (if stakeholders are not aware that such decisions are being made).[2] For instance, trade policy has a large and direct effect on private sector interests, and trade policymaking processes have tended to be much more secretive and less accessible to non-state actors, particularly those with fewer established ties and points of access to the ministries involved (Newell and Tussie, 2006).

The degree of openness and access to knowledge is important. Media systems play an integral role in shaping the pool of knowledge considered when policies are developed. Through the media, at least in theory, citizens learn how policies will affect them and provide feedback (in the form of 'public opinion') to government on their policies and programmes (Barker, 2005). Access to information can promote citizens' involvement in the policy process, by making them aware of how issues or decisions affect them and (potentially) how they might exert some influence over them.

Having said this, it is important to understand the environment involved in communicating and knowledge brokering facing intermediary actors. Even where those in charge of media organisations do not have an overt or direct influence on the messages carried, incentives and constraints at various levels can nonetheless militate against providing fair and balanced reporting. Focusing on the US context, Herman and Chomsky (2006) outline how material incentives such as competition for advertising can lead to internal self-censorship.

Chapter Five deals in more depth with the roles of knowledge intermediaries, but it is worth also mentioning here the roles that can be played by CSOs. Over the years, CSOs have seen their role shift gradually from that of service delivery to include policy advocacy, leading to a more prominent presence at the knowledge–policy interface. CSOs can help fill the gap between citizens and the institutions governing their lives (Gaventa, 2003) by representing their particular (often experiential) knowledge and perspectives in the policy process (see Chapter Four). As Selener (1997, p 2) argues:

> The inclusion of direct testimony in the development debate can help to make it less of a monologue and more of a dialogue, as people's testimony begins to require answers and as their voices force the development establishment to be more accountable for their actions.

CSOs can also play a key role in sharing knowledge to make citizens more aware of how policy issues affect them. This can be particularly crucial for marginalised groups that may lack the capacity to do this themselves (Tembo and Wells, 2007).

However, CSOs do not always play this positive role; their interests may be driven by the availability of resources on an issue, narrowing and biasing their role as an intermediary in the policy process. Sundet (2010) argues, for instance, that the rapid growth in Tanzanian civil society has been driven largely by the availability of donor funding. Donors expect CSOs to bolster the power of citizens to make demands on government, but if their agenda has been driven by donor organisations, this risks weakening the power of genuine political and social movements. A Tanzanian pastoralist land rights movement, for example, was encouraged by donor funding to professionalise and projectise activities in a manner that subsequently estranged the leadership from its constituents and diminished the extent to which the organisation effectively represented the interests of the people it was meant to serve (ibid).

Actors' interests: producing and codifying knowledge

Knowledge that informs policy may already exist, be produced independently or be commissioned by powerful policy actors to bolster their interests. Research priorities often reflect government priorities and interests and, in developing countries, those of international donors (see Jones et al, 2009c). It could be argued, for instance, that the focus of many donors on 'fragile states' reflects their need to serve their own national security interests more than the interests of people living in those countries.

In general, research organisations must compete for funding, which means they may shape their research activities to correspond to project or grant proposals. In doing so, they may find their work influenced by donor visions or perceptions of key issues and by prevailing language, concepts and buzzwords (see also Boxes 3.2 and 3.3). That said, researchers also have their own career path; the pressure to publish leads many to engage in stimulating debates on issues that do not align neatly with politicians' agendas and cannot be converted into workable programmes with priorities and specific actions (Kogan, 2005).

The private sector can also play a powerful role in shaping the research agenda by sponsoring research to back up its claims, publishing findings that put it in a good light (Angell, 2000) or threatening to sue those who criticise the evidential basis of their policy advocacy (Rosenstock and Lee, 2002). Promoting ambiguity, disagreement or uncertainty can have similar effects: industry may sponsor research with the direct goal of countering existing scientific opinion, in order to deflect attention from research findings and from the actions that are likely to follow these (ibid). This issue is particularly acute in relation to climate science. The task of modelling future scenarios around such a vast and interdependent system as our global climate is highly complex, and requires interpretation and value judgements about which models 'fit' the data. Generating scientific knowledge relies on honest and open intellectual discussion, and carefully qualified levels of uncertainty, but this fact may be seized on and exploited in political debates to show that the science as a whole is unclear (Jones, 2010).

Meanwhile, a lack of knowledge may be present where there is a 'collective action problem', such that the individual costs outweigh the benefits for any one actor to find out more about an issue, despite the fact that it would be in the collective interests of the group to do so. With many natural resources, the precise structure of the resource and the ways in which different actions affect it may not be well known, affecting its future sustainability. However important collective knowledge of the resource may be, the costs of acquiring it could outweigh the short-term benefits for any single actor (Ostrom, 1990).

Box 3.2: The role of interests in shaping policy knowledge uptake

Established in 2007, the UK Department for International Development's (DFID's) Child and Youth Working Groups aim to promote more coherent civil society–government collaboration on child and youth programming and development policy issues. The groups have had varying degrees of success owing to the differential resonance of their policy advocacy messages with DFID's broader institutional interests. Reflecting on their experience to date in these networks, several non-governmental organisation (NGO) participants were of the view that the key challenge lay not in forging evidence-informed arguments but rather in convincing DFID advisers of the fit between their institutional interests and the networks' social development aims. This was particularly challenging for the Child Working Group; while there was general buy-in about the linkages between youth employment and economic group and between youth exclusion, conflict and state fragility, overlap between child participation and protection goals and DFID's institutional mandate was seen as more indirect and tenuous.

Accordingly, while the Youth Working Group was able to respond to already existing demand within DFID at headquarters and country level, the Child Working Group faced the taller order of trying to promote demand for child-related information among advisers with already complex policy and programme agendas. Given more infrequent and *ad hoc* connections with DFID staff, the latter began to explore pressure-based strategies, such as the tabling of parliamentary questions, in an effort to prompt DFID officials to become more engaged in child-related policy and programming. However, this strategy met with mixed approval from within the group; certain members felt there were no other avenues at the time but others argued that such approaches could create tension and resentment. Indeed, some informants noted that the detailed evidence requested in some of the parliamentary questions (such as the number of dedicated and relevant projects relating to child rights) might have created a sense of burden among already time-pressured advisers.

Source: Key informant interviews for this book

Actors' beliefs and values

Although approaches focused on actors' interests have broad applicability, the specific guidance and nuance they can offer is limited, especially as they tend to be better at explaining persistence rather than change (Booth et al, 2009). Even if an actor does attempt to estimate rationally the costs and benefits of different options for any key decision, this calculation is based on certain assumptions about how the world works, about the important factors in understanding change and about what is of value (Ajzen, 1991). As such, there is growing recognition of the critical role that beliefs and values play in shaping policy decision making.

A **belief** is an idea an actor has about the world – a proposition they hold to be true ('the bridge will support my weight if I walk on it'). Beliefs can be explicit or implicit, actively considered or background assumptions and based on considerable scrutiny (for example scientifically tested knowledge). Psychologists have found that beliefs are influenced by a large number of factors, as people may internalise the beliefs of their peer group or take on ideas that are emphasised repeatedly in a particular society (GCN, 2009).

A **value** is a normative idea, that is, a belief in something that one takes to be 'good' or 'valuable'. This might entail seeing certain actions but not others as appropriate and permissible (for example respecting people's rights); holding a certain kind of outcome as of primary importance (for example welfare and wellbeing); or valuing a certain way of life (for example religious devotion).

Increasingly, a range of academic disciplines, including institutional and behavioural economics, point towards the critical role that people's attitudes, mental shortcuts and values have in shaping not only the way they interact with new knowledge sources but also the types of alliances they forge in a given policy context. The New Economics Foundation, for instance, offers a set of principles for this new 'behavioural' economics, where findings diverge from neoclassical assumptions of rationality (Dawnay and Shah, 2005), owing to the role of beliefs and values:

- Habits are important: people do many things without consciously thinking about them.
- People are loss-averse and hang on to what they consider 'theirs'.
- Many people are bad at computation when making decisions, putting undue weight on recent events, not calculating probabilities and worrying too much about unlikely events.
- People are influenced strongly by how problems/information are presented to them.

Political economists have also taken these ideas on board in the concept of different 'decision logics', which govern how particular actors understand and act in certain situations. For example, policymakers in many, especially developing, countries are involved in systems of patronage. Collier (2007) shows that these tend to be sustained by a renewable cost–benefit analysis, and the assessment that using public resources for patronage is both cheaper and more reliable than using equivalent resources to win support by providing public services.

Beliefs and values: using knowledge

Values and beliefs shape how knowledge is used in policy in a number of ways. First, they do it quite directly. The content of policies, including the underlying principles and reasoning, reflect political goals and choices, and in doing so express values and beliefs that are themselves important elements of 'knowledge'. 'Affirmative action' policies aimed at reducing inequalities between groups stemming from gender or ethnic differences are likely to be based on an underlying judgment that such inequalities are wrong and that what society values is greater equality between such groups.

   Second, actors (including policymakers) do sometimes act against their individual or group interests in the name of morals and values (Campbell, 2002) – such as Britain's costly 60-year campaign against the transatlantic slave trade (Kauffman and Pape, 1999). In the 1960s US policymakers – most of whom were white males – passed affirmative action legislation, favouring social groups other than their own and risking their electoral fortunes, since the majority of the public favoured the status quo over policies that granted preferential treatment (Skrentny, 1996). Actors can derive orientation from their values, as they provide a way of deciding between alternative paths of action according to their value framework (Scholtes, 2008). Thus, values can play a role in shaping interests rather than the other way around (Heclo, 1978), and in turn can influence decisions about the use of particular areas of knowledge or types of information.

Third, values and beliefs may constrain action. Values (including political ideologies, religion and cultural beliefs), along with social, political and cultural norms, have a strong influence on restricting actions and shaping the 'rules of the game' (Booth et al, 2009) (see also Box 3.3). In the face of incomplete or inconclusive knowledge about what will work best, policymakers often operate according to a logic of moral or social appropriateness (March and Olsen, 1989), attempting to carry out actions that fit within the values of core constituencies rather than systematically thinking through the consequences. Irrespective of the available evidence base, some issues may effectively be 'taboo' and hence will remain off the policy agenda. Thus, actors who play a 'moral leadership' role (religious organisations, cultural leaders) may act as key players in blocking or facilitating the use of particular sources of knowledge in policy dialogues. For instance, in Yemen, despite rigorous scientific knowledge on the linkages between early pregnancy and maternal mortality, many religious leaders oppose reforms to early marriage practices, arguing that these are part of Islam (Pereznieto et al, 2011a).

Box 3.3: The role of values and beliefs in shaping the influence of actors' knowledge in the policy process

In the DFID Child and Youth Working Groups, formal value and belief positions emerged as key drivers of knowledge–policy interactions. The Child Working Group's stated goals were underpinned primarily by a rights-based agenda, whereas the Youth Group was for the most part interested in youth participation and connecting boundary partners/beneficiaries. The implications of these different value orientations were significant. While there are unavoidable complexities in securing child-specific participatory inputs, motivating and incorporating youth views (particularly those of older cohorts) is structurally viable. A rights-based agenda, on the other hand, can be challenging to operationalise, given that it is open to interpretation and potentially very resource-intensive. Consequently, the Child Working Group faced a myriad of organisational challenges for which it lacked an adequate strategy.

In the early stages of the partnership, and supported by an NGO secondment into DFID, the Child Working Group was able to initiate a supply-focused piece of research on the 'child rights climate' within DFID. However, during the desk review and key informant interview stages, requests for information in DFID were frequently redirected to particular thematic silos, such as the education, reproductive health and orphans and vulnerable children programmes. This demonstrated that DFID, overtly or unintentionally, could not channel particular child rights enquiries through a centrally coordinated unit responsible for children, and that belief systems concerning the understanding of child rights were theme-related and fragmented rather than universal or cross-cutting. Moreover, some group members were of the view that DFID's approach to rights seemed to be based on an instrumental vision of rights, that is, avoiding 'getting it wrong' rather than being driven by the more deeply held value system intrinsic to the Child Working Group involving rights holders and duty bearers. As a result, the Child Working Group struggled to gain any significant policy traction with DFID.

Source: Key informant interviews for this book

Finally, while values and beliefs can positively shape the interface between knowledge and policy, they can also insulate actors against taking new knowledge on board unless it fits with pre-held beliefs and values. One recent study (Munro, 2010) shows that individuals presented with 'science' that confirms their beliefs often accept these findings, whereas when presented with 'science' or rational arguments that seem to contradict those beliefs, they may reject the arguments, possibly going on to take more extreme positions on the issue. Monaghan (2011) reports similar findings for UK drugs policy, showing that when issues are highly politicised, what is accepted as 'evidence' for policymaking depends on bureaucrats' deep core beliefs.

Beliefs and values: brokering and communicating knowledge

Values and beliefs are normative ideas about what is 'right' and good for the collective rather than just being individually beneficial, and as such have a role to play in enabling change. They are important because people's self-expectations influence how they behave, in trying to keep their actions in line with values and commitments (Dawnay and Shah, 2005). This affects the knowledge brokered and communicated on an issue, because arguments are often 'framed' to resonate with key constituencies or to move them to action. In this vein, the study of social movements shows that interpreting issues using a moral lens helps to mobilise action for change (Tarrow, 1995). Such collective realisation tends to come about when people begin to interpret their situation (or the situation of others) as involving injustice and unfairness.

How problems or potential solutions are framed is therefore crucial. The framing individuals use to make decisions depends partly on the way issues are presented to them (and is partly based on habits), and this can play a large role in determining their reactions (Tversky and Kahneman, 1981) (see Box 3.4). Lobbyists may frame the evidence base for policies to influence decision makers to define a problem in a way that would push them towards the lobbyists' special interests. Framing can, however, also be designed to stimulate change in a more inclusive way: framing problems in terms of social justice may help empower poor people by challenging underlying beliefs about 'naturalised' inequalities and power imbalances (see Escobar and Álvarez, 1992).

Normative ideas often function as **boundary concepts** that are flexible enough to embrace different rationales and interests (Scholtes, 2008 and see Chapter Five). Studies of coalition building show that, as well as instrumental judgements, the other two main factors motivating actors to join coalitions are identity (affinity with pre-existing groups, based on profession, ethnicity and so on) and ideology (a search for meaning in political life) – both of which are based more on beliefs and values than on rational self-interest. This may also be true of the forces driving and sustaining some organisations.[3] Keck and Sikkink's (1998) model of transnational advocacy networks highlights the power and robustness of coalitions based on shared values (gender equity, human rights) and the search for alternative sources of knowledge in effecting change nationally and internationally. In short, knowledge brokered around a particular policy issue is often shaped around the values of competing coalitions.

Box 3.4: Context-sensitive packaging of evidence

Packaging evidence to resonate with particular cultural values and narratives is a critical element of knowledge uptake. In post-authoritarian Korea, rather than adapt a framing of feminist ideas, which tend to focus on values of individual rights and freedoms, researchers and activists promoted culturally resonant messages which emphasised the collective (in line with Confucian ethics and values) and contributions to national development and progress. Accordingly, demands for equal employment rights were couched as: 'maximising women's human resources for national development and strengthening Korean industry' and 'male protection laws'. Demands for paid maternity leave were presented as 'women's right to healthy motherhood' and 'reproductive responsibilities are societal responsibilities'. In the same vein, demands to overturn Confucian patriarchal family law were framed as 'promoting family health and societal democratisation'.

Source: Jones (2006)

Actors that play a role in framing issues for the general public, such as the media or think-tanks, can be crucial in shaping policy processes by drawing in new audiences and provoking value-based responses from policymakers (Panos, 2006, 2008). Knowledge intermediaries who purvey new information and mediate knowledge on a problem and its consequences are in a unique position to influence stasis or change, by representing the main way for individuals to find out about the world outside their immediate experience (see Chapter Five). Recent work on the economic costs of sexual violence in schools (Pereznieto et al, 2010), for example, was taken up by the national media in the US, Brazil and India in 2010 and has spurred widespread debate about the need to address this too-often invisible problem. While the NGO community had been advocating for greater policy attention to be paid to this issue for a number of years, once a credible mainstream think-tank such as the Overseas Development Institute presented an economic model and related figures as to the direct and indirect financial costs of such violence, new audiences, including the private sector, were drawn into the debate.

Beliefs and values: producing and codifying knowledge

Knowledge generation is often motivated not through a self-interested cost-benefit calculation but by the belief that knowledge is itself valuable. Academics and scientists are frequently driven by the value of producing robust research for the sake of furthering knowledge of an issue (Choi et al, 2005). A recent study of DFID's use of research and evaluation showed considerable support for the idea that a portion of the research budget is spent on work that is not directly instrumental to DFID priorities but rather is carried out for the broader benefits it can bring (Jones and Mendizabal, 2010). In the same vein, Stiglitz (1999) argues that knowledge is a 'global public good', providing very broad benefits for both the 'haves' and the 'have-nots', and hence should be funded by the state.

However, sometimes knowledge is produced in order to protect beliefs and values. Sabatier and Jenkins-Smith (1999) show how advocacy coalitions – powerful transnational alliances brought together around a core set of values and beliefs – work to avoid having their beliefs questioned. While they may adjust certain 'periphery beliefs' based on new information, they are much less likely to change more fundamental beliefs about overall policy strategies or normative judgements that are defended from refutation. Contrasting the approaches of the Heritage Foundation and the Brookings Institute, two highly influential American think-tanks, provides a clear case in point (see Box 3.5).

Box 3.5: A tale of two think-tanks

The Brookings Institution and the Heritage Foundation are two prominent think-tanks in the US, the former liberal in orientation and the second socially and economically conservative. Their missions and reputations are poles apart, in part because of their approach to knowledge and the role of values therein and in part because of their approach to knowledge brokering. The Heritage Foundation is much more explicit about its value orientation and how knowledge can support this; while Brookings devotes most of its budget to research, Heritage puts a substantial portion into media and government relations. In 2004, Brookings spent 3% of its $39 million budget on communications; in 2002, the most recent year for which information is available, Heritage spent 20% of its $33 million budget on public and government affairs. Reflecting on this difference, Herb Berkowitz, Heritage's former Vice-president for Communication, observed: 'Our belief is that when the research product has been printed, then the job is only half done. That is when we start marketing it to the media.... We have as part of our charge the selling of ideas, the selling of policy proposals. We are out there actively selling these things, day after day. It's our mission' (Rich, 2004).

Brookings Institution	Heritage Foundation
Origins	
Founded in 1916 by industrial-era capitalists to be a source of neutral expertise for government	Founded in 1973 by former Republican congressional staff to produce and market policy-relevant research from a conservative perspective
Opening comment	
'It is essential for the permanent standing of an institute of economic research that it should early establish its reputation as scientific, impartial, and unprejudiced in its findings and presenting of the facts as to economic and social conditions.'	'We realized we not only needed a Republican Study Committee on the inside to help the congressman, but we needed something on the outside to promote ideas and do the longer-term research, but still research that is policy-relevant.'
Mission statement	
'The Brookings Institution ... is an independent nonpartisan organization devoted to research, analysis, and public education with an emphasis on economics, foreign policy, governance, and metropolitan policy.'	'The Heritage Foundation is a research and educational institute – a think-tank – whose mission is to formulate and promote conservative public policies ....'
Tributes	
'The men of Brookings did it by analysis, by painstaking research, by objective writing, by an imagination that questioned the "going" way of doing things....You are a national institution ...' (Lyndon Johnson, 1966).	'[The Heritage Foundation] is without question the most far-reaching conservative organization in the country in the war of ideas, and one which has had a tremendous impact not just in Washington, but literally across the planet' (Newt Gingrich, 1993).
Clout and credibility	
Ranked second-most influential and number one in terms of credibility in a 1997 survey of congressional staff and journalists about 27 think-tanks.	In the same survey, ranked number one in influence and ninth in credibility.

Actors' credibility

Credibility is the set of the beliefs and/or knowledge that are more persuasive to particular groups. It can help explain the weight different people give to different pieces of information. Actors can look to bolster their own credibility by co-opting networks to suit their personal preferences, or they can push particular pieces of evidence in order to strengthen the influence a particular network has on policy.

Perceptions of credibility, expertise and objectivity are a strong factor in shaping how knowledge is used in policymaking and implementation, as are the ways in which actors assess the robustness of claims used as a basis for collective choices. Power in all its forms – overt, covert, hidden – plays a key role. Not all perspectives are 'equal', and on certain issues particular actors may be able to draw on a loose group of people (possibly from a variety of disciplines and backgrounds) with a wider range of thought in order to act effectively (Haas, 1992). Such 'epistemic communities'[4] may be formal or informal; as with many other policy networks and coalitions, they share a set of normative beliefs, but most of these are technically informed and it is the particular form of knowledge this entails that sets them apart from other actors. Epistemic communities are typically global and transnational in character, but tend to be quite specialised, focusing on producing knowledge to clarify particular problems, specific policy enterprises or common sets of practices. Members often have formal training, and they share empirically informed causal notions of validity and criteria for the credibility of knowledge. Being a member of such a community grants a certain level of credibility, greater than that of an actor who is perceived to be a 'lone voice' on an issue.

Notions of credibility also vary from country to country. Jasanoff (2005) argues that policy debates are refracted by a 'civic epistemology' (the institutionalised ways citizens understand 'knowledge') as well as their shared and entrenched expectations about what authoritative claims to knowledge should look like and how they should be articulated, represented and defended. In any country context, how credibility is defined is thus affected by dominant styles of decision making (for example interest-based), methods of ensuring upward, downward and lateral accountability (for example legal), practices of public demonstration (for example empirical science), preferred registers of objectivity (for example consultative and negotiated) and accepted bases of expertise (for example experience).

Actors' credibility: using knowledge

Knowledge types that are more credible to key decision makers have a greater likelihood of being used in policy.[5] Depending on what those in power define as 'credible' knowledge on a topic, particular groups or networks will be involved in developing, brokering and using that type of knowledge – and be best placed to influence the content of policies. Networks of policy actors are often highly integrated within the policymaking process, flowing in and out of policy and advisory positions and academia and playing a key role in developing, testing and refining policy ideas that make it on to the agenda (Kingdon, 1984). These tend to coalesce around particular institutions and – operating independently of the wider political sphere – to be resistant to change. Think-tanks may train cadres of individuals who will one day play important roles in politics or the civil service (Mendizabal and Sample, 2009). While this may result in powerful coalitions for advocacy, there is a danger of issues and institutions becoming monopolised by a single profession (trade policy by economists, nutrition policy by epidemiologists) (Pomares and Jones, 2009). Over time, the credibility of certain understandings can become institutionalised in law or within bureaucratic procedures, programmes, departments and so on (Campbell, 2002). This creates constituencies of actors whose interests are tied directly to the veracity of these ideas and who will defend them strongly if needed.

In democratising countries, access to, and use of, credible knowledge sources can be a powerful way for new actors to increase their legitimacy in the policy process. A case in point is the way in which legislatures in a growing number of developing countries are seeking out alliances with non-governmental knowledge producers in order to obtain access to rigorous evidence that can help augment their political voice relative to the all-too-often dominant executive branch (Jones et al, 2011; see also Box 3.6).

Box 3.6: Developing country legislatures and use of research-based evidence to strengthen policy credibility

Legislatures can be categorised according to their role in shaping policy debates and their related need for, and access to, information and research. Four types can be identified:

Rubber stamp legislature: meets to vote in favour of the ruling party's programme of work; legislators have little need for independent information.

Emerging legislature: legislators need information to participate in the legislative process. A legislative library or research service, including reference materials and clipping services on current issues, may be created. The legislature may also provide some permanent staff for legislative committees.

Informed legislature: legislators have a small cadre of personal staff, professional committee staff and a legislative library and/or research service that actively distributes information on pressing issues to all members and may track progress on key legislation. Noted more for debate than for policy initiatives, the legislature succeeds in amending some bills introduced by the government and in enacting some of its own.

Transformative legislature: legislators can alter proposals offered by the government and develop policy options of their own. Transformative legislatures can also introduce fully developed proposals and enact them, and may undertake regular annual reviews of the extent to which the bureaucracy is implementing new legislation. A generous allotment of personal staff, strong and well-staffed committees, research and analysis at the party level and large central research groups capable of developing policy options is needed to make transformative legislatures work well.

Those working in the legislature can draw on knowledge from a range of sources: executive research services; legislative information and research services; arrangements between legislatures and external knowledge producers; political party-affiliated think-tanks and research centres; or informal links with university institutions, civil society knowledge producers and think-tanks for which they may once have worked or enjoyed close affiliations.

Source: Robinson and Gastelum (1998)

Actors' credibility: communicating and brokering knowledge

A narrow definition of credibility will limit both how knowledge is brokered within an organisation and who is allowed to act as a knowledge intermediary. Participation in certain dialogues may be limited to those with specific types of technical expertise, or organisations may be more receptive to certain types of argument. Rao and Woolcock (2007) argue, for example, that a 'disciplinary monopoly' of economists at the World Bank dominates the internal dialogue, restricts what is studied, delimits how issues are analysed and thereby promotes a narrow range of policy options and strategies.

To increase their credibility, members of knowledge networks can build up recognised competence or expertise in certain areas. Ideas communicated through such channels can be trusted more as well tested and examined. In the face of complex problems, knowledge networks can help shed light on problems and help develop policy responses. This is reflected in the role of 'sounding board' for new policies that think-tanks can play in national policy processes, with political actors testing the robustness of their ideas and developing programmes of change (Mendizabal and Sample, 2009).

Networks can have a more substantial influence on how knowledge is incorporated into policy during crises or upheaval or in the face of entirely 'new' problems. Here, it may be that the nature of the problems and the range of possible solutions are unclear. Uncertainty around distributional consequences can make it difficult to identify underlying interests, making normal modes of interest-based bargaining irrelevant. 'Experts' and others with credibility in the domain are then called on to offer interpretative frameworks and tools and normative ideas of potential goals, facilitating action, in particular collective action and coalition building (McKean, 2002).

It should be clear now that the perceived credibility some actors enjoy based on their position in knowledge networks affords them a degree of power in the policy process. For example, a review of the World Bank's interaction with civil society showed that consultative fora tended to be too technically framed, and that this also limited dialogues around poverty reduction strategy papers (PRSPs) in some countries to small networks of technocrats (Booth, 2003). Where policy issues are highly complex, requiring knowledge of particular language and theories and expertise on instruments and institutions, participation in knowledge networks may facilitate access to such knowledge resources, and in turn much-needed credibility.[6]

Knowledge networks, acting as knowledge intermediaries, can facilitate the transfer of explicit, codified knowledge such as publications or manuals (the 'boundary objects' referred to in Chapter Five), as well as tacit knowledge that is context-specific – woven into experiences and contexts in which it is generated. Network interactions help members build shared understandings and social capital that may foster coordination and collaboration, and further add to their knowledge base and credibility (see Box 3.7).

> **Box 3.7: The role of networks in strengthening actors' credibility**
>
> Networks have six functions that can strengthen actors' credibility: **filtering** (helping members find their way through often unmanageable amounts of information); **amplifing** (making little-known or little-understood ideas more widely understood); **investing/providing** (providing members with the resources, capacities and skills they need); **convening** (bringing together different people or groups of people); **community building** (promoting and sustaining the values and standards of the individuals or organisations within them); and **facilitating** (helping members carry out their activities more effectively and learn from their peers).
>
> *Source:* Mendizabal (2006)

Actors' credibility: producing and codifying knowledge

Different perceptions of credibility play a very direct role in shaping the (policy-relevant) knowledge produced in a country or on an issue. Actors subscribe to different 'epistemologies' – different approaches to inquiry (for example scientific observations versus practical questions of costs and benefits), standards of validation (methodological rigour and generalisation versus representativeness and resonance of community stories) and explanatory frameworks (causal and statistical analysis versus lived experience and sense of identity). These shape approaches to knowledge generation, as well as influencing the degree to which each type of knowledge is seen as being credible, salient and legitimate in policymaking. Members of the executive exert a degree of discretionary power when commissioning research, playing an active role in setting the agenda of research organisations (and therefore defining what is accepted as credible knowledge). However, knowledge is generated not only through formal research consultancies, but also through interaction. By sharing, discussing, testing and developing ideas, and working with others to link ideas to action, knowledge and 'expertise' become a mark of being integrated into a credible network. Thus while individuals may develop a high degree of credibility with key policymakers, it is the voices of network members that are heard above others on certain issues. The danger is that a strong network of like-minded individuals may self-limit the external challenge to its ideas, resulting in undue support for particular issues in spite of limited evidence of success (Molle, 2008).

Engaging with actors' interests, values and beliefs

We now turn to discuss the practical implications of the framework described above and give readers some tools to negotiate their way through the complexity of actors' behaviour. This section outlines the ways in which the policy process, and especially the knowledge–policy interface, differs based on actors and their interests, values/beliefs and registers of credibility. We use three simple 2 x 2 matrices to explore how each factor plays out in the policy process with particular attention to:

- how the distribution of interests around an issue affects styles of policymaking;
- the relationship between actors' values and the costs and benefits of action; and
- how different degrees of consensus about policy goals and the evidence affect registers of credibility.

In each subsection, we provide guidance about how policy is made and what this means for whom one should work with (or against) to secure pro-poor policy change;[7] how to improve the quality of debate in the policy process and make it more inclusive; and how to improve actors' engagement with knowledge and policy. Finally, we summarise the learning from the preceding sections, pointing out the need to build networks of actors, moving away from centralised, hierarchical policy processes to build capacity in an incremental manner and fostering an enabling environment for local, networked action.

How the strength and distribution of interests affect styles of policymaking

Questions this section will help you answer:
- How do different actor interests shape who is involved in a policy issue and how they use knowledge? What are the implications for less powerful or more fragmented voices?
- How do actor interests affect the degree to which knowledge is shared openly and transparently? How do they affect whether decisions are made openly or not?
- How do actor interests affect the boundary between neutral brokering and advocacy/influencing? What effect do the interests of the media have on how knowledge is transmitted to policy?
- How do the interests of government, international donors and the private sector affect what is prioritised for knowledge generation, what is published and how it is communicated?

Where interests are an important factor, policymaking is likely to be shaped by how these are distributed – that is, how concentrated they are among actors who are working towards a particular change and among those who will block it. If costs or benefits are concentrated on one side, it will be easier for groups to organise, lobby and influence the key actors (out of the public eye, if necessary). If they are diffuse, coalitions for or against change will face greater challenges; people may not even know about the costs and benefits, and marshalling effective political action will require significant publicising of issues and the organisation of larger, more diverse groups in a country.

These insights are at the centre of a typology developed by Wilson (1980), who argues that policymaking on an issue will have different styles according to the distribution of costs and benefits. The typology marks out where the crucial site for policymaking is likely to be and shows that different policy issues are likely to have different balances of these characteristics (see Table 3.2).

The typology presented above marks the key characteristics of policymaking processes on issues where interests are important. However, certain variables within the model can be influenced in ways that are likely to support more constructive, progressive outcomes (for example changing actors' perceptions of their 'interests'). Other features of the broader environment can also be influenced to shift an issue from one category to another (for example broadening public awareness and strengthening coalitions). Indeed, where benefits are distributed, it is likely that 'normal' political processes will provide sufficient checks and balances to allow broad conceptions of knowledge to inform policy by ensuring that all voices are heard. The challenge comes where benefits are concentrated – where the interests of a powerful group limit what is accepted as knowledge for policy, either through client or interest-group politics.

One way to deal with such client and interest-group politics is to accept that certain decisions will be made behind closed doors but look to change how key actors view their own interests. This may be impossible in heavily politicised areas where core beliefs are deeply held and lead to intransigence (Monaghan, 2011); for other issues, working 'within the tent' could change the attitudes of certain decision makers about what their 'interests' are and how different policy options stack up in relation to those interests. For example, systems of patronage tend to be governed by a perception of costs and benefits that sees using public resources for patronage as both cheaper and more reliable than using equivalent resources on public services to win support (Collier, 2007; Booth and Golooba-Mutebi, 2009). There are, however, two ways of changing these sorts of perceptions:

- **brokering credible accounts of the likely effects of certain problems on actors' own interests or on how reforms may bring about benefits:** this may involve using knowledge intermediaries to improve the robustness of evidence around an issue, appealing to values and beliefs or reducing uncertainty over the attractiveness of an option. Understanding what actors consider 'credible' will be important; elites have been known to take pro-poor actions where they are convinced of the links between poverty and their interests;
- **shifting the cost–benefit calculations of key actors through mediation and conflict resolution:** many complex issues give rise to conflicts of interest between different actors. If managed intelligently, these can be a positive force for change, as actors and norms of behaviour can be reorganised into more sustainable and equitable patterns. Collective and deliberative processes are a powerful way of resolving these sorts of issues. Encouraging rules that actors see

Table 3.2: Typology of policy processes according to distribution of interests on an issue

		Benefits	
		Distributed	Concentrated
Costs	Distributed	**Majoritarian politics** Where issues involve widely distributed costs and benefits, policy making is more likely to play out in public fora such as legislative debates or policy debates around an election. The public debate often addresses questions of whether social benefits exceed the costs, and basic ideological beliefs and values may come into play, in potentially partisan dialogues. These issues may be less frequent in countries where elites have reliable ways of capturing the benefits of policy programmes. *Examples:* pollution control on cars, civil rights.	**Client politics** Small groups or 'clients' benefit directly from policies where the general public is often the loser. Well-organised clients can secure political support largely in private; those who stand to lose out are often unaware of the issue, or hard to organise. This kind of behind-the-scenes politics might involve politicians using government spending to reward their constituents, or actors trading favours to allow the passage of special interests. This is quite regular in contexts with dominant elites or strong issue networks, or where there is an 'iron triangle' of consensus between groups in legislature, administrative agencies and interest groups. *Examples:* agricultural price supports, regulatory waivers.
	Concentrated	**Entrepreneurial politics** Here, the general public, or very broad groups in society, are pitted against concentrated special interests. This is likely to involve political entrepreneurs identifying (short-lived) opportunities and bringing together a large (and often transient) coalition of beneficiaries, framing and dramatising issues to capture the public imagination. These kinds of dynamics are quite rare, especially in contexts with significant entrenched interests or elite control of the media. *Example:* environmental standards on companies.	**Interest-group politics** This involves the competition of well-organised rival groups, similar to the 'pluralist' vision of policy processes. Policymaking takes place largely behind the scenes, in informal meetings and networks, or in closed spaces in implementing agencies or legislative committees. Processes are characterised by decision makers being forced to take sides, with shifting alliances and bargaining, with incremental changes rather than major confrontations, won depending on the energy and strength of groups. This is frequent in contexts with significant elite capture. *Example:* competition between different agricultural sectors.

Source: Adapted from Wilson (1980)

as legitimate can foster more meaningful participation and higher compliance. Issues can be transformed as actors develop shared concepts and perceptions, shifting the perceived patterns of costs and benefits and with it the deadlock. Warner (2001), for instance, investigates how agricultural cooperatives and village councils, as well as collaborative efforts between actors such as forest user groups and local government wildlife departments, have responded to external shocks and developments such as new irrigation technology, new legislation and increasing affluence among subsections of the local community. Facilitated processes of interest-based negotiation, aiming at underlying needs and values rather than immediate 'wants', have proved highly effective in promoting successful adaptation and continued resource management.

If well facilitated, such processes can foster social learning between actors, allowing them to move away from conflicts being seen as essentially 'zero sum', involving adversarial bargaining that can frequently cause deadlock, towards finding areas of mutual underlying interest beyond immediate demands. Chapter Five demonstrates how knowledge intermediaries can contribute to facilitation processes by:

- convening or brokering deliberations at various scales in order to provide a catalyst for collaborative efforts;
- commissioning action research to build linkages between actors and move towards consensus and shared ideas around a problem; or
- simply providing platforms for actors to hold discussions, giving them a chance to communicate, build trust and coordinate action.

How values and beliefs influence the costs and benefits of action

Questions this section will help you answer:
- How do actors' values and beliefs shape what they class as knowledge? What does this mean for what they include or exclude?
- What is the relationship between actors' values and beliefs, and their interests? Is one necessarily stronger than the other?
- Is it clear how actors' values and beliefs (and by extension their identities and ideology) shape how coalitions are built around an issue?

Where values and beliefs are important, the wider common interest is best served by building support from those groups implicitly losing out from the situation. This involves broadening the range of dialogue and knowledge sources, attempting to build broader public movements or create societal coalitions around shared values – and may be particularly relevant where well-organised groups secure the (concentrated) benefits of public policies, due to client and interest-group politics. Table 3.3 shows how we can visualise the likelihood of policy change by reflecting the relative costs and benefits to an actor, along with how well the framing fits with their values (Busby, 2005).

To overcome indifference, interventions can alter the interests of key decision makers by building awareness of issues; inaction or continued clientelism may have higher political costs if coalitions employ effective 'shaming' techniques and direct them at veto players (see Box 3.8). To overcome hostility, successful strategies

Table 3.3: Typology of likely actions according to costs, benefits and the degree of fit with actors' values

		Cost-benefit analysis	
		Net benefit to key actors (or neutral)	Net cost to key actors
Values	High fit	Low costs, high fit with values **Cheap moral action** Likelihood that values 'win'	High costs, high fit with values **Costly moral action** Success depends on veto players
	Low fit	Low costs, low fit with values **Indifference** Success depends on veto players (see Box 3.8)	High costs, low fit with values **Hostility** Costs 'win'

Source: Busby (2005)

might improve the perceived 'fit' with decision makers' values by introducing new or repackaged information and thus altering their cost–benefit calculations. In situations where both costs and moral 'fit' are high, research shows that policy change comes down to the support of key policy gatekeepers and effectively pinning messages to crises or 'focusing events' (Busby, 2005).

> ## Box 3.8: Veto players
>
> A 'veto player' is an individual or collective decision maker whose agreement is required for the change of the status quo. Different political structures have different configurations of veto players, but policy outcomes still depend on how these actors choose to act within the boundaries the structure provides (Tsebelis, 1995). This is a powerful tool for summarising and comparing the characteristics of different political systems – for example, the greater the number of veto players, the more difficult policy change may prove, but the more stable a commitment to a particular policy.

In order to foster change where values and beliefs are strongly held, changing perceptions of costs and benefits, and on whom they fall, will be an important priority. This will involve altering decision makers' views of the causal and distributive effects of problems or proposed solutions by producing credible accounts of where the costs and benefits fall. Wilson's typology (Table 3.2) makes it clear that identifying the actors affected by a reform is an important factor shaping policy processes and outcomes. It may be strategic for an actor to frame what they say about an issue in a way that seems to include as broad a set of actors as possible (for example 'taxpayers' alliance') in order to marshal a sizable coalition. But where the 'winners' or 'losers' from a proposed policy (or an existing problem) are more easy to identify (for example where they are connected by industry or clearly geographically demarcated),[8] they are likely to be a more powerful force. Clearly, too, working with the media is likely to be a central element of any strategy to alter perceptions of costs and benefits. Understanding how different media actors work in the particular context will be important, as will establishing which communication channels are most likely to reach the target population.

Improving the robustness and detail of information could also help strengthen reform coalitions, by identifying the specific groups that bear the costs and benefits. Developing disaggregated data about poor people in developing countries is likely to help in expressing their problems and empowering them to act. The fact that such data are relatively difficult to come by could be a collective action problem (see above), although it may also reflect that there are many more powerful people who gain from their absence.

How actors' credibility affects their role in the knowledge–policy interface

Questions this section will help you answer:
- How do we determine which actors are seen as credible, or 'experts' on an issue? What does this mean for those who are excluded?
- What efforts are being made to consider different types of expertise (for example experiential rather than scientific, different types of knowledge) and what are the implications of this being done poorly?
- Are there particular technical, scientific or social scientific disciplines that are currently more credible than others in policymaking? What does this mean for the types of knowledge most likely to be accepted by policymakers?

Actors' credibility plays a key role in shaping their role in the knowledge–policy interface. If we consider pro-poor policy change – an example of an issue that involves wide public debate – encouraging change may require working against not only entrenched values and beliefs but also notions of credibility. Issues that involve broad majoritarian politics or wide public debate will need to engage with processes to define and negotiate public values[9] or reconcile differences in ideology. These involve very different kinds of debate from a 'rational' model of policymaking (see Box 3.9).

Box 3.9: Defining public values at the knowledge–policy interface

One important type of value for understanding policy debates relates to fairness and equity: understanding how things are distributed in society (wealth, health, food, rewards, punishments) and judging whether the distribution respects the right kinds of principles in terms of the nature of the goods and the features of those to whom they are distributed (Jones, 2009c).[10] Most societies share a concern for equity and social justice, and this is integral to legal traditions as well as being a major concern of many religions (World Bank, 2005b). International surveys indicate that fairness in the distribution of resources is valued in a wide variety of cultural contexts (CPRC, 2008). Knowledge, information and opinion about how 'deserving' or 'in need' a group might be of different goods or services are likely to be central to policy debates with large distributional implications. For example, beliefs about welfare fraud or dependency play a major role in setting the acceptability for social protection systems (Slater and Farrington, 2010), irrespective of evidence of the efficiency or effectiveness of some systems (for example unconditional cash transfers).

Another important kind of value is that of 'rights'. These constitute the minimum entitlements due to any individual or group; they also impose constraints, forbidding or requiring certain actions. For example, political rights include freedom of participation in civil society and politics, and civil rights include ensuring people's safety and protection from discrimination. Rights are often invoked with respect to a particular group (such as ethnic group or gender) whose rights are (perceived as) being infringed; this can often play a big role in political debates, as it is key in 'identity politics', whereby political action or movements are organised around a marginalised group's beliefs and ideas about themselves. Such values then play a strong role in how these groups perceive their interests (Hall, 1993). This means that actors' beliefs about the (historical) treatment of particular groups are likely to be help shape policies that affect them.

Establishing such credibility may be challenging for two reasons. First, many actors may work against their own material interest to defend strongly held cultural beliefs – Box 3.4 on gender equality debates in South Korea gives an example of how to acknowledge their importance explicitly and present alternatives that are framed as in keeping with them.

Second, how actors are able to communicate aspects of public values will depend on the extent to which different groups consider them to be credible, but this will depend on the extent to which there is consensus on the policy goals and on the meaning of the different types of knowledge. As Figure 3.1 illustrates, drawing on 'experts', consultants and scientific analysis in the policy process is useful for issues where basic values and goals are agreed (Shaxson, 2009). But in attempting to improve the knowledge–policy interface on other issues, where there is no broad agreement on the definition of public value and there are competing interpretations of the appropriate goal of public policy (or, on a smaller scale, a clash of values between key stakeholders), there will be competing interpretations of who is the 'expert' and what is 'credible' knowledge. If this is the case, it may be inappropriate to pursue technically led solutions or attempt to bring consensus through scientific analysis.

Processes of contestation and argument may be important for informing and improving the foundations of policy and action for complex policy issues. Burawoy (2005) has famously argued that linking social scientific knowledge and policy requires approaches to be critical and 'reflexive', not just instrumental. Such discursive approaches problematise prevailing trends and discuss values, ideology and the underlying goals of policy; they do not simply draw on sources in order to understand how to fulfil specific goals. As well as aiming at an academic audience, it is important to engage the wider public in such discussions to communicate different perspectives in the public and policy dialogue in a relevant fashion (Livny et al, 2006; Harriss-White, 2007). The ideal situation would be to establish credibility processes that would allow alternative framings of issues and

Figure 3.1: Credibility as defined by availability of evidence and policy values

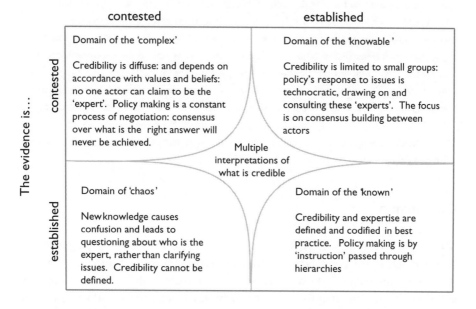

Policy values or outcomes are:

	contested	established
	Domain of the 'complex'	**Domain of the 'knowable'**
contested	Credibility is diffuse: and depends on accordance with values and beliefs: no one actor can claim to be the 'expert'. Policy making is a constant process of negotiation: consensus over what is the right answer will never be achieved.	Credibility is limited to small groups: policy's response to issues is technocratic, drawing on and consulting these 'experts'. The focus is on consensus building between actors
	Domain of 'chaos'	**Domain of the 'known'**
established	New knowledge causes confusion and leads to questioning about who is the expert, rather than clarifying issues. Credibility cannot be defined.	Credibility and expertise are defined and codified in best practice. Policy making is by 'instruction' passed through hierarchies

The evidence is...

Multiple interpretations of what is credible

Source: Adapted from Shaxson (2008; 2009) and Snowden and Boone (2007)

an exploration of where policy makers may share priorities with local people would be ideal (Powell, 2006; Morgan, 2008). Unfortunately, three factors mean that such work may be difficult to carry out in Southern contexts (although this is not a problem just for the South): political freedoms may restrict the operation of organisations that would carry out such work (see Chapter Two); funding may be more difficult to find; and the frequently highly unequal distribution of skills and resources in Southern societies may ensure that powerful groups maintain the upper hand in policy debates. Capacity building for NGOs and other actors who work to hold governments to account for how knowledge is used may therefore be important (see Chapter Five; also Jones et al, 2008, 2011), as could support for communities of practice that engage in collective processes of social learning, shared practice and joint exploration of ideas (see Box 3.10). And, as Chapter Four shows, knowledge incentive structures in government also condition what types of knowledge are considered credible in the core processes of policymaking.

Box 3.10: Networked transformative learning

Communities of practice may be useful in helping to build shared understandings of a situation and transform underlying views, attitudes and values (Munro and Jeffrey, 2006). Scartascini et al (2008) argue that building trust and cooperation between key actors can make space for necessary changes, even where issues are characterised by high numbers of veto players (which would usually present major barriers to progressive policy change). Genuine collaborative institutions and networks flourish or perish according to their own internal dynamics, because the potential for learning comes largely from the informal side rather than formal management and other structures. Any new interventions should therefore seek to work with existing networks rather than create new ones with often unrealistically optimistic goals or timeframes (Ruitenbeek and Cartier, 2001), so as not to disempower current or emergent local organisations. Rather than putting in place projects and programmes with their externally driven goals, funding for networks is better seen as 'seeding' emergent action via mechanisms developed to build capacity and action at the local level. The Netherlands Development Organisation's Local Capacity Development Fund represents pioneering work in this field, allowing demand-oriented support in a way that empowers local organisations and gives them services tailored to their needs (Tembo, 2008).

Conclusion

Much of what happens at the interface between knowledge and policy is affected by what actors are involved, how they are related and their different 'stakes' in the issue. This chapter shows it is possible to analyse all of this systematically and then to use this analysis to identify whom to work with (and how) to make improvements. The reader should therefore take away a number of key messages.

First, it is not enough to examine an actor's material self-interests in an issue: he or she will be motivated by a complex blend of factors, which also includes their values and beliefs and claims to credibility. Moreover, people's personal and professional decisions are generally related to decisions taken by those around them, meaning it may not immediately be clear what provides the motivation for a particular course of action being agreed on. While 'science' and 'facts' may be upheld in public as the basis for policymaking, cultural beliefs or patronage-type allegiances could constrain what is considered 'evidence' to the extent that whole avenues of possible action are closed down. However, the reverse could also be true: actors with a strong claim to credibility could use this to encourage openness to other voices and thereby increase the options available to policymakers. Having demonstrated that it is possible for actors to act in ways that are seemingly against their material interests, this chapter concludes that all actors are, in practice, open to influence. The tripartite framework we present in this chapter gives readers an understanding of:

- how to look at different actors' self-interest and the economic or political stakes actors may have in an issue in order to understand their stance and actions;
- why it is important to dig beneath broadly applicable rational choice frameworks to understand the core beliefs and values that drive actors and coalitions engaging at the knowledge–policy interface, and how these might be influenced;

- the reality that science and knowledge are rarely the single driving force of policy or the only form of 'speaking truth to power'. Different registers of credibility come into play at various stages of policy processes, and (if they are allowed to be recognised) these can provide the spaces and languages with which to negotiate an improved link between knowledge and policy.

Based on these insights, there are a number of ways to approach a particular issue and to work with actors in order to improve the knowledge–policy interface. Initially, it is important to assess how the distribution of costs and benefits on an issue helps shape policy dialogue and whether such dialogue reflects client, interest group, entrepreneurial or majoritarian politics (noting that the categories overlap and are not mutually exclusive). These in turn shape the processes by which policies are likely to be made, including whether they will be open or closed and with short or long windows of opportunity. Once these have been defined, it is then possible to understand how to devise and sequence actions so as to have the desired impact.

It is possible to change actors' perceptions of their interests and values, either by brokering credible knowledge of how reforms may bring benefits or by shifting the cost-benefit calculations actors make through mediation, conflict resolution and collective or deliberative processes. Broadening the dialogue and building wider public movements can also improve client- or interest-group-based politics; framing the issue to resonate with key constituencies helps alter the political costs of key actors holding different stances. Building coalitions for change can be achieved even against entrenched interests, but determining how to do this means developing a clear understanding of how the values held by decision makers affect their calculations of political costs, the role of veto players and (as set out in Chapter Five) how to work with knowledge intermediaries to construct broad, durable coalitions.

Some issues, such as those that involve broad 'majoritarian' aspects or wide public debates, need to move away from a narrowly rational approach to dialogue and action and instead engage with (rather than ignore) issues around values and principles (for example equity and rights). A key part of this process will be to improve the interface between knowledge and policy by building capacity to ensure that underrepresented voices and groups can participate at all levels of the debate.

Finally, where issues are complex, involving multiple perspectives and different types of knowledge, it will be important to recognise that credibility is likely to be dispersed between multiple groups of actor, not limited to technocrats or elites. This means that to address issues of wider common interest, it will also be important to embed learning and negotiation throughout the lifecycle of policy and implementation. Again, a simple linear approach to policymaking is less likely to work here. Instead, policies will need to be more decentralised and will need to be facilitated by ensuring that all types of knowledge are recognised, emergent knowledge networks are encouraged and links between different levels and communities are promoted to support greater collaboration. This is the subject of Chapter Four.

Notes

[1] For example Keeley and Scoones (2003); Nutley et al (2007); Jones and Sumner (2011).

[2] This draws on Gaventa (2006), who distinguishes between three dimensions of power: levels (global, national and local), spaces (closed, invited and claimed/created) and forms (hidden, visible and invisible). It should be noted that hidden or closed spaces are not necessarily illegitimate; the private sector often has issues of commercial confidentiality to protect, and hence even highly formal consultation processes have to be carried out behind closed doors.

[3] Lessons can be drawn from experiences of faith-based organisations, for which the norms and values underpinning their work serve to better mobilise human and capital resources and draw individuals and communities into global discourses of development and social justice (Clarke et al, 2007 and Jennings, 2008). Similarly, research into CSOs finds that shared values contribute to a unified organisation and provide a sense of purpose; create strong bonds with partners and other stakeholders; have a positive impact on recruitment and performance; improve organisational governance and strategic management; and provide frameworks against which to evaluate and reflect on progress (Jochum and Pratten, 2009).

[4] Networks of knowledge-based experts (Haas, 1992, p 3): 'what bonds members of epistemic communities is their shared belief or faith in the verity or applicability of particular forms of knowledge or specific truths'.

[5] Chapter Four discusses how this credibility arises and implications for how different types of knowledge may or may not be perceived to be credible by different groups of actors.

[6] Note, however, that Chapter Four shows that the level of technical sophistication required in a particular policy space may limit participation and means that various actors are unlikely to be able to take part in debates or may be discouraged.

[7] The presumption here is that development actors are likely to be aiming to reduce poverty, and hence working against the prevailing power differentials.

[8] Such as NIMBY – not in my back yard – groups opposed to particular issues, for example, the siting of landfill areas close to their home.

[9] Bozeman (2007, p 37) defines a society's public values as values 'providing normative consensus about (1) the rights, benefits and prerogatives to which citizens should (and should not) be entitled; (2) the obligations of citizens to society, the state, and one another; and (3) the principles on which governments and policies should be based.'

[10] For example, many people feel that some rewards or positions in society should reflect differences in effort and ability, based on fair competition (for example university professor), whereas other goods and services are seen as necessities (for example basic food, medical treatment) and should be distributed according solely to level of need. The idea of equal life chances means there should be no differences in outcomes based on factors for which people cannot be held responsible (for example seeing differences in life expectancy based on the place of your birth as unfair).

FOUR

Integrating different types of knowledge

Analysts of the policy process have advocated for strengthening links between knowledge and policy for decades (Head, 2010). A poorly functioning interface will give rise to policies and programmes that reflect the biases of certain individuals or groups (see Chapter Three); rely on untested views or speculative conjectures that may result in ineffective policy; or draw on pieces of knowledge selectively, covering up ideological standpoints or decisions made behind closed doors (Davies, 2004).

This chapter presents the conceptual and practical reasons for taking a broad view of what 'knowledge' is used in policy, on both theoretical and empirical grounds. It focuses in particular on three types of knowledge – research-based, practice-informed and citizen knowledge. It then analyses the power dynamics around each type of knowledge and some of the practical steps that can be taken to improve both the supply and demand for knowledge in policy.

By the end of this chapter, readers will be able to answer the following questions:
- What are the different ways of conceptualising knowledge?
- Why is 'knowledge' such a contested issue?
- What are the factors to consider in analysing the different types of knowledge used in policy?
  - » What does each type of knowledge bring to the policy process?
  - » What are the challenges to using them effectively?

The chapter starts with a discussion of the various conceptions of knowledge and how they affect our analysis of the interface between knowledge and policy. From this, we draw out a framework that distinguishes between three types of knowledge, which we use to analyse the factors affecting how knowledge is used, brokered and communicated, and produced for policy purposes. Finally, we look at some of the practical issues that need to be addressed to improve how each of the three different types of knowledge are incorporated into policy; paying particular attention to the institutional incentives that condition the demand for knowledge in policymaking.

Understanding the role of knowledge at the knowledge–policy interface

What is knowledge?

We do not aim to adjudicate between competing claims from the prolific literature to find a single neat answer to the question 'What is knowledge?' Even a brief discussion of the key ideas and arguments in these fields shows that we need to take a broad view of the nature and content of knowledge.

There are four main aspects to the **'content' of knowledge**:

- **Descriptive:** 18th- and 19th-century epistemology conceptualised knowledge as true, justified belief, that is, as a statement about the world that the speaker holds to be true. This developed into the 'positivist' view, which suggested that knowledge functions primarily to 'describe' the world, with greater or lesser degrees of success. The positivist conception of knowledge sees the quality or robustness of knowledge as tied to how it is justified, in other words, the rigour of the methodology that produces it. Although positivism is now widely regarded as flawed, the notion that description is a key function of knowledge remains uncontested.
- **Explanatory:** the positivist conception saw scientific knowledge as being built by proposing theories that make predictions that can be justified by empirical observation. However, Popper (1934) argued that individual beliefs and scientific theories could not be 'justified' or held to be true on the basis of any number of experiments because scientists could confirm only that observations to date fit with a theory or 'falsify' a theory where new observations were inconsistent. Similarly, Quine (1951) argued that the testing of beliefs must involve weighing up a whole interconnected system of ideas to decide which does not fit with the others (for example, did the experiment really produce a falsifying result? Was it undertaken poorly? Is there some new and unknown fault in the equipment?) The 'reliability' of knowledge was seen as relating to its connections with other beliefs or everyday experiences and the shared nature of these belief systems. These and other currents in philosophy tie the idea of knowledge to proven success at explaining (and sometimes predicting) phenomena.
- **Normative:** an even more radical departure from positivism resulted from Kuhn's (1962) work, which showed how underlying assumptions, accepted practices and theoretical structures 'frame' the logic of scientific progress. In some cases, more than one 'paradigm' compete, and shifts in knowledge do not come about as a result of straightforward neutral calculations that confirm or falsify a theory. Instead, collective judgements are made as to which framework fits better – and thus even science can involve interpretations and judgements. This re-linked the philosophy of science with other areas of philosophy, such

as ancient Greek ethics, which suggested that people held 'moral knowledge' about how the world *should* be as well as how it is.

- **Subjective:** post-modernism goes further, suggesting that the world is itself created and determined by our acts of cognition. Thus, the very act of describing the world in a particular way shapes what can be written or thought; hence 'truth' and 'knowledge' are both subjective and multiple. Knowledge and truth are also based on shared practices or 'forms of life' – inseparable from how we learn to follow rules and extrapolate them to new circumstances (Wittgenstein, 1953). Knowledge is linked inextricably to action, and 'understanding' is something that comes about from, and results from 'doing'.

Given these competing understandings, there is no single understanding of where and how **knowledge is held**. Some views emphasise that knowledge is something held by individuals; this leads to one conception, common in knowledge management, of 'knowledge' as information and data. However, others stress that beliefs are frequently collective, held by and transferred within large groups of people, and this affects what is thought of as knowledge.

There are also **tacit and explicit** aspects of knowledge. Explicit knowledge can be codified, written down or passed on; tacit knowledge is innate to each individual and more akin to 'understanding' – a belief that is relied on but not consciously recognised (though it could be if needed). Tacit knowledge is close to the idea of 'wisdom', related to making sound judgements in different contexts.

Importantly, knowledge can be thought of in terms of **stocks and flows**. Stocks of information can be built up by testing theories and passing them on explicitly in publications such as reports or manuals. However, the implications of information are often apparent only in the context of how it can be used to interpret different situations and instigate change – which is closely linked to how knowledge is shared and collective meaning is developed. Thus in analysing the construction of knowledge, flows of information are as important as stocks.

How can we understand the knowledge used in policy?

Influenced by the progress of empirical science, early studies of the policy process were based on the positivist approach to knowledge, conceiving of it in terms of 'high-quality' analysis providing apolitical inputs to improve policy in a neutral way. Policymaking was seen as rational problem solving, with knowledge production a quite separate domain. The function of knowledge and expertise was to 'speak truth to power' (Price, 1965); the priority was to ensure sufficient 'inputs' to feed into the different stages and to drive the policy process.

The relationship between evidence and policy is far more nuanced than this,[1] however. Policymakers draw on much more than strictly 'scientific' knowledge (see Figure 4.1). Analysts today reject the key assumption that processes move in a logical, problem-solving manner. Policymaking is not a single decision made by one actor at one time (Neilson, 2001b; Hogwood and Gunn, 1984), and the process does not stop once a decision has been taken on what *ought* to happen; feedback from what *actually* happens is a key source of knowledge on what does and does not work in practice, to channel into further decisions about whether or not to change the details of the policy so it achieves its goals. As such, policymaking involves negotiation with a wide variety of actors and pragmatic decisions taken in conditions of uncertainty.

To negotiate successfully, policymakers must draw on many types of knowledge from a variety of different sources. Lomas et al (2005, p 1) argue that policy decisions are based not only on 'scientific evidence' or knowledge gained through formal research, but also on colloquial evidence, or 'anything that establishes a fact or gives reason to believe in something'. Important sources of knowledge to guide policy include values; political judgement; habits and tradition; and professional experience and expertise (Lomas et al, 2005). Davies (2005) offers another set of factors (see Figure 4.1). Sometimes, policymakers will draw heavily on scientific knowledge for a specific purpose; at other times their use of knowledge will be opportunistic or reflect explicit efforts by other actors to promote its uptake. Even when scientific knowledge does inform policy, it is as one among many inputs.

Figure 4.1: The different influences on policy

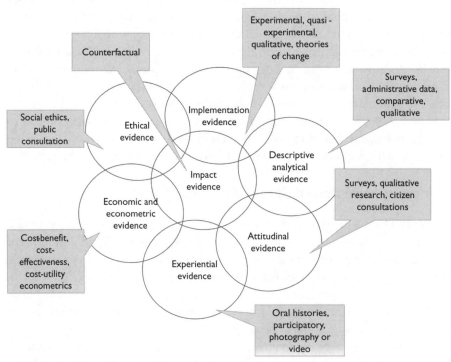

Source: Adapted from Davies (2005)

The type of knowledge used is linked closely to the politics involved. Foucault and others have shown how power infuses the knowledge process, from generation to uptake. Modern states deploy their power over the population chiefly through a collection of 'institutions, procedures, *analyses* and *reflections*' (emphasis added) (Foucault, 1991, p 102), in the process of which a series of 'knowledges' are developed. For example, demography and economics received their impetus from the interest of states in normalising their citizens, and concepts such as insanity and criminality, along with knowledge built up in the field of mental health and penal justice, are inseparable from the ways in which governments seek to treat those who do not fit within the prevailing 'rules'.

Politics will also affect when, where and why research influences the policymaking process. Rather than being universally useful or 'good' to use, knowledge will often reflect and sustain existing power structures, serving to add legitimacy to political action *after* the decision (Jasanoff, 2005). Investigating why different types of knowledge are used in policy can therefore reveal the structures and dynamics of power in a particular context, and be an important way of understanding how to improve the policy process. Work on policy processes (Kingdon, 1984; Sabatier and Jenkins-Smith, 1993) has revealed them to be the site of politics, contest, negotiation and marginalisation, with knowledge production and use entwined with these forces. Whose knowledge is used, and to what end? This question may be as revealing as examinations of the actors engaged explicitly in policymaking processes.

Three different types of knowledge

The literature on the knowledge–policy interface contains many interpretations of how different types of knowledge should be categorised, based on their source, the actors involved or their content. We outline two interpretations here to illustrate different approaches to this kind of taxonomy, and then draw on these to create our own categorisation, which we believe reflects the major trends in the literature on knowledge and policy, and serves the purposes of a practical guide to improving the knowledge–policy interface.

The first categorisation comes from Mollinga (2008), who distinguishes three key types of knowledge to help understand 'water control'. This is a managerial type of classification, based largely on the content of knowledge and the use to which it is being put: technical control, which focuses on guiding and manipulating physical processes (in this case around water resource management); organisational control, about commanding and managing people's behaviour; and socioeconomic and political control, involving the domination of people's labour and the regulation of social processes.

The second categorisation comes from Brown (2007), who develops a rich and comprehensive taxonomy and argues (based on a large empirical study) that five key contributors bring the knowledge necessary for long-term, constructive decisions: key individuals; the affected community; relevant specialists; influential organisations;

and those who can help develop a shared holistic focus. This gives rise to five different types of knowledge: individual; local; specialised; strategic; and holistic.

We draw on both of these conceptualisations, synthesising aspects of each to develop a practical framework that is still broad enough to allow deeper analysis:

- **research–based knowledge:** knowledge sourced according to the best protocols of research and the requirements of individual specialisations;
- **practice–informed knowledge:** knowledge from experience of implementing policy and practice. This includes strategic knowledge, forward-looking (appraisal), current (monitoring) and backward-looking (evaluation) knowledge. Practice-informed knowledge incorporates tacit and experiential knowledge, ideas around appraising and demonstrating impact, as well as ideas of value for money and cost-effectiveness;
- **citizen knowledge:** knowledge held by citizens, both individually and collectively, drawing on their daily lived experiences.

Table 4.1 outlines some key aspects of each of these three types of knowledge.

Table 4.1: Issues involved in using different types of knowledge in policy

Issue	Research-based knowledge	Practice-informed knowledge	Citizen/lay knowledge
Actors	Scientists, professional groups, academics	Organisations tackling specific issues, local groups or institutions	Citizens and their representatives (CSOs), indigenous groups
Source of knowledge: why is it trustworthy or useful?	Empirical observation, repeatability, independence, objectivity	Know-how, hands-on experience of what does and does not work	Experiential knowledge, beliefs, values, incentives
Where is the stock of knowledge held?	Mainly written: publications, reports, journal articles; availability depends on access by users as well as a commitment to open access on the part of knowledge producers	Some is explicit and written down (for example evaluation reports) but much is tacit in institutional memory, ways of working and precedents	Held as 'social capital' – inherently tacit, made explicit only when needed. Generally unwritten, and may be better communicated in non-written media (speaking, drama, active engagement on an issue)
How does knowledge flow?	Scientific practices, academic exchange, conferences, seminars, teaching	Decision-making spaces (for example meetings), mentoring	Common language, lived experience, communities and networks, everyday interactions

Issue	Research-based knowledge	Practice-informed knowledge	Citizen/lay knowledge
Main learning style	Theorising, validation, teaching	Hands-on, build-up of organisational behaviour and memories, work experience	Experiential, learning from peers either informally or formally through movements such as Campesino a Campesino or Farmer Field Schools
Tacit or explicit?	Codification produces explicit knowledge, but many tacit understandings and judgements remain hidden	Both equally important; can be made explicit via formal reporting systems, but tacit knowledge informs many decisions and working relationships	Almost completely tacit, making it difficult for outsiders to access (issues of trust can be an important barrier to making citizen knowledge explicit)
Why is it produced or made explicit?	Career incentives for academics and professional groups encourage publication. Within the policy process, commissioned consultancies produce reports and other dissemination tools	Mainly for accountability purposes; sometimes for learning. Practice-informed knowledge is distributed throughout an organisation or networks working on a problem and made explicit as a tool for helping to achieve organisational or individual goals	Made formal, for example in elections or other participatory processes. Often extracted by the other two types of knowledge to try to make it more explicit. Deliberative democracy approaches show that representative participation is insufficient for accountability, and ongoing inclusive deliberation is required
Specific use in policy	Helps clarify associations between issues; naming, describing, analysing and disentangling complex relationships. Tests ideas for relevance	Helps make comparisons between intended and actual; describing and situating actions within this. Tests ideas for feasibility	Helps describe opinions and values. Tests ideas for acceptability and coherence with local and individual understandings

Issue	Research-based knowledge	Practice-informed knowledge	Citizen/lay knowledge
Normative content (how it incorporates values)	Normative content of research is often implicit, which means that the knowledge tends to be used instrumentally	Normative content of practice-informed knowledge is determined by organisational goals and mandate. Depending on what these are, values are sometimes explicit, sometimes implicit	Values are explicit: some see this as the main purpose of integrating citizen knowledge
Positive content (types of data used)	Statistical data collection imperative; the ability to distinguish between variables and collect information on discrete issues	Data collection primarily for decision making, combining statistical data with other types (costs, performance, unanticipated results)	Data are wrapped up in local experience and issues are not discrete; it is difficult (if not impossible) to distinguish between them
Timeframes	Research proceeds according to its own (disciplinary) timeframes, often relatively long (years or even decades)	Timeframe may be long or short depending on the nature of the issue and how politicised it is	Reflects what is currently important to a community
Potential challenges to its use	Irrelevance to lived experience, inaccessibility because of highly technical content, silo mentality defined by academic structures	Dominant appraisal, monitoring and evaluation frameworks force practice-informed knowledge into a particular format that can become meaningless or irrelevant to decisions that need to be taken	Rumour, high levels of subjectivity, power structures and taboos may obscure issues. Citizen knowledge may also be so context-specific as to make scaling up difficult or impossible

While we recognise that there are some aspects to knowledge that we have not explicitly covered (see Box 4.1), our three categories mark out clear themes in the developing country-oriented literature and link to strong currents in the field as a whole. They also allow us to illustrate the different dynamics in play at the knowledge–policy interface[2] and to examine how to value multiple types of knowledge simultaneously and the practicalities and power dynamics involved in linking them with policy.

Box 4.1: Alternative knowledge typologies: feminist and holistic knowledge

Feminist knowledge: while a single, uniform 'feminist methodology' does not exist, a number of common concerns in the work of feminist scholars raise questions about the nature of social science knowledge and of social reality. Scientific methods and practices vary, but feminists have been particularly wary of the application of a scientific method loosely known as positivism, which is based on the idea that 'reality is directly accessible given the correct methods' (Ramazanoglu, 2002b, p 45) and that it is possible, and desirable, for research not to be affected by the researcher's social position and values. The feminist critique is that apparently value-free social science can arrive at only limited and biased accounts of social reality because the personal experiences of the researcher and dominant discourses 'only permit certain question to be asked, in certain ways, within male-centered frameworks of explanation' (Ramazanoglu, 2002b, p 45). Feminist academics and advocates have used a variety of strategies to introduce feminist knowledge and research into mainstream policy and research agendas. Some adopt an empirical approach, objectively using the methodological tools of positivist social science. Others choose strategies that celebrate subjectivity – particularly the subjective experiences of women. Overall, these methodological variations hide a common unifying theme – a political commitment to tackling unequal gender relations. In other words, advocates of feminist knowledge production are of the view that, as all research is permeated by values and political ideologies, the fact the feminist research is fuelled by a commitment to gender equality does not make it less valid than research guided by other worldviews.

Holistic knowledge: Brown (2007) notes that different types of knowledge have their own internal modes of synthesis, defining 'holistic knowledge' as knowledge dealing with 'the core of the matter, a vision of the future, a common purpose, aim of sustainability' (Brown, 2007, p 143), arguing that it interprets an issue as part of an interconnected system. For the purposes of analysing the interface between knowledge and policy, we see this holistic knowledge as being communicated via actors' values and beliefs (Chapter Three) and via the political system (Chapter Two). Additionally, we view it as being crucial to the work of knowledge intermediaries (Chapter Five). Having said that, it could be argued that the increasing use of theatre, song, art and dance in communicating knowledge for policy purposes shows recognition of the need to consider separately how holistic knowledge can help shape policy and action.

Research-based knowledge

Research aims to further theoretical and empirical knowledge of an issue. It is often scientific in nature, carried out by those working in established disciplines and professions with their own subsets of practitioners and practices. Research-based knowledge is felt to be trustworthy because of the rigorous and systematic methods employed. Scientific practices work around empirical observation and according to set norms of scientific enquiry: working with 'organised scepticism' of their own work and that of others; judging it with an open mind and according to impersonal criteria; and ensuring that results are accessible by the whole scientific community.[3] Much of this process aims at making judgements, assumptions and assessments explicit, in order to make the reasoning clear and available for examination and critique.

These factors mean that research-based knowledge can contribute significantly to policy. It is often presented as the remedy to more partisan, politicised decision making, helping policymakers function in a 'problem-solving' mode according to reason and logic by improving their understanding of how and why issues may have developed. As we have outlined, this is only a small part of policymaking, but research-based knowledge nonetheless has high credibility with many actors, who argue that its quality can be assessed according to specific criteria (see Table 4.2). Methods deemed acceptable vary according to a 'hierarchy of evidence', from opinions at the bottom of the scale to systematic reviews at the top (Monaghan, 2011), although, as will become clear, this hierarchy needs to be treated with caution once we accept that research is not the only type of knowledge needed for policy.

Table 4.2: Criteria for assessing the quality of research

Traditional criteria (most suitable for quantitative approaches)	Alternative criteria (better for qualitative approaches)
Validity: a correspondence between data and conceptualisation	*Credibility:* a set of findings is believable
Reliability: observations are consistent when instruments are administered on more than one occasion	*Transferability:* a set of findings is relevant to settings other than the one or ones from which they are derived
Replicability: it is possible to reproduce an investigation	*Dependability:* a set of findings is likely to be relevant to a different time from the one in which it was conducted
Generalisability: it is possible to generalise findings to similar cases that have not been studied	*Confirmability:* the researcher has not allowed personal values to intrude to an excessive degree

Source: Becker et al (2006, pp 7-8)

We can distinguish two broad types of relationships between research-based knowledge and policy. Independent research is often produced for academic audiences, primarily to further knowledge. As such, the chosen topics tend to reflect the career incentives of scientists and professionals rather than current policy issues (Burawoy, 2005). In the UK, the Haldane Principle enshrines the independence of research from government interests via the setting up of independent research councils to manage funding decisions.[4] Policy-oriented research focuses on issues of relevance to policy and uses systematic methods to examine policy problems, often analysing or synthesising existing academic knowledge. Researchers will often be commissioned or consulted by policymakers to provide answers to specific questions relating to current issues. The line between the two is somewhat blurred, however; Table 4.5 shows that there is a spectrum of policy relevance that depends both on the coincidence of interests between researchers and policy, and on the degree to which research and policy are both targeted at specific local issues.

The '*stock*' or positive content of research-based knowledge for policy is a global and (in theory) common knowledge base, building on past achievements including carefully constructed explanatory frameworks, and set assumptions, methodologies, questions and theories. There is a great deal contained in scientific journals and texts, technical assessments, commissioned analyses and systematic reviews of existing research-based knowledge. As scientific research is often carried out independently from social or political interests, it is regarded by some as 'value-free', although the fact that some work is well suited to certain ends, for example nuclear power, may lead some analysts to differ. However, when research is carried out for a policy audience this is not the case – policy research is valued instrumentally, that is, it is produced as a means to better achieving the aims of the organisation commissioning or carrying out the work. Even where this research seeks to give impartial advice, its content is implicitly normative; drawing on this kind of policy research will help actors achieve some goals but not others.

How research knowledge *flows* through policy is the subject of much heated debate; there is a very large literature setting out different routes via which research is thought to have an impact on policymaking (see, for example, Nutley et al, 2007; Carden, 2009; Jones, 2009a). The nature of these flows and their effectiveness in ensuring that research exerts an influence on policy depends on three factors:

- the type and extent of individual contact between researchers and policymakers, and whether the points of contact are formal or informal. Formal seminars, workshops, conferences, project or programme meetings and expert advisory committees all provide formal forums for learning about research results. Care needs to be taken to ensure that these are not set up simply as lectures, as the technical content of research can be too challenging for non-specialist policymakers to absorb. Providing additional formal opportunities to debate meaning and clarify the implications for future policy development and implementation can be more helpful in embedding research knowledge in ongoing policy debates. Informally, policymakers do build up networks of research contacts to whom they may turn for interpretation or clarification of a current issue. These may be particularly effective when the need for knowledge is urgent, but the danger is that policymakers fail to seek out alternative opinions, developing a cosy consensus based on a limited view of the issue;
- the extent to which the core processes of policymaking (strategy, policy appraisal and business planning, for example) are designed to be informed by research knowledge. This will depend very much on internal processes within government departments; whether they actively encourage policymakers to read research reports, attend seminars or other research-based events and how they then support a process of open debate and discussion within the

organisation. Described in fuller detail later (see the section on knowledge incentive structures) this is an under-studied aspect of the knowledge–policy interface; and

• how well research is communicated to policymakers has a strong effect on whether the messages it contains are retained and ultimately used. There is a long history of research on research communication[5] and while Chapter Five discusses the topic in relation to the role of knowledge intermediaries, it is beyond the scope of the book to cover the topic in any depth.

Practice-informed knowledge

Practice-informed knowledge is gained by organisations and individuals working to tackle a particular issue. It is represented by those with expertise in a specific area, those with a track record of implementing projects and programmes or, more generally, those who have had a hand in influencing change on an issue or in a particular context.

While practice-informed knowledge is often tacit, it can be made explicit for two purposes. First, it can inform organisational decision-making processes and structures, such as project and programme approval, in order to improve cost-effectiveness. It has a key role to play in improving accountability by, for example, providing external stakeholders with information on progress. It is also often encapsulated in performance management frameworks, which put in place incentives for success, as proposed by the 'new public management' approach to policymaking (Pons and van Zanten, 2007).

The second purpose is to improve individual and organisational learning by generating useful knowledge for future policy and practice (Powell, 2006). Effective interventions cannot be shaped fully by research carried out elsewhere, and it is difficult to predict in advance the best strategies for success (Guijt, 2008; Jones, 2011). This may be the case particularly for complex problems with context-dependent dynamics and change processes. Rather than prior technical training, practice-informed knowledge for policy comes through a process of 'learning by doing' (on the part of individuals, teams or organisations).

Practice-informed knowledge is often arranged around the impact-to-outcome causal chain (Table 4.3), and helps provide a 'reality check' on policy models and implementation strategies. Some argue that this is the most common use of practice-informed knowledge – to test the feasibility of potential policy ideas and better situate a problem within the logistical, ideological and management constraints where it is to be addressed (Delvaux and Mangez, 2008).

Stocks of this knowledge are found in documents produced for planning (for example log frames, *ex ante* impact assessments, strategy papers, regulatory budgets), monitoring (for example information on spending and activities for auditing purposes, or 'key performance indicators') or evaluation (for example a formalised, systematic assessment of the intended and unintended, positive and negative, effects of an intervention). The 'normative' content of this knowledge

Table 4.3: Practice-informed knowledge in a causal chain

	Definition	**Example**
Inputs	Resources (human, financial, technical and material) necessary to carry out project activities	Staff, budget
Activities	Actions or series of actions undertaken, using inputs, to produce planned outputs	Construction work
Outputs	Products or services, tangible or intangible, resulting directly from implementation of activities	Schools built
Outcomes	Changes resulting from use of outputs during project period or soon after	Greater educational achievement
Impact	Lasting and significant changes in people's lives to which project contributes, directly or indirectly	Reduced poverty
Sustainability	Capability of maintaining over time the positive outcomes and impact obtained or of continuing the promotion of such changes in future	School maintained by local community

Source: ACT Development (2008)

is determined by the goals and mandate of the organisation. As well as meeting formal goals and objectives, certain values and judgements may underlie much of the information produced, such as how the categories used for data collection (for example gender-disaggregated or not, see Box 4.2) reflect what individuals or the organisation believe is significant about an issue. Similarly, planning and evaluation documents reflect underlying rhythms and political expediencies of the organisation, carried out periodically or sporadically in reaction to particular events or circumstances.

Box 4.2: Gender statistics

The history of gender statistics goes back to the First World Conference on Women held in Mexico in 1975, where a general plea was made for governments to invest in the collection and dissemination of sex-disaggregated data so as to better support gender-sensitive policy and programme development. By 2005, the UN noted that the majority of countries were producing sex-disaggregated data on a burgeoning array of demographic, human development and service-use indicators at least once every decade and also undertaking gender budgeting (analyses of government budgets from a gender perspective to highlight the gendered impacts of public expenditure decisions). These have been complemented by the creation of a variety of internationally comparable gender indices. The UN's Gender-related Development Index, for example, adjusts the mainstream Human Development Index for gender inequality, effectively discounting a country's score as women's and men's performance becomes more disparate. The UN Gender Empowerment Measure complements this focus on human capital indicators with a composite index on empowerment in the political and workplace spheres, while the

Organisation for Economic Co-operation and Development's (OECD's) Social Institutions and Gender Index seeks to measure the role of social norms and institutions (such as son preference and family codes) in perpetuating gender inequalities. The OECD also produces the Development Assistance Committee gender tracker, which allows funders to ascertain how much aid given to a country goes to enhancing gender equity.

Nevertheless, many gender statistics from the developing world – including those on gender-based violence, informal sector employment and time poverty – are still collected at best in an *ad hoc* manner – outside national statistics offices, whose capacity for both collection and dissemination is often limited. Lack of rigorous data impedes advocacy on many women's rights issues, with arguments too often seen as 'feminist advocacy, rather than objective/scientific arguments backed by facts and figures' (Razavi, 1997, p 1117). Even so, some analysts argue that the reasons behind the uptake of some types of evidence and not others are more political and ideological in nature. Certain methodologies of knowledge production, such as those of neoclassical economics, can easily legitimise the status quo and thus are more acceptable to those in power (for example Folbre, 2001). Accordingly, many feminist scholars have turned to qualitative and participatory methods to help plug some of the data gap, partly because quantitative data are simply not available and partly as a commitment to going beyond headcounts and including indicators that reflect qualitative change in gender power relations (Folbre, 2001).

Analysing the flows of practice-informed knowledge in policymaking is challenging because, as noted above, a good deal of such knowledge remains tacit and hidden. Organisations often work with a 'shadow system', an informal side of organisational life that can be just as crucial to their functioning as as their official aspects (Stacey, 1996); and which are difficult to share with organisations that do not have a similar mandate or are staffed by people with different skills (such as analysts in one organisation, practitioners in another). Institutional memory and well-known 'precedents' are important, as are shared 'rules of thumb', understandings and judgements. Much tacit knowledge is passed on without being codified formally, and it is easily lost when staff leave organisations or move to new positions.

Strengthening relationships between implementing staff and other organisations can improve the retention and sharing of tacit practice-informed knowledge, as can strengthening the institutional arrangements essential to the development effort (Mosse et al, 1998). This may need to be handled informally (for example through discussions with partners), either because of sensitivities in reporting such issues or because of a lack of 'fit' with prevailing reporting formats. In many cases, learning occurs and changes are made in the process of an evaluation rather than being made explicit in a report – not only for the staff evaluated but also for those who engage in dialogue, dispute and debate over the findings (Patton, 1998).

Citizen knowledge

Citizen knowledge is built through interactions in communities and wider social networks. While practice-informed and research-based knowledge tend to be held by those 'outside' the lived experience of any changes,[6] this type of knowledge highlights the value of experience; the personal and shared understandings of ordinary people can have a number of benefits when given a proper voice in policy dialogue. Jones and Sumner (2007), drawing on concepts of participation from Chambers (1997), argue that local people need to be able to enhance, share and analyse their knowledge of life and conditions, and to use this knowledge within policy processes.

Citizen knowledge is valuable for its descriptive content – people's own lived experience of issues. Chambers' (1994) description of 'rural development tourism' provides a vivid caricature of the ways in which staff of development agencies or central government ministries are often entirely blind to local circumstances and realities, consequently misdiagnosing the causes of poverty and implementing policies that are simply not relevant. Local understandings of problems are in many circumstances less likely to be fitted artificially into organisational or disciplinary frameworks and hence can give a more holistic and resonant picture of some of the key dynamics (Brown, 2007). They also have considerable value as a way of understanding and influencing change, as an instrumental input with the potential for considerable 'quality' or reliability. Citizen knowledge can also serve an important normative function – it relates to the uncovering of citizens' values and norms. Delvaux and Mangez (2008) argue that the role of public knowledge and opinion is to assess which social problems, or aspects of problems, are worthy of attention, and to decide where potential policy responses are acceptable (through coherence with local values). Less well-recognised, but equally important, values and norms in citizen knowledge are important in shaping what is an acceptable process: Jasanoff (2005) shows how policy processes in different countries are shaped by preferences for different styles of collective decision making – consensus-based, competitive or adversarial.

Both stocks and flows of citizen knowledge tend to be highly tacit in nature, residing in people who have individual or collective experience of a place, culture or practice. Communities have their own local history, tied to collective identities and understandings of their society and environment, often shared through oral traditions or other shared symbols or practices and encapsulated in the concept of 'social capital' within and between individuals and groups.

Citizen knowledge can be made formal and explicit through a number of processes: via elections or through the work of Civil Society Organisations (CSOs) such as resource user groups or indigenous organisations. However, some analysts and practitioners argue that more needs to be done to link citizen knowledge to policy and action, especially where complex decisions or implementation processes may require a variety of trade-offs between different values and ideals not foreseeable in advance (Laderchi, 2001). Many 'participatory' tools and approaches have been designed to help bring out and make explicit citizen knowledge, most famously participatory rural appraisal (Chambers, 1994), but representative participation may be insufficient for proper accountability, and legitimate decision making may require fair and inclusive deliberation. This would ideally entail bringing about a new and autonomous 'discourse' to the policy process, letting citizens hold government to account for their actions (Goetz and Jenkins, 2005) and exploring where policymakers or development agencies may share priorities with local people (Powell, 2006; Morgan, 2008). Some citizen knowledge has to be treated with caution, however. Indigenous technical knowledge has long been studied in agriculture and natural resource management. Often unique to a given culture or society, it is passed on through generations and evolves through local experimentation (done, for example, by farmers). While indigenous innovation can result in real progress (see Chapter Five, Box 5.6), Bentley's (2001) observation that 'what farmers don't know can't help them' highlights the importance of ensuring that indigenous knowledge is not based on a lack of understanding about crucial issues (such as plant pathology) leading to a misdiagnosis of problems.

The supporting role of data

All three types of knowledge have their own reasons for collecting facts and statistics. These 'data' are often thought of as reflecting a positive view of the world, but they do not emerge of their own accord; rather, data represent knowledge whose form must be decided in advance in order to be created. The way a scientific experiment is constructed, for example, will affect the types of data that emerge from it; *how* information is gathered from local people will influence *what* is gathered (participatory assessments versus statistical survey techniques give rise to very different types of information). Data are thus shaped by the normative view of the world of whichever type of knowledge they are intended to support (see Box 4.2). This means thought needs to go into ensuring that the methods used to collect the data are a good reflection of norms and that they are built on the highest disciplinary standards. Professor Sir Roger Jowell, Head of the European Social Survey at City University, notes that 'bad data are not simply less good than good data: they can be positively mischievous'[7] – giving rise to a misleading picture of a situation, inaccurate reasoning or analyses that reflect the normative framing of the dominant type of knowledge. Having said that, there is a danger that creating the perfect dataset becomes a goal in its own right.

The power dynamics underlying the uptake of different types of knowledge in policy processes

Having examined what constitutes each of the three types of knowledge, we now turn to discussion of how the power dynamics associated with each type affect its production and use, and consequently the interface between knowledge and policy.

Linking research-based knowledge to policy

Improving the uptake of research by policymakers is not simply a matter of improving its supply: there are a number of practical issues, many of which give rise to, or are affected by, power dynamics between the different actors. While research-based knowledge has a key role to play, issues exist that present a challenge in terms of how it is used and the influence it has.

The different 'cultures' of academic researchers and policymakers construct some of these barriers (Neilson, 2001b). Scientific research projects are often more narrowly focused than policy issues, and researchers who work in 'silos' may not comprehend the breadth of policy's needs (Scott, 2006). In addition, career incentives often push academics to specialise, to take their time to produce new and interesting results and to focus on internal consistency. Whereas policymakers need quick and clear answers to current issues, researchers may be able to provide only partial answers that are inconclusive, ambiguous, contradictory or quickly out of date (Scott, 2006). Researchers and policymakers also frequently use different languages and hold quite different values and affiliations, and such differences tend to be even more acute in Southern contexts (Jones et al, 2008).

At worst, this may mean academic research will have little relevance for pressing societal problems or that ideas will take a long time to filter into the policy sphere and fulfil the 'enlightenment function' of knowledge outlined by Weiss (1977). Meanwhile, when research whose results are ambiguous or uncertain meets a simple, abstract and powerful policy idea, policymakers may cherry-pick information to support their (pre-decided) policy position (Jones et al, 2008). While a focus on interpreting research results for policy can help (see Chapter Five), there are likely to be a number of trade-offs to make to produce information that is credible and sufficiently robust while also being salient to policy decisions (Cash et al, 2003), and in reality the actor providing this interpretation is thus afforded a substantial amount of discretion.[8] For example, relying on policymakers alone to interpret research results means that any such interpretation may be done poorly because of capacity issues or because the dominant policy discourse leads to a high degree of selectivity and bias. In many cases, researchers themselves provide this interpretation; with scientific findings that involve caveats or ambiguity, and conclusions that are heavily qualified with statements of uncertainty and risk, policymakers may frequently ask the scientist 'what is your best guess on this issue?'[9] Presenting research results accompanied by suggested policy options is seen as a standard element in linking knowledge and policy. Indeed, a large international survey showed that policymakers in developing countries definitely welcome scientists and researchers providing them with opinions on issues where there may not yet be strong evidence (Jones et al, 2008). However, this may sometimes be difficult to promote systematically, as researchers often lack the mandate, funding or career incentives to link research to action (Livny et al, 2006).

Moreover, some argue that, in offering policy interpretations, researchers undermine the neutrality and 'objectivity' that is the basis for scientific influence on policy, and risk undermining the link between the two (Scott et al, 2007). In some contexts, scientists have used their research to advocate personal positions on policy issues based on their own agenda (Lackey, 2006). Meanwhile, politicians may critique the personal biases and motivations of scientists or funding organisations whose research findings conflict with their priorities. The response to research into genetically modified varieties of cotton in India was highly politicised, with some political factions painting the scientists as 'puppets' of a Western 'totalitarian' science, sowing mistrust and discontent. The Indian government subsequently disregarded the research, pushing some state governments to ban biotech cotton varieties based on flawed evidence of agronomic failure (Herring, 2007). However, if researchers retreat from policy debates entirely, this issue is unlikely to be resolved, as it leaves a 'vacuum' that risks being filled by politically motivated parties that offer their own interpretations biased by prevailing values or discourse, or based on vested interests committed to a predetermined outcome of the evidence.

In addition to politicians, actors who are committed to a predetermined course based on their interests, values, beliefs or perceived credibility with a sector of society (see Chapter Three) may apply pressure to influence the findings of scientific research and how it is disseminated, reported or interpreted. With sufficient media attention, this can create real pressure on politicians to react, particularly since unusual hazards that pose relatively little danger to wider society often take up a disproportionate amount of coverage. This was seen, for example, in the British coverage of the measles, mumps and rubella vaccine, which was linked erroneously to autism in children (see also Box 4.3).

Box 4.3: Measures to stem the misrepresentation of science in policy debates

Science advocacy groups are beginning to be more vocal about the dangers of misrepresenting science and research methods. In the UK, the non-governmental organisation (NGO) Sense About Science actively responds to what it sees as the misrepresentation of science and scientific evidence by politicians and the media, and several high-profile individuals blog or write for the national press (such as Dr Ben Goldacre with his column and blog *Bad Science*). This strengthens the voice of scientific research in public debates and, although it does not make the debates any less politicised (Monaghan, 2011), it does contribute to greater transparency and greater understanding of the limitations of poor data and poor research.

Rigorous research is relatively expensive, often resulting in a supply-side gap on issues important to poor people and disadvantaged groups, particularly in developing countries where research capacity is low and there is little financial sustainability for policy-oriented research (Livny et al, 2006). The increasing reliance of research centres on paid consultancies can contribute to the 'commodification' of knowledge, whereby research is produced in a quasi-commercial manner (Harriss-White, 2007) or sponsored by industry, with the topics, framings and even outcomes determined by the priorities of the richest actors, reducing diversity and creativity in the knowledge base and hence in the array of policy options (Rosenstock and Lee, 2002; Nowotny et al, 2003). Delaying or withholding research results that are inconvenient (for example by threatening or undertaking libel action) can contribute to gaps in the knowledge base, and commissioning research with the direct goal of countering existing scientific opinion can be used to undermine a perceived consensus on issues (Rosenstock and Lee, 2002).

The examples above focus on independent research, but many of them apply equally to policy-oriented research. Policymakers may lack the skills and capacities to engage with researchers through organising research tenders and managing consulting processes (Livny et al, 2006).'Getting the question right' is an important part of the commissioning process; if the research is directed too heavily towards a specific policy goal, it can fail to question a policy's underlying theoretical and explanatory frameworks, meaning that assumptions and value judgements are hidden and context-sensitive policy judgements become harder to make (Cleaver and Franks, 2008).

Actors who have the power to fund this research can weight it in favour of certain outcomes or rule out the possibility of truly independent analysis or 'good science' by framing the research questions to their advantage (Waterston, 2005). This 'scientisation of politics' can be purposeful – to remove the scope for investigating certain assumptions or questions by glossing over political preferences or value judgements and presenting questions as a 'technical' matter for apolitical dispassionate analysis. Environmental research is often used, for instance, to depoliticise natural resource issues in poverty reduction strategy papers; the studies 'project an illusion of natural resources that require better management and enhanced legislation to ensure that poor people benefit, while overlooking highly political struggles over environmental control and rights to resources' (Waldman, 2005, p vii). KNOTS (2006) found that in Honduras environmental issues were framed around a 'crisis narrative', blaming poor people's behaviour and lifestyles for the mismanagement of public goods and ignoring the fact that environmental resources often form the basis of material wealth – which would lead to questions of power, inequality and the role elites have played in environmental degradation.

Linking practice-informed knowledge to policy

There are a number of difficulties involved in making the most of practice-informed knowledge for policy. To begin with, although donors are increasingly emphasising rigorous evaluations and ongoing monitoring, much practice-informed knowledge is tacit or implicit. Compared with explicit or formalised knowledge (as embodied in evaluation reports and manuals), it is 'stickier' – harder to transfer between individuals and organisations, particularly where there is high staff turnover (Greenhalgh et al, 2004). This is particularly true where participatory approaches to monitoring and evaluation depend on the strength of personal relationships, but may also apply where it is formalised, as the best learning opportunities are not easily predictable or repeatable (Kurtz and Snowden, 2003).

Second, implementers frequently lack the capacity to put in place systematic planning, monitoring or evaluation activities that make active use of practice-informed knowledge. Undertaking experimental impact evaluations requires a high level of technical sophistication, often lacking in the field of applied development. Many appraisal and evaluation frameworks used by international organisations are alien to staff working in developing countries. For example, Southern organisations often find it difficult to understand and use the logical framework approach, as it requires significant investment in time and effort to use it well (Bakewell and Garbutt, 2005).

Third, the processes, frameworks and resources needed to produce and use practice-informed knowledge are more likely to favour more powerful actors. Impact evaluation expertise is concentrated among a limited number of institutions, largely in Northern contexts (Levine and Savedoff, 2006), from which most frameworks for codifying practice-informed knowledge originate. Added to the fact that many development agency staff cannot speak local languages, this means many in-country staff or partners become disenfranchised. In addition, information and communication technologies, a key element of managing this kind of knowledge, are less prevalent and more difficult to use in some Southern contexts. As codified practice-informed knowledge becomes more significant in the everyday functioning of public policy and development, this 'digital divide' can amplify unequal power relations (Ferguson et al, 2008).

Finally, practice-informed knowledge is often produced around a particular decision context, shaped by the various incentive structures within implementing organisations. A significant amount of research shows that decisions facing staff in public policy organisations are often fairly incremental in nature, a matter of making small changes around the edges of existing approaches rather than being able to revise fundamental principles, assumptions or modalities (Neilson, 2001b). The information produced for these decisions is unlikely to be used to test assumptions or question principles, since there will be no space to act on the lessons learned. Moreover, when individuals or organisations are in competition with each other, they are unlikely to be forthcoming in sharing the real 'secret of their success'. A background of competition can also lead to a bias towards proving 'success' and a great deal of information produced largely in order to legitimise a preferred set of options, such as with NGOs, which often need to maintain good public profiles in order to secure funding. One study of the logical framework approach (Bakewell and Garbutt, 2005) shows that staff tend to report expected outcomes as laid out at the start of the project rather than to make genuine observations about progress; nearly all databases of experimental impact evaluations published were found to contain favourable results (Jones, 2009a). This process of legitimisation may also be seen where pressure to avoid the publicity bad news brings inhibits the commissioning or publishing of studies (Mosse et al, 1998; Ravallion, 2005). In a context where failure is not tolerated, incentives are institutionalised against finding and learning from unexpected results. Monitoring and evaluation can slide into 'symbolic' use – promoting an image of credibility and accountability in order to fulfil contractual obligations without taking on board findings in a more meaningful way. The adversarial process of policymaking and government tends to mean that politicians seek to avoid publicity from negative results, which can often be amplified or distorted into 'bad news' by the media, affecting the long-term sustainability and credibility of the organisation.

Ensuring that practice-informed knowledge contributes to learning and innovation is a constant challenge, often seen as taking valuable time and resources away from 'real' work, particularly where impact may take years to come about and results may not be available until long after programmes are completed (Foresti, 2007). This may be worse in bureaucratic organisations, where a high degree of formalisation and standardisation, along with an academic bias, inhibits innovation (Lam, 2000).

How all of these trends play out is very context-specific, but it is possible to draw together several implications for policy and practice. The greater the pressure to use set frameworks, the more likely it is that policy and practice will be skewed towards work that fits into the way these tools frame the development process. For example, experimental and quasi-experimental impact evaluations require a 'dosing model' (with interventions modelled as delivering discrete and homogenous output, like the distribution of pills) and a plausible counterfactual (finding a group large enough to represent a case similar to those receiving the intervention in all relevant variables). These sorts of evaluation can demonstrate impact for discrete initiatives in a specific contest (such as the provision of vaccines or cash transfer-based social protection), but are less amenable to work on advocacy and capacity building, where many complex, interacting factors produce change (Jones, 2009a). The implication is that, as donors increasingly demand these types of impact evaluation to legitimise programmes, they will skew funding towards issues that can be measured in this way. Project and programme staff often find themselves managing a system of representation and interpretation of information as much as a project itself (Mosse, 2006). This reduces the value of the practice-informed knowledge gained from implementing the project and constrains local institutional flexibility and adaptive capacity.

These trends mean that formalised and explicit practice-informed knowledge is only the tip of the iceberg, and hence only rarely provides the driving force for decisions. A great deal of data are collected to measure 'performance' according to criteria set out by frameworks such as results-based management, but these are actually used rarely (Thomas, 2007). Information on performance and progress often has 'no discernible effect' on decision making or budgetary allocations (for example in the UN system – UNOIOS, 2008). Similarly, work on the utilisation of evaluations concludes that these are not used because stakeholders see little or no value in the findings, because they are not aware of the results or because the context has changed dramatically (Sandison, 2005).

Linking citizen knowledge to policy

We can analyse the power dynamics affecting the role of citizen knowledge in policy by referring to Stirling's (2008) classification of normative, instrumental and substantive imperatives.[10] There may be some level of each in any policy process, but separating them out helps to crystallise their relative merits.

The **normative** reason for incorporating citizen knowledge in policy relates to the democratic imperative: to provide space for the broad-based expression of citizen desires. In many cases, however, the political context does not provide this sort of space. Although its intellectual origins lie in ancient Greece, substantial and meaningful political systems of representative democracy are only a relatively recent arrival to developed countries. Elsewhere, such systems are non-existent or in their early stages, and allow very little expression of voice in public policy at all, let alone more direct incorporation of citizen knowledge into policy or practice (see Chapter Two). In these situations, any experiential or lay knowledge of issues incorporated in policy is likely to be representative of policymakers and elites, which may be a vicious cycle, as inequality is frequently reinforced by beliefs that it is in some way the natural order of things (Bebbington et al, 2006). In a similar vein, politicians often frame policies in terms of prevailing perspectives and values of groups that could function to support or hinder the progress of decision making or implementation (see Chapter Three), which again could serve to reinforce biases and inequalities.

The tacit nature of citizen knowledge means that significant trust is required in order to draw on it, especially by 'outsiders', as government actors and development agencies frequently are. This means formalised outputs of participatory processes designed to generate citizen knowledge often reflect the political economy of the context in which they were generated as much as any underlying insight about a policy issue or solution. This could give rise to locals giving outsiders the answers they think are needed in order to secure funding, or reflecting and reifying 'local culture' and thereby reaffirming the agendas of local elites. Unless there is a clear appreciation of local power dynamics, the existing interests, networks and the political, economic, social and cultural interactions of participants can end up steering processes to generate citizen knowledge.

Policymakers also use citizen knowledge **instrumentally** to help them achieve their goals, such as a Nepali initiative to consult focus groups about the need for political reforms following the end of a decade of conflict (Jones et al, 2009b). From this perspective, the main function of local participation is to increase the efficiency and effectiveness of aid agency interventions by drawing on local resources, improving the targeting of project expenditure and reducing costs. Care needs to be taken with assuming that instrumental participation will deliver real impact, however. In the example above, the initiative operated under the implicit assumption that citizens already understood why the reforms were needed, which was not in fact the case (Jones et al, 2009b).

There are other challenges to the instrumental use of citizen knowledge. Such knowledge is often excluded from policy made under the rational paradigm, where the emphasis on 'high quality' often leads policymakers to conclude that research-based knowledge is the only means of formulating and implementing policies. While national governments are often at fault for this misconception, international development agencies may have been equally culpable, operating under the view that science and technology will provide a 'universal fix' that has a far-reaching impact on poverty (Leach and Scoones, 2006). Indigenous technical knowledge is often cast as 'outdated' or in need of 'modernisation' in relation to 'knowledge transfer' policies and agricultural extension, or deeply embedded cultural values and understandings are violated on the basis of them being seen as 'occult' practices in need of reform (Lansing and Miller, 2003). This disregard of citizen knowledge may contribute to the destruction of long-accumulated and treasured stocks of knowledge.

Participatory approaches have been incorporated into processes without altering the associated ways of working (Rudqvist and Woodford-Berger, 1996); in fact, they are often seen as a set of measures to be used *after* the scope and objectives of a project have been defined, in order to help meet its predetermined goals. Poor and vulnerable people rarely have the chance to question project objectives or scope, as major decisions have been taken elsewhere and their voices often have little purchase in terms of making aid agency interventions more representative or fostering genuine learning.

Citizen participation also takes time and money to carry out well, and incorporating citizen knowledge requires a variety of skill sets and capacities (such as facilitation) that are often lacking in government departments (Chambers, 2008). It can also involve considerable costs on the part of poor people in terms of their time and labour. Meanwhile, participation is often simply 'consultation', with views collected without any commitment to take them on board, or as a means of simply informing locals about upcoming or ongoing projects. This means it is difficult to use citizen knowledge effectively in other programmes or projects and (as already outlined with regard to practice-informed knowledge) it often does not contribute effectively to organisational learning and planning (Beardon and Newman, 2009).

Finally, citizen knowledge is often incorporated into policy to help improve the legitimacy of programmes with key constituencies; it has long been accepted, for example, that local 'ownership', in terms of involvement, is an essential ingredient to effective implementation. However, this can slip into desultory consultation, where participatory processes are simply a tool to ensure compliance with decisions taken elsewhere in advance, and the main drive is to foster a perceived legitimacy (Cooke and Kothari, 2001) or to 'tame' opposition and smooth the way for predetermined objectives to be achieved.

A **substantive** approach to incorporating citizen knowledge in policy uses it to help achieve outcomes, but these are not determined instrumentally in terms of particular values or interests. Instead, citizen knowledge is incorporated into policy *because* it can help define better outcomes, design better policies and evaluate progress according to better and more relevant criteria. Work on participatory evaluation addresses some of the issues involved in incorporating citizen knowledge substantively into policymaking (Guijt, 2008), and there are examples from developed countries where citizen knowledge on particular issues has been used to make substantive improvements to policy. Gavelin and colleagues (2007), for instance, report on the work of the UK's Nanotechnology Engagement Group, which involved citizens in a series of ground-breaking discussions on the development and governance of nanotechnologies. However, there is much still to be done to develop policy processes that regularly take a substantive approach to incorporating citizen knowledge, as shown by the examples in Box 4.4. We also discuss this later in the section on knowledge incentive structures.

Lastly, there are some difficulties in the nature of the 'stock' of citizen knowledge. It may be that other factors about the subjective and cultural nature of this type of knowledge will hamper its utility. Bentley and Gonzalo Rodríguez's (2001) work on indigenous technical knowledge shows that farmers in Honduras had a highly detailed understanding of plant species and stages of development, but know less about insects (especially with respect to their reproduction), and less still about plant pathology and its causes. Ease of observability and cultural importance are likely to play a large role in shaping these strengths and weaknesses (Bentley and Gonzalo Rodriguez, 2001). Things that are easy to observe and of great cultural importance are likely to represent areas of deep knowledge, but things that are difficult to observe but of high cultural importance are characterised by 'mistaken knowledge', where farmers know something exists but misunderstand it. For example, farmers believed that pests came inside bottles of insecticide, when in fact it was the case that the chemical killed the pests' natural enemies, allowing them to flourish. In these cases, mythico-religious explanations may hinder effective responses to problems.

Box 4.4: How excluding citizen knowledge may result in substantive deficits in policies and programmes

Asking poor and excluded people matters for shaping effective policy and programmes because, without reflecting their knowledge, interventions risk missing out on the true needs of their target beneficiaries. Social protection for youth in Ghana entails a number of community-based employment programmes for under- and unemployed young people. However, programme designers have done relatively little to tap youth knowledge while shaping these national initiatives. The overall emphasis in Ghanaian social protection on economic vulnerabilities means these programmes may well be missing out on tackling a host of often equally important social vulnerabilities facing young people. These include lack of status, lack of direction, gender-based discrimination, sexual harassment and rape, and time poverty, among others. In addition, youth are in general ill informed about existing programmes and how to access them.

'If you don't know anybody in the place, it is difficult to get a job.... Someone who had worse grades will be taken just because he or she knows somebody at the place.'
(Young female focus group discussion, Mamobi, 2010)

'You always see the guys hanging around. Because of idleness, most of them engage in fights.' (Young male focus group discussion, Chorkor, 2010)

In Nepal, research into poor people's priorities following the long-awaited Peace Agreement in 2006 suggested these were quite distinct from donor assumptions about the importance of policing and constitutional reform, for instance. Interviewees from different regions instead highlighted in particular the need to address the social vulnerabilities poor and excluded people in Nepal face. These include entrenched social hierarchies; multi-layered inequalities; limited representation; illiteracy or a mother tongue other than Nepali; community disunity; lack of awareness of the language of citizen responsibilities; regional inequalities and isolation; and poor access to information, among others. Such issues were consistent with research from 1999 as well as with several more recent qualitative research initiatives. This is of concern, as it suggests that many of the original sources of conflict remain unresolved and had not been integrated into donor or policymaker understandings of this fragile state context.

'[One of the barriers is] outmoded ways of thinking. Our way of looking at women is very traditional – we doubt them, question them, we don't educate them because they will marry into another house anyway. We haven't updated our thoughts but this needs to change.' (Chepang men, Makwanpur, 2007)

Similarly, a multi-country study on gender and social protection in Asia, Africa and Latin America found that, despite a broader commitment to gender equality and women's empowerment at policy level in a number of countries, in most cases there is a substantial disconnect between these goals on the one hand and social protection programme objectives and implementation on the other. Listening to what women themselves say about their own strategic interests would likely broaden the conceptualisation of gendered vulnerabilities, and also empower women to contribute to the transformation of gender relations within the house and community. This includes not only economic vulnerabilities but also social vulnerabilities.

'Women get sicker....They are responsible for household chores and take care of lots of things. Husbands and children get food first when supplies are limited – wives don't eat if the husband is uncaring and he doesn't share what he is eating.' (Married woman, Shibhta, Ethiopia, 2009)

'Husbands are the ones who take care of great matters [such as loans], so I can't say much.... I didn't talk to him about the [loan repayment] deadline or the interest because it would make my husband's family worry too, and I was afraid it would upset him. He says I don't know anything so I couldn't ask. I was too afraid to ask him.' (Married woman, Coc Cot, Viet Nam, 2009)

In short, there is an urgent need to balance knowledge from 'experts' with that of local grassroots knowledge from men, women, youth and children in order to create a more balanced evidence base and maximise the effectiveness of scarce development resources.

Source: Jones et al (2009c); Holmes and Jones (2010); Pereznieto et al (2011)

Practical implications: using different types of knowledge in policy

Improving the use of different types of knowledge in policy is not simply a matter of commissioning more research, conducting more evaluations or consulting more widely. Nor can one type of knowledge substitute for another: different types of knowledge are used in policy for different reasons, as we have seen. The power dynamics inherent in each of the three types will affect how they are used: the difficult task in front of policymakers is to exercise reasoned judgement in the face of competing knowledge claims, uncertain knowledge, continuous change and the political imperative to 'do something' to make change happen. Very rarely do they take rational calculated decisions based on a clear understanding of what is 'right' (Albaek, 1995), but strengthening the stocks and flows of each type of knowledge could facilitate a more reasoned approach, as outlined in the simple needs assessment described in Table 4.4.

The next section outlines some of the ways this can be done, before turning to important questions of where and how to mesh the three types of knowledge together.

Diagnosing the effects of different types of knowledge

Questions this section will help you answer:
- Is there a dominant narrative for your policy issue?
- Are there deeply embedded types of knowledge that shape relevant policy dialogues?
- Do central and local policymaking processes use different types of knowledge?
- What are the dangers associated with not recognising these differences?

The policy process can look very different across different issues depending on the types of knowledge involved, and the interaction between them. Highly technical issues are likely to be those dominated by research-based knowledge. One discipline may hold the monopoly over the definition of the problem, the goals to be achieved and the means of achieving them. This gives rise to deeply embedded registers of credibility that – as discussed in Chapter Three – can exclude some actors from being able to understand, or contribute to, key debates and decisions. At the same time, they offer privileged access to members of the dominant knowledge networks. The underlying logic and assumptions of the prevailing profession or discipline are likely to become unquestionable principles of policy responses, treated as 'objective' truths. For example, environmental issues are often technically specialised; key issues are decided under the guise of technical 'impact assessments' and affected communities are unable to fully grasp or challenge the process.

Table 4.4: Strengthening stocks and flows of different types of knowledge

For each type of knowledge (research-based, practice-informed and citizen knowledge), consider:	
Stock	Flow
How much of each type of knowledge is available on this issue? What is its quality? How accessible is it? Does technical language make it difficult for non-specialists to understand?* Where are the gaps in the stock of knowledge for policy? In attempting to fill the gaps and produce knowledge that enables policymakers to make reasoned judgements, what balance should be struck between quantity, quality or accessibility?	Who 'holds' the knowledge and what are the power dynamics between them and policymakers?* How does the knowledge held by each actor reflect its values?* What are the implications of this? When is the knowledge most likely to be needed? What affects this? What are the forums where knowledge can be transmitted to policymakers? Do the processes used help ensure all voices are heard, or are they dominated by elites? Where are the weaknesses in the flow of knowledge into policy? Which processes need to be strengthened and how?
Cross-cutting issues	
Is the *supply* of knowledge appropriate for where policies are made? Where is the most effective interface between knowledge and policy (central or local)? What are the implications for the types of knowledge needed, and how do prevailing power dynamics affect how this knowledge is supplied? What are the factors that affect *demand* for the different types of knowledge? How do knowledge incentive structures (skills, organisational capacity and core policy processes) influence policymakers' knowledge-seeking behaviour?	

Note: * Covered in more detail in Chapter Three.

Some issues are characterised by the strength of structures built up around (formalised) practice-informed knowledge, which can coalesce into a dominant policy narrative: stories about change with a beginning, middle and end that interpret certain physical/social phenomena (Sutton, 1999). Such stories define a problem, explain how it came about and show what needs to be done to improve the situation; in other words, they contain explicit and implicit ideas about what is 'wrong' and how to put it 'right', interpreting physical and social phenomena in the process. Narratives can become embedded in implementing organisations, allowing decision makers to simplify and (seemingly) tame complex problems. As a result, they can become self-sustaining if organisational structures and mandates are built around them, and can dominate policymaking in spite of mixed relevance and applicability. Powerful narratives often function as organising principles for knowledge and action on the issue and become embedded in key organisations (KNOTS, 2006), limiting the range of what is accepted as credible knowledge. Molle (2008) examines, for example, how the 'free water' narrative generated a vast swathe of literature and formed an epistemic community around price-based incentives for irrigation, taking on a hegemonic character in the development establishment despite limited evidence of success.

Issues can be dominated by citizen or lay knowledge, leading to 'populist' policymaking, where policies are made in order to resonate with perspectives of large constituencies to win their support. In some cases, policies may reflect the underlying interests, values or perspectives of the ruling elites (see Chapter Three), overriding evidence that they may be unsustainable or ineffective or further reinforcing and entrenching social inequalities. In some countries, fuel subsidies are maintained because of their populist appeal, despite the fact that they tend to benefit the better off in a country and contribute to a very large budgetary burden.

Whichever type of knowledge is dominant, policymaking can be improved by working to strengthen the links between the other types of knowledge and the policy issue. The first step is to increase the credibility and salience of other forms of knowledge, opening up windows in core decision-making processes for other types and perhaps using knowledge intermediaries and boundary objects to help sort through knowledge claims to establish what is accepted into the body of knowledge policymakers routinely draw on (Clark et al (2010), and Chapter Five). Another approach could be to work within the dominant type of knowledge, but in a way that broadens horizons and definitions, actively critiquing the prevailing ideas in order to promote learning.

Other issues may not involve a single dominant type of knowledge, but rather a deep level of contestation. If an issue is heavily politicised, actors' deep core values will shape their definitions of what counts as legitimate knowledge (Monaghan, 2011), and it may be impossible to change them. In this case, increasing credibility and salience of other knowledge types will at least serve to open up wider debate on the issue and ensure exchanges based on robust knowledge. Creating spaces within policy to draw on and combine multiple types of knowledge in an integrative manner (for example through inclusive, fair deliberations) may also serve to help.

These ideas can be built into an understanding of the policy context in a country. The knowledge–policy interface is clearly influenced by where knowledge is produced, where policy is made and any context-specific structures and institutional incentives. Understanding how these interact is an important part of any process of diagnosis and should be done before putting in place interventions to improve the uptake and use of knowledge in policy. However, there are other implications. In centralised policy environments, care will need to be taken to recognise which form of knowledge dominates, because attempts to strengthen other sources may upset the prevailing political economy of the system. This is not to say that this should not happen, only that it must be done consciously. As Figure 4.2 demonstrates, it is possible to distinguish some broad relationships between the extent to which multiple types of knowledge are used and where policy is made.

Figure 4.2: The relationship between where policy is made and the types of knowledge used

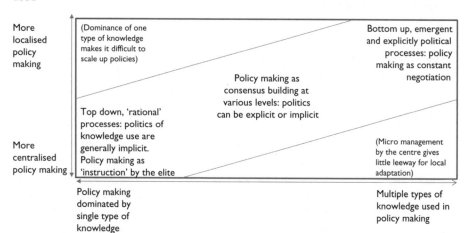

Where policymaking is centralised and dominated by a single type of knowledge, we are likely to see more top-down processes, which the dominant elite will define as 'rational'. If research is the dominant form of knowledge, rationality will be defined by the scientific process. Because the political economy of policymaking will be implicitly defined by the elite, a centralised policymaking process can be characterised as one of 'instruction', with a focus on best practice, regulation, standards and formal agreements. Examples of this could include highly technical policymaking processes such as international trade negotiations or situations where politics are dictatorial. If citizen knowledge is dominant, policymaking processes are likely to reflect the 'rationality' of the political elite and result in populism, as described above.[11]

At the other end of the spectrum, policymaking can be decentralised and make extensive use of all three types of knowledge. For this to happen effectively, the politics of the issue will need to be explicit, with bottom-up processes contributing to an emerging set of institutions and relationships that define and redefine the issues that need to be addressed. Policymaking processes here are characterised by constant negotiation. While this may look like an effective way to promote the voices of marginalised groups in policymaking, it can make central government uneasy, as effective local political processes can upset the established political order. In addition, as outlined in Chapter Two, decentralised government structures can have significant capacity issues that prevent them from making full use of all types of knowledge.

In the middle is a complex mix of policy processes, where different types of knowledge may dominate at different stages and where policymaking processes will be a mixture of instruction, negotiation and consensus building (see Box 4.5). Depending on the prevailing local politics, the consensus is more likely to be built around the dominant type of knowledge, mediated by contributions from others. Policymaking processes have begun to draw on the considerable body of work on local participation, making use of different tools such as focus groups, citizens' juries and others. This may take place at several levels simultaneously – national, regional and local – depending on the context and the actors involved (see Chapters Two and Three).

Box 4.5: Deliberative processes and their value in the policy process

In the context of attempting to combine multiple types of knowledge, spaces for drawing on knowledge may need to be structured as 'deliberative processes'. This involves carefully designed processes where different types of evidence are combined and weighed up in a reasoned fashion, through an inclusive and transparent dialogue (Lomas et al, 2005). The aim is to make decisions that are relevant, feasible and implementable by combining different perspectives and building consensus prior to a decision (Culyer and Lomas, 2006). Key stakeholders should be brought together to discuss and consider appropriate action and policy responses, sharing knowledge, considering different perspectives on an issue and reaching reasoned, consensual decisions where possible. Generally, they require face-to-face meetings, typically combinations of workshops, consultations and roundtables (and so on), at which actors convene to discuss and debate pressing issues. They require detailed and in-depth discussion and carefully structured and managed processes, allowing groups of people to engage in reflection, interaction and learning. Deliberative processes must be action-oriented rather than functioning as just a 'talking shop'. They need to be aimed at an explicit decision, or at a decision context on which they will have a direct bearing (Cash et al, 2003), so as to address specific problems in a clear-cut and managed way rather than simply being a source for generating ongoing perspectives on an issue (Michaels, 2009). As such, while deliberation specifically requires a departure from straightforward majority rule, it is important to embed within it mechanisms to combat the danger of discussions stalling and failing to reach a consensus, and also the conservatism that can sometimes be inherent in consensus approaches.

While the area between the two lines in Figure 4.2 represents the spectrum of prevailing policymaking processes, some challenges remain, as set out in the top-left and bottom-right corners. If a single type of knowledge is too dominant in local policymaking, it will be difficult to scale up policies to the national level. This may not pose a problem if national politics are heavily federalised, but it is something to bear in mind when designing local pilots for possible scale-up afterwards. The reverse can also be a problem: centralised policymaking is likely to micromanage and stifle local adaptation and innovation if it tries to incorporate all types of knowledge into the same top-down processes.

Improving the supply of research

Questions this section will help you answer:
- What can be done to improve the supply of research to policy?
- How important is research communication?
- How can the policy relevance of research be improved?

There are three main approaches here. First, government departments can be allocated budgets specifically for commissioning research, evaluation evidence or evidence from citizen and stakeholder opinion. Second, knowledge can be built by publicly or privately funded academic institutions, sometimes via research councils that hold large research budgets to allocate to universities and individual researchers via various funding modes.[12] Finally, research can be generated by a variety of organisations, such as CSOs, philanthropic foundations, think-tanks, NGOs or interest groups, often in networks with academic institutions. However the new research is generated, quality assurance schemes are important, with disciplinary peer review playing a critical role, via project and programme advisory boards or through high-level advisory committees that provide expert advice to government departments (such as the system of scientific advisory committees in the UK).[13]

Although research commissioned directly by government tends to be focused more on questions of immediate policy interest, it is also important to promote more fundamental scientific research. While scientific research tends to deal with academic questions rather than policy problems, it can affect policy through the building of human and intellectual capital, with spill-over effects on the culture of policy and government, because such professional knowledge is specifically needed in order to develop holistic policy solutions (Livny et al, 2006; Harriss-White, 2007) and to provide expert advice. In addition, the supply of fundamental scientific research can give rise to new policy issues – nanotechnology, stem cells and climate change are three examples where science has led to policy development by pointing out the absence of policies to deal with chaotically emerging issues. It is not as simple as expanding the budget for research funding and letting researchers decide how to spend it, however; Chapter Three shows how actors' interests, values/beliefs and credibility affect how knowledge is produced and codified, and how this may affect what is ultimately used in policymaking. Also, in the face of complex, multidimensional problems, knowledge generation needs to be oriented to the problems it addresses rather than confined to 'silo-ed' disciplines. Therefore, policy-relevant research is likely to require multidisciplinary research, mixed methods and *trans*-disciplinarity (Nowotny et al, 2003), mobilising a range of theoretical perspectives and practical methodologies that are not necessarily derived from pre-existing disciplines, nor necessarily contribute to the formation of new disciplines.

It is also important to communicate, translate and disseminate existing knowledge to the appropriate policy audiences. There is a large literature on research communication[14] and on knowledge intermediaries (see Chapter Five), but it is worth reiterating here the importance of demystifying key messages and increasing their perceived policy relevance by carefully considering reports' language, objectives, timeframe, contacts and mediums of communication. Meanwhile, building the capacity of both policymakers and researchers to engage with each other is key, enabling researchers to better understand the policy process and improving policymakers' skills to interpret scientific evidence and use external expertise. In resource-constrained environments these training costs may be prohibitive, and it may be more cost-effective to focus on building up a cadre of external advisers to provide the necessary support.

A key part of improving the policy relevance of research is to improve 'policy pull' (Bielak et al, 2008) by clarifying policy goals and communicating them regularly to the research community – allowing researchers to take strategic decisions about the extent to which their organisational mandates encourage them to address issues that are directly relevant to policy. Table 4.5 distinguishes five categories of policy relevance, to allow individual researchers and funding

Table 4.5: Five categories of policy-relevant knowledge

Description	Detail
E: non-aligned	The broad research topic is the same as the policy issue (for example maternal and child health) but there is no further alignment with policy priorities or active dissemination to policymakers. Quality of research and monitoring is assessed solely on academic merit.
D: policy interest	Research broadly addresses topics of interest to policymakers, but the specific issues research projects or programmes address are not aligned with policy's identified priorities and needs, and project dissemination is not targeted at policymakers. Research quality is assessed solely on academic merit, but there is a sufficiently broad understanding of policy needs to frame calls for research.
C: high-level policy alignment	The topics of research and monitoring activities are aligned at a high or thematic level and reports contain evidence that is set in the broad policy context, but interaction with policymakers is limited to the dissemination of project reports. Policy relevance is increasingly important in assessing research quality, but interpreting the implications of research is done by researchers alone.
B: explicit policy relevance	The choice of topics for research and monitoring activities is driven explicitly by policy needs. Policymakers are closely involved in prioritisation activities, in scoping the specific researchable questions and in interpreting the resulting evidence for current policy development processes. Policy relevance is an explicit quality criterion for research; interdisciplinary research is likely to be particularly useful.
A: co-produced knowledge	Research and policy collaborate on the production of knowledge in the context of specific, large-scale, interdisciplinary and participatory interventions. The quality of research is defined jointly by academics, policy professionals and stakeholders/citizens and is likely to be more transdisciplinary in nature.

Source: Adapted from Shaxson (2010)

bodies to make a choice as to how much they want to focus on the production of research as a global public good alone (Category E) or move towards full engagement and policy relevance (Category A). As Chapter Five describes, knowledge intermediaries may play an increasingly important role as the degree of policy relevance is improved.

Improving the policy relevance of research is not without its pitfalls, however, most notably in the degree to which prevailing politics and power dynamics can affect both sides' ability to engage with each other over a sustained period of time. Moreover, it does not follow that improving the relevance of a piece of research will automatically improve its impact on the final policy decision, particularly where issues are heavily politicised (Monaghan, 2011; see also Chapter Two).

It is also important to be ready to produce research that broadens a dialogue or challenges prevailing paradigms. Processes of contestation and argument are important for informing and improving the foundations of policy and action, and implementation should look to build and work with critical voices, rather than avoid them. Burawoy (2005) has famously argued that linking social scientific knowledge and policy requires both critical and 'reflexive' research as well as more 'instrumental' consultancy-type work. This could problematise prevailing trends (for example research looking into the role and impacts of a contract culture in the production of knowledge for development agencies), or it could discuss values and ideology and the underlying goals of policy (for example questioning whether market-led solutions should hold sway in a particular sector versus 'coping without growth'), rather than simply drawing on different sources of knowledge in order to understand how to fulfil specific goals (Livny et al, 2006; Harriss-White, 2007). Especially in situations where different perspectives compete for the definition of a problem, or where issues of the distribution of costs and benefits are at stake, it may be crucial to build the capacity of relevant stakeholders (or their representatives) to participate in negotiations and collaboration. For example, discussing scientific findings may help parties develop stronger arguments or test the claims of those with whom they disagree (Michaels, 2009).

Improving the use of practice-informed knowledge in policy

Questions this section will help you answer:
- What are the main issues in improving the use of practice-informed knowledge?
- What is the role of performance management frameworks and knowledge management?

Strengthening practice-informed knowledge in policymaking does not happen by just increasing the number of evaluations commissioned. It is important to be clear whether the knowledge is needed for audit purposes (building a true and fair picture of the state of an issue), for value-for-money purposes (to demonstrate accountability and cost-effective expenditure of public money) or to support ongoing decision making and learning. Clarifying this at the outset will help ensure knowledge is targeted at the appropriate decisions (Guijt, 2008).

Improving the supply of practice-informed knowledge can be addressed directly, by building capacity to collect it or ensuring that sufficient resources are available. Many aid agencies and government departments, in both the North and South, now include budget lines for planning, monitoring and evaluation in all project and programme funding, and a number of initiatives worldwide have been set up to improve funding to these activities. It is widely recognised that, where possible, knowledge production may need to address the question of impact, the direct effects of programmes on their surroundings, other effects they have and how they contribute to people's lives (Riddell, 2008). The idea is that carrying out this kind of reality check in a rigorous or independent way will allow organisations to truly understand the determinants of effectiveness, overcoming the tendency for evaluations and formalised programme knowledge to avoid tackling difficult questions or to question underlying principles.

Just as important, however, is the question of *how* these assessments are carried out. Intended users are more likely to use evaluations if they understand and feel part of the process and findings (Patton, 2008). This means it is important for evaluators to involve intended users from the outset, setting the purpose and focus, deciding on the methods, analysing findings and disseminating results (Patton, 2008). The ability of the evaluator to build trust and establish constructive relationships with key users is relevant here; knowledge intermediaries may help in this process (see Chapter Five).

Using knowledge in this way may best be done with adaptive management techniques. These recognise that our knowledge of how change happens is necessarily incomplete, that there is no single 'right' answer to questions about what needs to be done and that competing knowledge claims are influenced by actors' beliefs, values, interests and claims to credibility. They emphasise that policymaking is a matter of choice, exercised by a variety of people throughout the decision-making process, and that it is the sum of these choices that finds its final expression in 'a policy'. Conventional policymaking defines predetermined policy outcomes and sees any drift from this as an error that needs correcting. Adaptive management approaches focus instead on ongoing cycles of evaluation, assessment and learning, redefining goals as knowledge of the issue changes and as the network of actors involved in each issue evolves. They have a long history of being used to manage natural resources and address challenging environmental issues such as urban adaptation to climate change (Gray et al, 2008), but are increasingly being applied to social issues, including the field of 'adaptive governance' (for example Folke et al, 2005).

Knowledge management also plays an important role in improving the use of practice-informed knowledge. Knowledge management approaches have, over time, moved from a focus on formalising and codifying knowledge and distributing it using technology, towards a more people-centric, practice-based approach, focusing on the knowledge processes embedded in organisations (Ferguson et al, 2008). Within an organisation, sharing tacit knowledge depends partly on a culture of reciprocity, on staff's personal fulfilment and on positive social relationships (Greenhalgh et al, 2004). Organisational governance will also play a key role, such as transparent decision making, accountable decision making, public availability of information and data, and formal and long-term planning mechanisms.

Finally, the different incentive structures in public policymaking mean frameworks transferred from the private sector have not had the same impact in the public sphere. There is increasing recognition that rigid performance frameworks manage only what can be counted and do not in themselves contribute to organisational learning and changed behaviour. More reflexive approaches to monitoring and evaluation (for example Guijt, 2008; Patton, 2010) emphasise the need to let the culture of the institution inform the techniques used to collect performance management information, putting in spaces for reflection and social learning (Ferguson et al, 2008) and encouraging communities of practice to adapt lessons to local contexts and spread knowledge by focusing on implementation. Monitoring and evaluation techniques that use critical path analysis, actively incorporate discussions of unintended outcomes and focus on indicators of behaviour change (such as outcome mapping and its variants) are more likely to be able to deal with the way complex projects often appear to drift off course, seeing this drift as a necessary response to a complex environment rather than something that needs to be corrected (see Hallsworth, 2011).

Improving the use of citizen knowledge in policy

Questions this section will help you answer:
- What are the challenges to improving the use of citizen knowledge in policy?
- What techniques are there to better link citizens to policy makers?

Improving the use of citizen knowledge in policy can be done through direct consultation, by working with representative organisations such as CSOs or by conducting research whose aim is to codify and disseminate knowledge that would not be covered by conventional survey techniques.

Direct consultation with citizens is often not cost-effective for policymakers, particularly given the need to think carefully about the politics of engagement outside what is supposed to be a neutral bureaucracy. Focus groups offer opportunities, but these are often short-term and issue-driven, rather than broad-based attempts to improve the incorporation of citizen knowledge into policy.

Aid agencies and national governments have made efforts to facilitate participation by working with organisations seen to represent citizens, particularly those who are generally underrepresented. This process began by integrating 'user groups' into programmes (particularly in forestry, health, education and drinking water). In the 1990s, this evolved into engagement with CSOs, which were seen as working to articulate the interests of citizens and thus providing a channel enabling them to participate in government and national and local institutions without depending on state agencies.

Increasing recognition of the importance of citizen knowledge has led to an explosion of methodologies for participatory engagement. Many empirical research tools, such as participatory rural appraisal (later participatory learning and action), are now well established and widely used. Such methodologies have generated practical ways of incorporating participatory principles into development practice, and since the 1990s debates have been less about *why* to 'do' participation and more about *how*.

Citizen knowledge needs to be integrated into policy at multiple levels and at many different junctures. There are some recent developments in this field, such as locality-based methods for participatory democracy. International NGOs and other agencies have achieved considerable success by building the capacities of CSOs in methods such as participatory budgeting, participatory approaches to monitoring expenditure and service delivery, and participatory budget tracking (Chambers, 2008). One example is methods for beneficiary feedback, a systematic approach to collecting the views of key stakeholders about the quality and impact of work undertaken by an agency, generating quantitative data (Jacobs, 2010). These have the potential to achieve success in some contexts – for example, a randomised controlled trial attributed large, concrete changes in service delivery to the facilitated use of report cards and public meetings (Bjorkman and Svensson, 2009). Transparency and accountability initiatives designed to put relevant information in the hands of local people are also mushrooming, and have been shown to increase responsiveness and improve service delivery in some contexts (McGee and Gaventa, 2010). Other initiatives, such as citizens' juries and social audits, have successfully revived and enhanced institutions of local governance and collective action. There have also been a number of initiatives to feed in participatory knowledge at an earlier stage of the policy process. Participatory Poverty Assessments and studies such as 'the voices of the poor' are based on significant levels of field research in order to feed the views of poor people into national poverty reduction policies and elsewhere in policy processes.

Central to these frameworks is an understanding of the political economy of knowledge creation; participatory methodologies aim to help generate popular knowledge and stimulate critical reflection, free from the biases of aid agencies or other powerful actors. These tools have enabled illiterate, poor and marginalised people to represent their own lives and livelihoods through (for example) visual methods and rankings; to carry out their own analysis to come up with their own solutions; to provide training to each other; and thereby to increase the legitimacy and credibility of the knowledge on offer. The Campesino a Campesino movement, which began in Latin America in the 1980s, was one of the early examples of embedding participatory methodologies into the processes of creating and transferring knowledge. It was an inherently political process: Holt-Giménez

(2006, p xii) notes that the movement increasingly saw this form of development as 'an interface for political negotiation'.

There can be systemic barriers to these participatory approaches, however. Being able to articulate needs effectively may be a matter of organisation and capacity, but it also may involve deep power imbalances between actors and require effort to empower groups and amplify their voice. While building this voice may involve cooperative relationships, it may also involve conflict, as initiatives to empower grassroots actors and promote their access to resources and opportunities for voice in general community decision making meets with opposition (Jones et al, 2009c). Therefore, it is particularly important to promote research and advocacy by organisations that can speak for groups that are systematically excluded (Powell, 2006; Morgan, 2008).

Knowledge incentive structures: improving demand for knowledge in policymaking

Questions this section will help you answer:
- What affects the demand for knowledge by policymakers?
- How do skills, resources and other incentives influence the types of knowledge that are sought?
- How do policy processes shape policymakers' knowledge-seeking behaviour?

The structures and incentives given to policymakers to acquire and use knowledge have been neglected by analysts and practitioners alike, in the literature and in practice. This section therefore focuses on the structures that influence *demand* for knowledge in policymaking, which we believe are as important as those that influence its supply, particularly given the growing internationalisation of knowledge through knowledge hubs, communities of practice and more formal structures such as pan-African research councils. Demand for knowledge in policy is conditioned by two factors: the capacity of policymakers to acquire and interpret it; and the core processes of policymaking, which affect how knowledge is used to develop, appraise, implement and monitor policies. Figure 4.3 shows how these are linked.

Capacity can be split into two components. First, *skill levels* will affect the ability to source and interpret different forms of knowledge. This is closely related to human resource policies for civil servants and whether there is a prevalence of one particular discipline in a department that may affect the types of knowledge it seeks. Capacity also reflects whether continuous training is encouraged, either internally or by secondment to external organisations. While training budgets are notoriously small for civil servants, it is possible to analyse the political economy of capacity development by examining how porous the civil service is to secondments into and out of academia, think-tanks, NGOs or industry. This may

Figure 4.3: The components of knowledge incentive structures

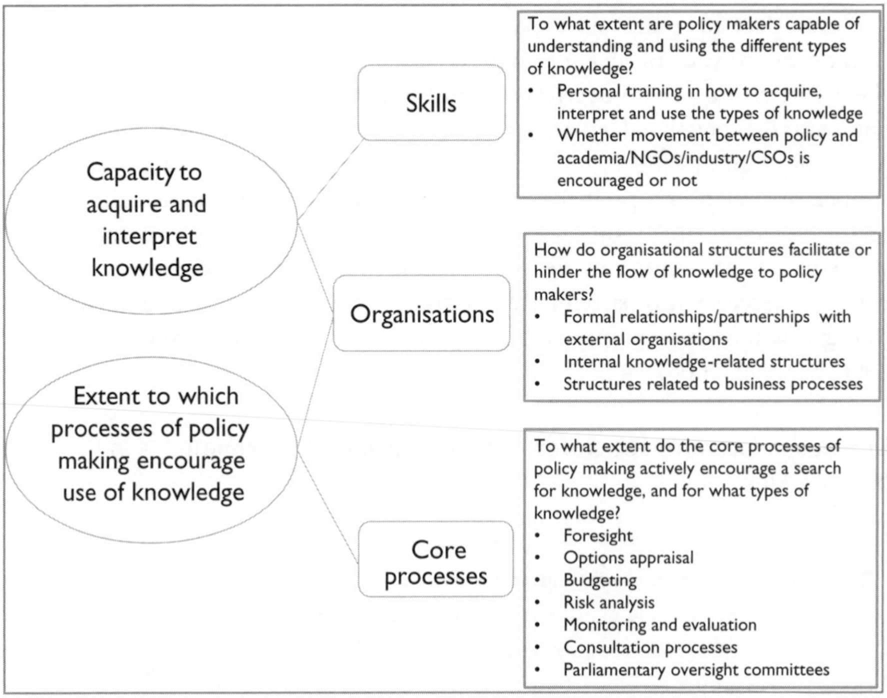

To what extent are policy makers capable of understanding and using the different types of knowledge?
- Personal training in how to acquire, interpret and use the types of knowledge
- Whether movement between policy and academia/NGOs/industry/CSOs is encouraged or not

Skills

Capacity to acquire and interpret knowledge

How do organisational structures facilitate or hinder the flow of knowledge to policy makers?
- Formal relationships/partnerships with external organisations
- Internal knowledge-related structures
- Structures related to business processes

Organisations

Extent to which processes of policy making encourage use of knowledge

To what extent do the core processes of policy making actively encourage a search for knowledge, and for what types of knowledge?
- Foresight
- Options appraisal
- Budgeting
- Risk analysis
- Monitoring and evaluation
- Consultation processes
- Parliamentary oversight committees

Core processes

Source: Adapted from SPARC (2010)

reflect the prevailing political context (see Chapter Two); an influence–network approach to policymaking in consolidated democracies may see these sorts of loans or secondments happening at many levels of the civil service, based on open, transparent recruitment processes and with clearly defined terms of reference.[15]

Efforts to combine many different sources of knowledge must tread particularly carefully in order to give genuine space to different perspectives. Datta et al (2010) note that, while some think-tanks are non-partisan, many provide support to political parties and legislators, and those that originated within the political space may end up as the source of expertise from which high-ranking officials (up to and including ministers) are drawn. In more autocratic contexts, the degree of politicisation may extend further down the structures of the civil service, making hiring and firing mechanisms less transparent and more open to manipulation by incumbent politicians.

The second component of capacity is *organisational*: whether organisational structures facilitate or hinder policymakers' ability to source and interpret a wide range of knowledge. There are internal and external components to this. The existence of formal relationships with external knowledge providers can ensure that policymakers know whom to turn to for information on key issues.

Internally, the existence of teams within government departments that focus on acquiring, interpreting and communicating knowledge, can be taken as an indication of the emphasis departments put on different aspects of knowledge. They may be in strategy units, evidence teams, research programme teams, disciplinary hubs such as economic intelligence units or formal policymaker networks (see Box 4.6); they may favour one type of knowledge above others, but their existence demonstrates that resources are being devoted to the systematic acquisition, assembly and interpretation of knowledge.

Box 4.6: Internal structures for improving the use of knowledge in policy

A **strategy unit** is generally located towards the top of the organisation. Its mandate is to provide synthetic overviews and stimulus to top management to aid its strategic decision making. **Research programme teams** focus on the procurement aspects of commissioning and quality-assuring research, although increasingly they also work on communicating research results to different audiences. **Evidence teams** have a broader focus on all the different types of evidence, focusing less on procurement of research and working more as knowledge intermediaries to improve the way policy questions are scoped and the ways existing and emerging knowledge is assembled, and to support the joint interpretation of knowledge for policy (Shaxson, 2009). In 2010, the government of Lagos state in Nigeria created an **economic intelligence unit** to provide 'environment scanning and impact assessment' for the economy and the detailed analysis on which state budgets are based (Akabueze, 2010). Coordinating across departments and across countries is also important, and there are increasingly moves to create **policymaker networks** around issues that demand specific knowledge about a pressing concern and where there is a need for that knowledge to be updated regularly. For example, the multi-donor-funded Africa Platform for Development Effectiveness has a closed networking site accessible only by registered policymakers,[16] and the Rockefeller-funded Asian Cities Climate Change Research Network links cities in Asia so they can develop robust plans to prepare for, withstand and recover from the predicted impacts of climate change.[17]

Knowledge incentive structures are also concerned with the *processes* policymakers must follow as part of the legislative or business procedures of government and the organisational structures put in place to support them. The question here is to what extent do the core processes of policymaking actively encourage a search for knowledge, and for what types of knowledge? While knowledge may be supplied from multiple sources and be of multiple types, these core processes affect how knowledge is actually used to make policies. They may include foresight, strategy and planning, options appraisal (such as economic modelling), budgeting, risk analysis, monitoring and evaluation, consultation, parliamentary oversight committees (technical and budget/finance) and legislative review processes. Some of these may be included in mandatory processes as part of the traditional 'policy cycle' approach, which disaggregates policymaking into a number of functional components (Sutcliffe and Court, 2006).

It is important not to limit the analysis to the conventional policy cycle, however. Budgeting and business planning are fundamental departmental processes that affect what can and cannot be spent on developing and implementing policies. Petkova (2009) notes that the transition from input-based to outcome-oriented budgeting has been difficult for developing countries. Medium-term expenditure frameworks (MTEFs) and medium-term sector strategies are intended to make budgeting processes more policy-oriented and credible by structuring the budget 'around broad programmes which are defined along government policy objectives and linked to specific outcomes, thus aiming to integrate policy, planning and annual budgets' (Petkova, 2009, p11). For these to be implemented, policymakers from ministries of finance and/or planning and budget need to work together with those from line departments to develop a budget that truly reflects policy priorities. If MTEFs (for example) are not clearly directed by the need to monitor progress towards strategic policy priorities, they will tend to be driven by the needs of those whose concern is with budgetary control rather than the need to make more inclusive policies (Petkova, 2009).

Legislative review processes are another potentially powerful way of strengthening the interface between knowledge and policy, but only if legislators are equipped to understand what makes knowledge robust and have the resources to commission their own work (Jones et al, 2011). Programmes under the auspices of organisations such as the Parliamentary Centre in Pan Africa tend to focus on improving understanding of legislative and budget processes and increasing transparency, voice and accountability, rather than on specific work to improve understanding of the knowledge base for policy. Some programmes exist to promote the use of particular types of knowledge (the South African Indigenous Knowledge Systems Policy, adopted in 2004; the Federation of Australian Science and Technological Societies' annual Science Meets Parliament training session), but currently few initiatives train legislators in the breadth of knowledge needed for making policy. Supporting parliamentary select committees to source, assemble and interpret knowledge could make an important contribution to the way they operate. Greater training and resources would encourage them to use their cross-party status to counterbalance any party political use of knowledge by government, check the authenticity of competing knowledge claims and take a longer-term view of the knowledge needed to make substantively better policies.

Conclusion

This chapter has made the case for thinking of knowledge for policy as falling into three broad categories: research-based, practice-informed and citizen knowledge. Each has its own characteristics that give rise to particular power dynamics, and this means the knowledge–policy interface for each issue is not affected simply by the political context (Chapter Two) or the network of actors (Chapter Three) – it is clearly influenced by the contributions each of the different types of knowledge can make. Our analysis has also shown it is important to consider whether the knowledge–policy interface is central or local, and the implications this has for the different types of knowledge that can be used. Finally, the chapter outlines what can be done to improve supply and demand for knowledge.

It is rarely the case that there is simply a gap between knowledge and policy that requires bridging. Different types of knowledge emerge from various sources and are embedded in policy in complex ways. Not all research needs to be immediately policy-relevant; not all local contextual knowledge can be accessed easily; and weak feedback loops mean that not all practice-informed knowledge is incorporated into ongoing decision making. The real questions are whether the stock of knowledge is sufficient for policymakers to make reasoned judgements on how to move forwards, and how inclusive and transparent the flows of knowledge (in bridging processes) have been (see Table 4.4).

The location of the knowledge–policy interface differs depending on the policy issue. This means it is important to consider both central and local processes for using knowledge, examining the incentive structures that condition policymakers' knowledge-seeking behaviour. We identify this as a major gap in the literature, and suggest that a considerable amount of work needs to be done here. This also means considering how politics and normative values may be concealed by a 'rational', centralised approach to policymaking, reinforcing the perspective of the dominant elite. Conversely, it also means understanding that stimulating the use of citizen knowledge at a local level will inevitably become an explicitly political process. Deliberative processes at decentralised levels will need to be supported if we are to improve the way we incorporate all types of knowledge into all policy processes.

Finally, a general theme running through the chapter is the importance of enhancing the legitimacy, saliency and credibility of each of the different types of knowledge to all actors, enabling them to make their choices in a more transparent and open way (also a key theme addressed by Cash et al, 2003). While researchers, evaluators and citizen organisations can do this for the knowledge they produce, it is very difficult for them to step out of their own perspective and provide sufficient support to the other types of knowledge. Chapter Five shows how to address this by focusing on an emerging group of actors – knowledge intermediaries.

Notes

[1] See Nutley et al (2007), Head (2010), Chapter Five, and many articles in the journal *Evidence & Policy*.

[2] Some of the most interesting approaches to knowledge generation could be seen as a mixture of two different types, for example action research as a mixture of citizen and research knowledge, rigorous impact evaluation as a mixture of practical and research knowledge, and professional knowledge as somewhere between research-based and practical knowledge.

[3] Taken from Merton's (1938) formulation of scientific norms.

[4] In fact, in an interesting example of how collective knowledge morphs over time, the Haldane Principle is not a single article or Act of Parliament. Instead, it is a collective understanding of how several different arrangements for research have adapted, merged and reinforced each other; see Edgerton (2009).

[5] See www.researchtoaction.org for a comprehensive set of examples of good practice in research communication and for further reading on the subject.

[6] The exception is farmer-led research and participatory evaluation; see Box 5.6 and Guijt (2008).

[7] Personal communication (2011).

[8] The concept of 'traducture' (as opposed to translation) is important here (waGoro, 2006). This highlights the power dimensions of translation, pointing out that dominant discourses can distort reality, reinforcing existing discourses and biases.

[9] The UK's Marine Climate Change Impacts Partnership report card presents these 'best guesses' by considering the level of confidence in the science. These high/medium/ low assessments can represent complex (and uncertain) scientific knowledge in a condensed way that is very visually appealing. See www.mccip.org.uk/annual-report-card/2010-2011.aspx

[10] Normative: because involving citizen knowledge is the 'right thing' to do in a democracy. Instrumental: because it helps achieve certain outcomes, as defined by a particular group or organisation. Substantive: because it achieves better outcomes as defined through the democratic process.

[11] If value for money is the overriding imperative, then practical knowledge which focuses on cost-efficiency may dominate, but this is likely to be the case only for single issues and is unlikely to dominate the general approach to policy making.

[12] In the UK, research councils use three main funding modes. Directed funding guides resources towards a specific purpose, such as funding an institute or large programme: proposals are assessed on a mixture of academic quality and policy relevance. In responsive funding mode, the broad direction of calls for proposals is set by the individual research council's corporate strategy: ideas which do not align with this will not be funded, but there are no other restrictions and proposals are assessed solely on academic quality. National capability funding covers monitoring activities and other work in support of long-term need (not statutory monitoring), support for infrastructure and technical equipment and giving advice to government (Shaxson, 2010).

[13] See www.bis.gov.uk/go-science/science-in-government/independent-scientific-advice

[14] See www.researchtoaction.org/

[15] See, for example, www.civilservice.gov.uk/jobs/Secondment-Opportunities/Secondment-Opportunities.aspx

[16] www.africa-platform.org/discussion_forums/policymakers.

[17] Specifically, it seeks to improve cities' capacity to plan, finance, coordinate and implement climate change strategies; generate and test a range of actions, models and processes to build resilience; develop human resources, resources and institutions to produce and update resilience strategies; and share experiences with other Asian cities, networking with a wide variety of actors including the private sector, NGOs, civil society and donors.

FIVE

Facilitating knowledge interaction

It is now well established that policy processes do not follow an orderly, linear path from conception to appraisal, implementation, monitoring and evaluation. Rather, they involve many different sets of actors (Chapter Three) and types of knowledge (Chapter Four) set in varying political contexts (Chapter Two). Determining the different types of interaction between knowledge and policy is therefore a complex process. Within this complexity, we attempt to disentangle the roles of knowledge intermediaries, that is, individuals or organisations that act between the producers and users of knowledge with the intention of improving the supply, demand and use of knowledge and smoothing the path between the two. As this chapter shows, it is not necessary to be badged a knowledge intermediary to act like one. All actors can function as knowledge intermediaries even if they draw on different sources of knowledge and use it at different times in different ways. Meanwhile, any individual or organisation that functions as a knowledge intermediary is not politically neutral. Intentionally or not, they have considerable potential to reconfigure the social and organisational relationships (such as understandings, rules and agreements) that underpin the use of knowledge in support of innovation and change (Leeuwis and Aarts, 2011). A final point is that no two knowledge intermediaries are the same; their work is entirely context-specific, which means that, while it is possible to draw general lessons as to how they *could* choose to act, it is impossible to develop a standard set of rules as to how they *should* act.

> **By the end of this chapter, readers will be able to answer the following questions:**
> - What is the definition of a knowledge intermediary?
> - Who can be a knowledge intermediary?
> - What functions can they perform? Which function is appropriate in which situation?
> - Can intermediaries ever be truly neutral? If not, what does this mean for how they work?
> - How can we measure the effect of knowledge intermediaries on policy and practice?

Table 5.1 reviews the roles various actors play at different stages of the policy process, showing that their roles may change through the policy process, as does their need for knowledge. Importantly, understanding why actors engage differently at different stages of policymaking will help us make sense of how they can most effectively act as knowledge intermediaries. This chapter begins with an analysis of the different approaches to knowledge interaction, outlining some key terms in the literature. It then uses a framework developed by Michaels (2009) to examine the relationship between knowledge interaction and social learning, outlining six core functions of knowledge interaction. The chapter illustrates these functions using examples from a think tank and two non-governmental organisations (NGOs) that work at the interface between knowledge and policy.

Translating knowledge into policy has been a central concern of much of the literature on knowledge–policy relationships (see, for example, Nutley et al, 2007). In the 1950s, the concern was to develop rational and 'scientised' policymaking, whereby policy decisions would draw explicitly on the latest research (Nutley et al, 2007). In the world of international development and aid agencies, this gave rise to the idea that technical assistance would aid the process of transferring knowledge to policymakers and practitioners alike to fill the perceived gap in knowledge. However, from the 1980s onwards, it became clear that communicating the results of research to policy and practice worked better if there was a greater appreciation of the user's needs for knowledge, both in form and in content (for example Röling, 1988). As Lavis et al (2003, p 83) note, 'pushing or pulling evidence into policy is far from sufficient'.

With greater emphasis on the interface between knowledge and policy came a deeper appreciation of the multiple spaces for interaction between knowledge producers and users (Gibbons et al, 1994; Nutley et al, 2007). While there is still a role for simple messages to be conveyed from knowledge producer to knowledge user, in many cases what work better are partnerships that recognise the co-construction of policy knowledge (Lavis et al, 2006) and forge a shared understanding of what questions to ask, how to go about answering them and how best to interpret the answers.

This social constructivist approach to knowledge production (Yakhlef, 2007) acknowledges that knowledge contexts and content overlap and move, and in doing so shift the interfaces between knowledge and policy. This means there is a politics of interaction where discourses overlap, compete and merge to create new forms of knowledge that are welcomed and confirmed just as others are avoided and refused (Freeman, 2009). Moreover, the relationship between supply and demand for knowledge is characterised by 'communication and politically mediated feedback undertaken in the context of a dynamic decision-making process' (McNie, 2007, p 18). If this is the case, analysing power relations between all actors at the knowledge–policy interface becomes an important part of the process of understanding the relationship between what we know, the values we assign to that knowledge and how it is applied in the pursuit of public value (Moore, 1995).

Before we can understand these relationships, however, it is important to review the terminology used in this chapter. We focus on six key phrases that describe the various processes and mechanisms through which these knowledge–policy relationships can be explored: knowledge interaction; knowledge intermediary; boundary spanner; boundary concept; boundary object; and boundary process.

Table 5.1: The roles of actors and knowledge during policy development, implementation, alteration or close-down

Stage in policy process	Limits of the stage	Likely actor set and reasons for involvement	To implement policy, these different groups will need to know about:
Development	Period between political idea for a course of action and sign-off (for example development of a White Paper, passage of a bill through parliament, agreement with a delivery body, new set of standards or results of negotiations on codes of conduct)	*Politicians* set goals, targets or intentions to act *Policymakers* interpret politicians' goals, targets or intentions into programmes of action *Delivery bodies:* government or NGOs charged with implementing policy interpret goals in light of their mandates, capacity and capability to act and negotiate around cost-effectiveness *Civil society and its representatives, including NGOs and advocacy coalitions* advocate for their particular interests and interpretations of broad goals *Private sector organisations* advocate for their particular interests and interpretations of broad goals *Academic researchers (including think-tanks)* provide various types of evidence on various aspects of goals and potential paths towards them *Media organisations* communicate goals and knowledge with varying degrees of alignment with particular citizen groups	• The current state of an issue, why it is unacceptable and what needs to change • What the goals, targets or intentions are and why they have been set in this way • The potential paths to goals, their likely cost-effectiveness and distributional effects • What different actor groups value about the various goals and paths that are being proposed • What has worked elsewhere, why, and what elements could inform this specific case • How resilient policy is likely to be to specific changes, and what is likely to push it off track

Stage in policy process	Limits of the stage	Likely actor set and reasons for involvement	To implement policy, these different groups will need to know about:
Implementation	Period between sign-off and policy being altered or closed down	*Delivery bodies* implement policy with various different actor groups (civil society, NGOs, private sector) *Civil society, NGOs and advocacy groups* may be engaged in delivery, or may continue to advocate for alternatives, particularly on politicised issues *Academic researchers (including think-tanks)* monitor progress via research and/or expert advice *Private sector organisations* are involved to varying degrees depending on nature of policy and prevailing politics on role of the state in delivering public services *Media organisations* continue to communicate goals and progress (or lack of) depending on their political affiliation and degree of politicisation of issue *Politicians* may be directly involved if issue is, or becomes, politicised. As members of parliamentary review bodies, they may also be involved in scrutinising progress or spending *Policymakers* may still be involved in monitoring policy progress; some will have moved on to next urgent issue	• Whether the policy is on track to achieve its stated goals cost-effectively • Whether alternative paths to the goal have emerged and their relative costs, benefits and distributional effects • Whether goals need to be changed in light of new knowledge on the issue; this could be because unforeseen events mean that the initial framing of the policy goals was mistaken, or because political change has resulted in a shift towards a different set of core values

Stage in policy process	Limits of the stage	Likely actor set and reasons for involvement	To alter or close down policy, these different groups will need to know:
Alteration or close-down	Stage at which policies are altered to take account of new goals, new knowledge or increased capacity (or, rarely, when they are stopped altogether)	*Politicians* give their reasoning for altering or closing down policy (which may owe to emergence of new evidence, election of a new government or increased politicisation of issue) *Delivery bodies* change their activities or stop functioning altogether *Civil society and its representatives* advocate for alternatives if policy change or close-down affects them *Private sector organisations* advocate for alternatives if policy change or close-down affects them *Academic researchers* provide evidence or reasoning for alternatives *Media organisations* communicate rationales for policy change, new goals and new evidence – depending on their political affiliation and degree of politicisation of issues	• Why the policy needed to be altered; what the old policy did or did not achieve • What will emerge in its place (returning to the policy development phase) • Any effects on other, linked policies (for example changing policies relating to prison overcrowding may have a knock-on effect on policies relating to the functioning of courts system)

Knowledge at the boundary – some key terms

The terms we explore bring out some of the issues of power dynamics inherent in knowledge–policy processes with which this book is centrally concerned. Their importance derives from the fact that knowledge may be used in instrumental, conceptual or symbolic ways: instrumentally by acting in a specific or defined way to solve a particular problem; conceptually by providing a general and more indirect form of enlightenment; or symbolically to justify a particular position, action or reason for inaction (Lavis et al, 2003). It is not simply a matter of understanding where and how the knowledge intermediary works. The terms they use and the history of their intervention are all equally important.

The well-used term 'knowledge translation' has been defined as 'a dynamic and iterative process that includes the synthesis, dissemination, exchange and ethically sound application of knowledge' (Graham et al, 2006, cited in Tetroe, 2007, p 1) to focus on multiple intended outcomes. It is about more than simply providing knowledge to enlighten administrators (Weiss, 1987). Knowledge translation highlights the importance of a two–way flow of knowledge and focuses on interpreting it in context. Having said that, there is a growing recognition that the terms 'knowledge translation' and 'knowledge transfer' may be too technocratic and need to be rethought to account for the complex and contested nature of applied social research (Lemieux-Charles and Champagne, 2004; Dopson and Fitzgerald, 2005). In recent years, a wide variety of terms have been used (knowledge brokering, mobilising, translating, bridging, facilitating, transferring, mediating) for the act of intervening between knowledge producer and user to improve the supply and demand of knowledge and to smooth the path between the two, as this has emerged as an important part of the process of knowledge production, uptake and use in policy. It has even become part of official government guidance in the UK, which accepts the need to draw on 'individuals and organisations adept at working in the "knowledge brokering" capacity' (Government Office for Science, 2010, p 13). Because of the 'messy nature of engagements between actors with diverse types of knowledge' (Jones, 2009a, p 25), and the potentially political nature of any attempts to act as a go-between in relation to knowledge producers and users, we consider the most appropriate term to be **knowledge interaction**.

There is an emerging actor in this space – **knowledge intermediaries**. They can be distinguished from those whose mandate is simply to produce knowledge or those whose focus is just on using knowledge in the policy process. Sometimes referred to as **boundary spanners**,[1] they are organisations or individuals who operate across an interface, either by design or by default. Knowledge intermediaries operate in a system within which many different actors can play multiple roles, managing the 'boundaries between knowledge and action in ways that simultaneously enhance the salience, credibility and legitimacy of the information they produce' (Cash et al 2003, p 8086). Individuals or organisations that badge themselves as intermediaries may emerge of their own accord in response to a gap in the market (such as some consultancy organisations or think-tanks), or they may be created in response to a need to bridge a perceived divide (for example the Canadian Health Services Research Foundation, which links research and policy in health service provision in Canada). How they operate and what incentives drive them is the focus of much of the rest of this chapter.

While think tanks and consultants may be the most clearly identifiable knowledge intermediaries, it would be wrong to assume that intermediaries can exist only in the space between knowledge producers and knowledge users. Researchers and other 'knowledge producers' may also be interested in having a greater impact on policy; policymakers may also want to improve their links with knowledge communities and be searching for a structured approach to allow them to do this systematically. For these reasons, this chapter looks broadly at the *processes* of interaction between knowledge producer and knowledge user, with the intention of helping all readers identify when and where they themselves could act as knowledge intermediaries.

Two tools used by intermediaries to span boundaries and amply discussed in the literature are boundary concepts and boundary objects. A **boundary concept** is a term that enables communication across borders by creating a shared vocabulary (Star and Griesemer, 1989). It could be a term such as 'sustainability', 'resilience' or 'poverty' that means different things to different actors (see Box 5.1).

Box 5.1: Boundary concepts: 'poverty'

'Poverty' is a good example of a boundary concept. Maxwell (1999) sets out nine different terms used to describe poverty: income or consumption poverty, human (under)development, social exclusion, ill-being, lack of capability to function, vulnerability, livelihood unsustainability, lack of basic needs and relative deprivation. There is no clear-cut definition of any of these terms, and indeed they all overlap with each other to an extent. Discussing the terms and how they relate to a specific policy, programme or project will help create opportunities to learn from others' interpretations and shared understandings about what is important.

Discussing the meaning of a boundary concept helps uncover the implicit values and understandings that shape an actor's response to a question or issue. A **boundary object** is more concrete – a model, map, report or other form of assessment, or a picture, game or media programme that can be understood and adapted by different viewpoints but does not lose its particular identity when being discussed. Boundary objects are used to share understanding, overcome barriers to interaction and build the knowledge needed to deal with complex issues (see Brown et al, 2010). It is important that their use is not limited to technical or scientific issues; we need also to consider how boundary concepts and objects can be used to improve the use of citizen and other types of knowledge in policy as outlined in Chapter Four. Care needs to be taken in using boundary concepts or objects; if they are used too loosely, it can be difficult to separate opinion from established facts, and the particular value of each of the different types of knowledge can be hard to distinguish (Clark et al, 2010).

Finally, the literature appears to have neglected what we suggest are the **boundary processes** through which knowledge is integrated actively into policy. These are the core processes through which policy is made and for which knowledge is essential, not only the formally recognised 'policy cycle',[2] but also the processes of sector and poverty reduction strategies (PRSs), medium-term expenditure frameworks (MTEFs), internal budgeting and business planning and international negotiations on trade issues (for example) – what Chapter Four terms 'knowledge incentive structures'. The ways these processes are developed and implemented within government departments and the weight given to different types of knowledge within them will depend on the complex set of relationships between economists, natural scientists, lawyers, generalist policymakers and statisticians (for example).

Knowledge interaction: six different functions

Because the interface between knowledge and policy is socially constructed, managing the boundary between the various actors to stimulate the flow of knowledge is essential – and a spectrum of strategies may be possible. We argue that looking at the functions of interaction (as opposed to the different actors) can help us understand how knowledge interaction processes can make use of boundary spanners, concepts, objects or processes to foster engagement on policy issues. It also helps determine whether a specific firm or individual should act as a knowledge intermediary in a given context, or whether change is best achieved by encouraging a social, organisational and institutional framework that fosters knowledge exchange among all actors.

Interactions between knowledge producers and users are complicated by the different sites at which knowledge is produced (Gibbons et al, 1994), but may also vary in intensity, complexity and level of engagement (Tetroe, 2007), depending on the user's needs, the nature of the evidence and the level of resources that either side can commit. How these play out in practice will depend on the power dynamics between the actors, in particular the weight each side gives to a piece of knowledge. The policymaking process is not a value-neutral or objective one (Sutcliffe and Court, 2006); judgements about what knowledge to use and when are often embedded fairly deeply within assumptions about the validity of the knowledge, its interpretation in light of current events and the relative power of those producing and using it (see Chapter Three). This may be more obvious with evidence that has high scientific content (such as that around climate change – see Chapter Four), but can also be an important factor in how 'lay' or 'non-expert' knowledge is used in policymaking. The distinction between lay and expert knowledge is essentially a political judgement; a restrictive definition of expertise can have a powerful influence on whose knowledge is considered legitimate for decision making (Juntti et al, 2009).

This means the knowledge interaction process is not simply one of neutral facilitation, with implications for actors' degree of participation, the relative weight accorded to each type of knowledge and thus the potential for innovation and social learning (Leeuwis and Aarts, 2011). Michaels (2009) provides a clear framework of the spectrum of these knowledge interaction functions,[3] one that makes it possible to relate different interaction strategies to different issue types and policy settings. From our point of view, this framework is important because it does not begin with either the producer or consumer of knowledge but takes as its frame of reference the knowledge interaction process itself.[4]

Table 5.2 shows Michaels' framework of six functions of knowledge interaction, updated with the outputs of an international workshop in 2010 that analysed measures that could be used to assess the impact of knowledge intermediaries (Shaxson, 2011). It is clear that knowledge interaction can range from simply providing information to fully engaging with the process of social learning and transformation, building the capacity of all institutions to adapt to changing environments and new issues. However, Michaels' framework does not explore the potential power differentials between actors, implications for the quality of decisions made around a policy issue and the resulting degree of social learning. To do this, we set the framework against three well-recognised 'ladders of participation',[5] viewing these through a critique of the idea of a hierarchy of participation (Collins and Ison, 2009) and an understanding of the need for multiple knowledge types in policy making (Brown, 2003, 2007). In doing this, we begin to address calls for social learning processes in which stakeholders learn together 'and recognise that their own participation and presence in the process will affect the outcome of the entire system' (McNie, 2007, p 26).

Figure 5.1 represents these differences between ladders of participation and social learning. Collins and Ison (2009) criticise the idea of linear hierarchies of participation, whose goal of citizen control is achieved by reducing the power of the state and that recognise only weakly that participation is a collective process within which a high degree of social learning takes place. Of the three ladders, Kanji and Greenwood's (2001) version takes the idea of collective action closest to social learning, but does not take it further to understand that collective engagement with others fosters learning on an issue and, in so doing, changes how the issue is framed and how it can be addressed.

Michaels' knowledge intermediary functions approach shows how the nature of knowledge interaction changes as knowledge generation and use increasingly contribute to the processes of social learning. At one end (informing), a fixed form of knowledge is applied to a defined problem. At the other end, knowing occurs 'within the act of constructing and managing the issue' (Collins and Ison, 2006, Figure 3). As the element of social learning increases, the role of the knowledge intermediary becomes one of 'sharing problem definitions and monitoring, negotiation, conflict resolution, learning, agreement, confronting power asymmetries, creating and maintaining public goods ... (and fostering concerted action) ... amongst multiple, interdependent stakeholders' (Collins and

Table 5.2: Six functions of knowledge intermediaries and preferred descriptions used in this chapter

Michaels' original six functions	Additional aspects/preferred descriptions
Informing: disseminating content to targeted decision makers and decision influencers	**Informing:** disseminating content, targeting decision makers with information, making information easily accessible and digestible. Examples include factsheets, research synopses, web portals, databases, end-of-project seminars
Consulting: seeking out known experts to advise on problems specified by the user of knowledge, identifying who would benefit from expert advice, what advice is needed and the most appropriate forms of communication	**Linking:*** linking expertise to need for a particular policy area or within a particular discipline, helping policymakers address a specific policy issue by seeking out the necessary experts. Examples include project or programme advisory committees, focus groups, LinkedIn
Matchmaking: introducing each side to people or organisations in other knowledge domains; identifying the expertise needed, who can provide it and how best to foster communications	**Matchmaking:** actively networking to match expertise to need across issues and disciplines, helping policymakers think more broadly about a topic, and finding experts with relevant knowledge from another discipline, helping them take a strategic overview to address the fullness of the issue. Examples include departmental expert advisory committees, general conferences, university internships in government, mapping the evidence base for an issue
Engaging: helping frame the discussions and ensuring that all appropriate actors are involved for the life of the decision-making process	**Engaging:** framing issues inclusively to bring a common understanding to the decision-making process, contracting people or organisations to provide knowledge as needed. Examples include contracted research programmes, electronic knowledge networks, working groups, wikis, citizen juries, focus groups
Collaborating: helping both sides of the discussion jointly frame the process and negotiate the substance of the issue to address a particular problem	**Collaborating:** lengthening and deepening the collaborative process, strengthening relationships and formalising the process of ensuring that all sides jointly negotiate the questions to be asked around an issue. Examples include joint agreements where the emphasis is on equality in the relationships between actors, such as memoranda of understanding, joint agreements, communities of practice
Building adaptive capacity: stewarding long-term relationships, fostering organisational learning, co-producing knowledge	**Building adaptive capacity:** deepening the collaborative relationship to the extent that all parties jointly frame the issue; broadening institutional capacity of institutions to adapt to multiple issues simultaneously. The focus is on co-production of knowledge and joint learning from doing; the arrangements are self-sustaining in terms of both funding and function, with all sides contributing resources. Examples include co-management arrangements, local enterprise partnerships, self-sustaining consortia

Note: Michaels calls this a 'consulting' relationship, but the term is intended to cover a wider range of relationships than simply contracting independent consultants. We use the broader term 'linking' to avoid confusion.

Sources: Michaels (2009); Shaxson (2011)

Figure 5.1: Comparing a functions approach to knowledge intermediaries with conceptions of ladders of participation and of social learning

Ladders of participation			Functions of knowledge intermediaries: Michaels (2009)	Conceptual framing of social learning: Collins and Ison (2009)
Arnstein (1969)	Pretty (1994)	Kanji and Greenwood (2001)		
Aspects of social learning that are not covered by the ladders of participation. See Collins and Ison (2009)			Build adaptive capacity	Social learning
Citizen control	Self-mobilisation	Collective action	Collaborate	
Delegated power	Interactive participation	Co-learning	Engage	Participation
Partnership	Functional participation	Cooperation	Matchmake	
Placation	Participation for material incentives		Link	Consultation
Consultation	Participation by consultation	Consultation		
Informing	Participation in information giving		Inform	Information provision
Therapy	Passive participation	Compliance		
Manipulation				

Ison, 2006, p 11). Increasingly, then, knowledge intermediaries themselves become a force for innovation and change (Leeuwis and Aarts, 2011).

This functions approach also helps shed light on the power relationships with which knowledge intermediaries must deal. There are many challenges entailed in maintaining legitimacy and objectivity (Juntti et al, 2009) and, because social learning implies drawing on multiple knowledges to address complex problems,[6] it is important to ensure two things. First, any use of boundary spanners, concepts, objects or processes must be able to deal with issues of complexity, uncertainty and controversy at appropriate levels of participation between knowledge producers and policy makers. Second, it is important to be aware that, while intermediaries have an important role to play in ensuring all voices are heard, there is a danger they may become new power brokers in the system (Ramirez, 2008) and introduce their own biases or preferences for change. This means that, as social learning leads to the emergence of stronger local capacity, intermediaries may need to change their roles or remove themselves from the scene altogether. Likewise, in heavily politicised areas, it will be difficult for intermediaries to remain completely neutral, but they still have a role to play in improving the legitimacy and credibility of all voices so that debate is better informed and more transparent.

The next subsections explore the six different functions in more detail, but build on Michaels' original descriptions by focusing on how the aspect of social learning increases with each function. Note that there is no reason to suggest there should be any particular balance between different functions or any specific timeframe for their application to a policy issue. The framework is non-judgemental in this respect, but it offers a valuable structure to help readers analyse how best to develop and manage their own knowledge interaction processes to improve policymaking. In the final section of this chapter, we discuss whether or not there is a specific role for an independent knowledge intermediary to perform each of these functions.

Informing

Definition

Informing is disseminating content in a form that is appropriate to a specified audience. Knowledge producers create or share knowledge about an issue; users are seen as passive recipients of that knowledge and can absorb or reject it as they see fit. Improving the knowledge interaction process means understanding the needs of the target audience, then packaging and disseminating what has been produced in ways that retain its objectivity but make it easy for the audience to assimilate it.

Who is involved?

Anyone can be a knowledge producer and *inform* others; who is involved and to what extent will depend on the nature of the problem and the communication expertise of the intermediary. Researchers, NGOs, communities and policymakers can all be knowledge producers; they can do the *informing* themselves or make use of specialist communicators. Citizens, too, can be knowledge producers, although clearly a great deal of care needs to be taken to ensure the voices of those who are poor and marginalised are given adequate support so they can make themselves heard.

Strengths

Dissemination: disseminating knowledge is a basic function at the knowledge–policy interface. Some *informing* techniques target the needs of particular interest groups closely; the internet, on the other hand, allows vast numbers of people to have access to knowledge, increasing the likelihood that it will be appropriate to someone, somewhere.

Weaknesses

Minimal exchange between producers and users of knowledge: while a great many people can be reached, there is little contact between supply and demand, which means it is difficult to attribute impact to a particular piece of knowledge. Understanding user demand for different types of knowledge or different formats in which to present them is not a move away from the *informing* function – it is simply good practice (Adolph et al, 2010). How that knowledge is used is beyond the influence of the intermediary, who disengages from the process once the user has received it.

Limited transparency: if the *informing* function is simply the dissemination of content without any claim to participation or social learning, for ideas to penetrate deeply it needs to happen in an open, stable, legitimate, recognised and professional domain for decision making – where the goal is clear, processes are transparent and the need is for information to fill recognised gaps. This is not always the case. Policy goals change over time, and all organisations have their own internal political economy that affects how information is received and acted on. Understanding this will help determine which other types of intermediary activity could also be brought into play to increase the impact of specific pieces of knowledge

Competing cultures of knowledge: *informing* assumes that the knowledge producer has correctly understood the problem, has the necessary information and knows to whom the knowledge will be most useful. Often, this is not the case – different epistemic communities will define the problem differently and claim authority over the types of knowledge most aligned with their beliefs. Simply *informing* one community with knowledge from another will serve little purpose (Bentley and Gonzalo Rodríguez, 2001), unless the knowledges are brought alongside each other and interpreted jointly to develop useful solutions to specific problems. In addition, complex policy issues tend to be transdisciplinary, change over time and affect different stakeholders in different ways (Campbell and Schofield, 2006). Merely *informing* this diverse set of people about the results of research will not necessarily improve social learning across the community unless the different types of knowledge are integrated with what has been learned from the research. Other actors may pick up issues and draw on them in their own work, but it will not be possible to anticipate how information will be used and its likely effects.

Linking

Definition

Linking is the action of seeking out known experts to advise on a particular problem delineated by the policymaker. Rather than simply providing information, the person or organisation provides advice in response to a clear remit. This may be verbal or written, a one-off request or part of a long-term relationship. While users are still passive recipients of knowledge, they have played a part in framing the question and thus the types of knowledge that may be admitted to the process.

Who is involved?

Large organisations often employ external consultants and researchers to improve their knowledge of an issue, or bring together experts to help quality assure their work. However, this should not be considered an activity exclusively for those outside the policy arena; informal *linking* can be done inside the policy sphere by those who have a good overview of an issue (senior policymakers or those in a more strategic position). The *linking* relationship may be formalised with terms of reference or be part of the informal network all policymakers operate in their search for knowledge. This form of relationship is not always characterised by paid consultancy; instead, *linking* describes all situations where individuals or organisations are asked to provide specific findings or more general expertise in response to a specific series of questions.

Strengths

Speed and focus: the benefits of *linking* are that it can be relatively quick and cheap and is targeted at policymakers' perception of the important question. Because the relationship is instigated by knowledge users, they can set various parameters within which the work will be conducted – such as budget, timeframe and variety of expertise. For policymakers with a broad understanding of an issue, it is a way of ensuring that multiple perspectives are incorporated. It is also a way of getting a 'best guess' answer to a question where the emerging evidence is contested or uncertain and where knowledge producers are loath to release the final results of their work. *Linking* works well where the question of who is an expert in the field is relatively uncontested and where policy goals are fairly well aligned with those of both citizens and the relevant experts.

Weaknesses

Limited scope: this is an 'invited' process, controlled to a great extent by the person using the knowledge; the policymaker decides who to consult, how to frame the questions and how much budget to allocate. This means that, without suitable precautions, evidence that challenges current thinking may be ruled out and the search for knowledge may be limited by preconceived ideas of what the main issues are. If decisions are taken behind closed doors, this form of linking – as consultation – will likely be perceived as being carried out to co-opt radical or dissenting views. The value of formal consultation is largely a function of the engagement that precedes it; while a formal process is of value if regulations are being changed (for example, lawyers need written evidence from which to work), care needs to be taken to ensure formalising the *linking* function does not limit the sources of expertise.

Matchmaking

Definition

'Matchmakers introduce people to each other who would not otherwise meet' (Michaels, 2009, p 997). *Matchmakers* seek to identify useful knowledge from disciplines, countries and organisations the policy maker would not have thought to search in, and thus create networks across domains. In doing so, they broaden and enrich the scope of the evidence base a policymaker can draw on, possibly changing the framing of the policy question and certainly bringing a new depth to the analysis. This differs from *informing* and *linking* in that the matchmaker purposefully seeks out this new knowledge (rather than simply suggesting the policymaker attend another seminar, for example) and uses his or her expertise to interpret it for the policymaker's current needs. Developing a shared understanding between the different actors will be important, and *matchmakers* may find boundary objects and boundary concepts useful tools with which to work.

Who is involved?

Matchmaking can be accidental (a by-product of interactions) or purposive (the result of a specific focus on cross-issue engagement). It may happen of its own accord at a conference or seminar that helps decision makers connect with other spheres of action that hold valuable lessons or insights. This may work particularly well where issues have traditionally been considered sectorally or within organisational silos; cross-sectoral events that discuss some underlying principles or issues (for example gender, equity, governance, horizon scanning, futures) may be particularly useful for fostering the sort of engagement likely to lead to broad learning. More purposive *matchmaking* could involve the use of strategic expert advisory committees; strategy units whose remit is to spot cross-cutting issues and foster linkages to strengthen programmes; or even internships within government departments to strengthen relationships between government and academia.

Strengths

Acknowledging reciprocity: *matchmaking* is the first of Michaels' functions to explicitly acknowledge the two-way exchange of knowledge, and the consequent need to build relationships; influence and negotiate; build trust; resolve conflicts; and value alternative framings of an issue. An independent *matchmaker* can identify and build relationships between very diverse communities of actors to address complex policy problems.

Weaknesses

Concerns about trust: while accidental *matchmaking* cannot be planned and is therefore difficult to do cost-effectively, purposive *matchmaking* can judge which actors need to be connected to whom and thus be more effective. However, without a remit (as part of a strategy unit, say), it may be difficult for *matchmakers* to nose their way into discussions; once relationships are established, it may be hard for them to play a constructive role in maintaining and monitoring progress. And if not all participants trust the remit, it will be hard for the *matchmaker* to maintain the necessary degree of objectivity and impartiality. At a personal level, much will depend on the individual credibility of the *matchmaker* – but it is not simply about personal attributes. It is also possible to develop tools and techniques to help ensure this sort of boundary-spanning analysis is well structured (Bielak et al, 2008). Without such rigorous analysis, *matchmakers* too may begin to interpolate their own biases into the power relations between knowledge producers and users.

Engaging

Definition

Engaging is collaboration around a predetermined issue. Michaels (2009, p 997) defines the relationship as 'one party frames the discussion ... for the life of the required process, [involving] other parties in the substantive aspects of the problem on an as needed basis'. Whereas *informing*, *linking* and *matchmaking* could well happen informally, *engaging* is more about one party giving direction to both the type of relationship and the actor set, which will not happen without a clearly identified need. Note that, because the decision maker frames the process, *engaging* has a contractual nature – a point whose implications we bring out below.

Who is involved?

Engaging begins to formalise the processes begun in *linking* and *matchmaking*, meaning the set of actors involved is very similar. However, the knowledge interaction process is more long term than in *linking* or *matchmaking*; examples might include technical committees, secondments and short-term employment contracts (as distinct from those for research projects and programmes). Informal examples are less easy to categorise but might include longer-term relationships with 'friendly' knowledge producers to whom policymakers turn for general advice and information.

Strengths

Openness of the decision-making process: inviting knowledge producers into policymakers' space begins to open the space up and help knowledge producers see more transparently where their knowledge is being put to use, even if it is not possible to rigorously define the impact they have had. It also enables knowledge producers to actively seek out decision makers and instigate further engagement processes themselves. Opening up relationships this way begins to break down the distinction between 'lay' and 'expert' knowledge (Juntti et al, 2009).

Weaknesses

Barriers to openness: it can be difficult to open up relationships if the issue is perceived to be highly technical, or if policymakers feel intimidated by the expertise of the person or organisation they are engaging with. It can also be difficult to engage local knowledge, since the value of doing so lies in understanding the different framing put on an issue (which negates the somewhat contractual nature of this type of relationship). Participants may also be excluded by definition; processes to address chronic poverty may find it difficult to engage poor and marginalised people who do not have the resources to attend meetings or may be actively excluded through social discrimination or criminalisation (Johnson and Start, 2001; Harriss-White, 2005). Processes such as participatory budgeting, for example, where council budgetary allocations are co-defined through local-level community negotiating, often exclude those who are poorest (Brautigam and Knack, 2004). These sorts of relationships are also expensive to construct and time-consuming, and may become bureaucratic.

Collaboration

Definition

Collaboration lengthens and deepens the process of interaction between actors, responding to the power dynamics between them to improve the equality of relationships and beginning to build institutions able to respond to more than one issue at a time. Unlike *engaging*, where the issue is predefined by one party, *collaborating* allows all sides to frame the questions jointly. The process begins to explicitly address aspects of social learning emphasised by Collins and Ison (2009), as well as the need for actors to interact reflexively with each other and to respond to emergent issues.

Who is involved?

Various actors are involved in *collaboration*. Depending on the nature of the issue, these may include policymakers, practitioners, local communities, researchers and other advisers and national and international NGOs, often brought together around specific projects or programmes. Collaborative relationships can be informal (for example communities of practice) but are often formalised to various degrees via memoranda of understanding or joint agreements. The emphasis in these agreements is on equality in the relationship between actors. Again, boundary concepts, objects and processes are likely to be important tools to help actors develop a shared understanding of an issue.

Strengths

Ability to transform relationships between actors: there are many benefits to collaboration; the process can be truly transformative for all actors in the process. Policymakers may benefit from new knowledge of the issue and others may be given a real voice in how the issue is framed, addressed and understood. Some argue that collaboration is the only way to address 'wicked issues' (Williams, 2002).[7] A robust process of collaboration can build relationships that are resilient enough to deal with competing values, goals and knowledge bases or situations of crisis or chaos – using these to create opportunities for social learning rather than seeing them as threats to a perceived order.

Weaknesses

Time and financial constraints: collaboration is expensive and demanding in terms of the time commitments needed to sustain relationships. Indeed, it may not be possible to create truly collaborative relationships if the prevailing power dynamics are too unbalanced to begin with; powerful actors may still push through their points of view, favoured knowledge types or preferred processes. True collaboration with policymakers is notoriously difficult – they are often distracted by issues emerging in the political sphere that cannot be predicted.

Building equitable relationships: from an intermediary's point of view, structuring a collaborative process means putting in place safeguards to ensure a degree of balance between the different types of knowledge, values, interests and credibility, encouraging those with a weaker voice to play a real part in the process and to demonstrate accountability to all actors.

Building adaptive capacity

Definition

The difference between *collaboration* and *building adaptive capacity* is that the idea of social learning covers multiple, rather than single, policy problems – with a corresponding increase in the complexity of interactions. All actors work together on multiple policy problems to jointly frame the process of interaction, negotiate the substance and apply their joint learning to future issues. In doing so, they are co-creating their operational space, managing relationships and sharing power by continually negotiating claims to participation and ideas about the desired outcomes.

Who is involved?

Building adaptive capacity needs to involve all actors – community organisations, policymakers, researchers, funders and others need to work together to ensure that institutions' ability to anticipate and cope with change is sustainable. For example, it is not sufficient simply to ensure that new knowledge is fed constantly into a community organisation, without ensuring that it can continue to function over the long term and respond to whatever issues arise. The organisation needs to have regulations allowing it to operate, be socially legitimate (rather than simply existing to serve an elite), be able to weather political storms and be environmentally benign or beneficial. It must also be financially stable, which can be difficult if local tax-raising powers are needed to fund it. This is a challenging set of requirements, but does not mean that *building adaptive capacity* is too diffuse an idea to be codified. It can be enshrined in agreements such as co-management arrangements, local enterprise partnerships and self-funding consortia of organisations that address issues of concern to local communities.

Strengths

Building capability to respond to a variety of emerging issues: this concept underpins the whole notion of sustainable development: communities at all levels being able to develop and maintain the set of institutions they need to respond to their particular needs. This includes political, fiscal and organisational sustainability, not as a fixed series of organisations and relationships but instead as arrangements that are able to adapt to the nature of emerging issues.

Weaknesses

Cost and governance challenges: as well as the cost implications of *building adaptive capacity*, the process raises governance challenges. These are more obvious in Southern contexts, where democratic institutions and customs are often precarious. Policymakers may also have low degrees of autonomy resulting in greater implementation challenges and reliance on personal relationships leading to misgovernment. These deficits are often compounded by a dearth of hard data and strong intermediary institutions able to facilitate the transfer of evidence to policy (Carden, 2009).

Understanding the roles of knowledge intermediaries

It is clear from the above analysis that there is no single 'knowledge intermediary function'. Instead, a variety of functions need to be performed at different stages to improve the interface between knowledge and policy. It follows from this that it is not possible to identify a single type of organisation or individual as the ideal knowledge intermediary. The choice of who fulfils which role needs to follow the old adage that 'form follows function' – that it is important to identify which functions are needed for a particular issue at a particular time, and only then to choose who is best placed to perform them. This section helps readers decide which functions are most appropriate to their current needs, their relative strengths and weaknesses and whether or not there is a specific role for an independent knowledge intermediary.

As should be clear from the preceding analysis, it is by no means always the case that knowledge intermediaries should be hired independently. It may well be that people and organisations currently involved in an issue can be encouraged to undertake knowledge interaction functions themselves by realigning existing structures and incentives.

Choosing **where** to make these changes needs careful thought. In complex systems, problems occur over multiple interlinked levels. Delivering a national maternal healthcare system, for example, may involve the department of health, regional health authorities, hospitals, doctors, community midwives and nurses. Focusing on delivering services to the end user means the intermediary's priority will be to facilitate action at the lower levels, rather than relying on a command-and-control approach directed from the centre with little real understanding of who needs to be involved and the local knowledge about how local institutions really work. To decide where intermediary functions are needed, it will be important to consider:

- the vertical hierarchy of organisations (central and local government, head offices and regional/local outposts) and how intermediaries can contribute to ensuring delivery happens at the most appropriate level;
- the legal and regulatory barriers to self-organisation and how intermediaries can work to overcome these by facilitating the flow of knowledge across boundaries;
- how intermediaries can contribute to the process of negotiating the framings around an issue and understanding power dynamics between actors; and
- adopting an incremental approach to intervention that entails an understanding of how intermediaries can support the flow of knowledge between all actors to ensure they have a clear shared understanding of what impacts are needed and how to deliver them cost-effectively.

Choosing **when** to strengthen knowledge intermediary functions is not a simple process. When policy is complex, it may be difficult to determine the boundaries between discrete sets of activities. For example, a perfectly planned project may be thrown into confusion because institutions have not fully understood what is being asked of them, or because the reality of getting organisations to work together is more complicated and time-consuming than initially thought. Strengthening knowledge intermediary functions may therefore be appropriate at several different stages, as follows:

- in planning:
  - convening actors around shared identities, values and beliefs (see Chapter Three);
  - supporting the flow of knowledge to articulate shared theories of change between actors, including foresight and other visioning tools;
  - mediating between conflicting visions or identities and ensuring that any adjustments to plans are widely agreed;
  - involving policymakers in the design stages of a project or programme to improve political buy-in to the initiative and contributing to its longer-term stability;
  - developing innovative approaches to boundary processes such as foresight, strategy development, planning, appraisal and budgeting;
- during implementation:
  - facilitating the use of innovative approaches to boundary processes such as monitoring and evaluating, including making sense of unintended outcomes and using them to rework plans;
  - closing feedback loops between knowledge and policy by promoting lesson learning;
  - understanding the implications of variation and redundancy, and how they contribute to incremental interventions. Large programmes are often implemented according to a single master plan, but this works well only where there is no local variation. In complex systems, it makes more sense to encourage a large programme to run several small-scale pilots, which may differ significantly between localities. The results will be very different; the programme would pursue those that have the desired effects and revise those that do not. Instead of revisions being seen as a failure of the master plan, they become an essential part of the learning and localising process;
- exiting from the intervention, either because the intervention has ended or the intermediary function has become redundant:
  - ensuring that local capacity is well enough built to cope with additional issues, and that the intermediary's leaving does not compromise the project or programme's sustainability.

Understanding **how** to act as a knowledge intermediary means choosing from many different techniques:

- convening and integrating multiple types of knowledge and developing techniques to ensure all types of knowledge contribute to the story of change and to assessments of progress, at all levels from strategic to local;
- strengthening relationships between actors, using facilitation, mediation and consensus-building skills that ensure all voices are given equal weight;
- facilitating collaborative sense-making and deliberative processes, particularly for complex or fast-moving issues;

- opening up dialogue to actors outside the formal political economy, ensuring interventions are based on an understanding of informal systems; and
- mediating, convening and resolving conflicts that may arise, seeing them as part of a complex process of change rather than a reason to halt an intervention.

Careful attention needs to be paid to choosing which mix of techniques will best support each function at any given time. It will also be important to understand the prominence intermediaries may have as they use the techniques. If they are too conspicuous, they risk compromising their neutrality; if they are too inconspicuous, they risk being ineffective. There is no single answer to this (and it may change over time); it will be a matter of analysis, judgement, experience and intuition as to what will be most effective for each particular issue at each particular time.

Planning, implementing and monitoring knowledge interaction

Having identified where knowledge intermediaries could contribute and at what stages of the process, this section outlines the four steps involved in developing a clear implementation plan. These are summarised in Table 5.3 and detailed below; they are intended as a guide rather than a prescription and readers are encouraged to adapt the steps to suit their particular needs.

Table 5.3: Planning to implement knowledge intermediary functions

Step	Description	Comments
1	Undertaking a needs assessment	Review what information is available and how well it is targeted at various actors. On the basis of this, decide which types of knowledge should be involved to improve the knowledge–policy interface. Examine the roles of different actors and the wider political context to understand how they might influence the roles of intermediaries.
2	Understanding organisational mandates	Many different organisations could act as knowledge intermediaries: understanding their different mandates will help identify where any gaps could be filled by developing new partnerships or expanding roles for existing actors.
3	Sequencing the choice of intermediary functions	Review the six intermediary functions and decide which institution or individual is best placed to fulfil them, and how.
4	Interpreting the results and monitoring progress	Develop indicators of impact for each intermediary function that make sense to the institutions and individuals involved.

Step 1: undertaking a needs assessment

Availability of information

The first step in any knowledge interaction process should be to review the extent to which information is available on the issue and to make a judgement about how well it has been targeted at the people and organisations that may need to use it. At this point, we are simply looking at what variety of information exists, bearing in mind that different audiences will need a range of formats. It is also important to note that information is needed before knowledge can be constructed. Accordingly, this step relates simply to whether or not information is available, regardless of whether it is turned into knowledge and applied to an issue. Subsequent questions focus on the broader conception of knowledge. Key questions to ask in this step include:

- Who needs information about this issue? Why?
- Is there ample information about the issue we are dealing with? What sort of information? Who has it? In what format?
- How well is it disseminated to the various organisations and individuals involved in related issues? What media are currently used:
  - paper, email, electronic newsletters;
  - television, radio and theatre;
  - word of mouth (extension services, training courses, other interactive processes)?
- Where are the gaps, both in the breadth of information that is disseminated and in the media through which people are *informed*?

Types of knowledge

Understanding how to make best use of the different types of knowledge means understanding what they bring to discussions, but also how they affect (and are affected by) the prevailing power dynamics:

- How can the legitimacy of all types of knowledge be improved? For instance, what could be done to encourage greater acceptance by scientists of the validity and relevance of indigenous knowledge producers, and vice versa?
- Should the knowledge be used for general enlightenment, to support specific decisions or to feed into negotiations? Which of the six knowledge intermediary functions would be most effective at doing this?
- What boundary concepts, objects or processes could be used to explore knowledge on the issue? How should they be used – to translate generalisable results from scientific research into local context and application; to encourage local people to help shape future scientific research; or to engage all actors in a shared understanding of what progress means?

- How do knowledge incentive structures, such as the business processes of government, affect the demand for knowledge from policymakers?

Readers should also refer to Chapter Four to help answer these questions and analyse how to incorporate different types of knowledge into policymaking processes.

Roles of different actors

Some of the functions of knowledge intermediaries explicitly seek to alter the power relations between actors (see Box 5.3 below). Indeed, the act of *not* acting to rebalance relationships (such as not intervening to improve the use of indigenous knowledge in policymaking processes but instead relying on technical knowledge) could be seen as an implicit way of reinforcing the status quo. Questions include:

- What are the different interests and how do they shape who is involved in (or excluded from) an issue? What are the implications for the establishment of policy priorities?
- How do actor interests affect the openness of decision-making processes?
- To what extent do wider values and beliefs constrain or shape what different actors are able to do and whether they are open to new knowledge?
- Which actors are currently seen as credible, or as experts, and what are the implications for whose knowledge is used? Does the degree of technical knowledge needed to engage on a policy issue limit who is able to participate?

Readers should refer to Chapter Three to help answer these questions and understand what influences different actors at the interface between knowledge and policy.

Wider political context

The contours of different political processes will influence the possible scope and type of intermediary function that can be considered. Important factors include the roles of formal and informal political processes, and the capacity of a particular political system to absorb change.

Key questions regarding the political economy of the knowledge–policy interface include:

- Where are the checks and balances in the policymaking system that encourage policy scrutiny? To what extent can the executive and the legislature challenge the quality and quantity of knowledge used in policymaking?
- To what extent do political processes allow for – and even encourage – incorporation of knowledge types? Is decision making closed or relatively open, technocratic or participatory?

- Where are decisions about an issue really taken – in central policymaking organisations or at a more devolved level? How well do evidence providers respond to the need for a decentralised supply of knowledge?
- What is the balance of formal and informal politics, and what are the implications for whose knowledge is recognised as a legitimate basis for policymaking?
- To what extent is the issue affected by international pressures, such as international agreements? How do these influence how national policies are developed, and what knowledge is accepted as relevant?
- What are the implications of all of these for how openly the knowledge intermediary function can be performed?

Readers should refer to Chapter Two to understand how the wider political context can affect the flow of knowledge in policy.

Step 2: understanding organisational mandates

It is also important to reflect on the mandate of the organisations involved in the issue, so as to take sensible decisions about how each can best contribute to strengthening the knowledge intermediary functions needed. For instance, a research communications organisation is best suited to the informing, linking and possibly matchmaking functions but is likely to be going beyond its mandate by getting involved in collaboration activities. On the other hand, an NGO focused on strengthening local institutions would want to identify and work with an organisation whose strength is linking and informing and then to focus on engaging and collaboration activities. The checklist in Step 3 helps in answering the following questions:

- How far does the organisation's mandate extend through the six knowledge intermediary functions?
- How far could other organisations address the various functions of knowledge intermediaries for the current issue?
- What is missing? How could this gap best be filled – should we ask existing organisations or individuals to expand their current roles, or should we seek out new partnerships?
- To what extent could knowledge intermediaries fill the gaps? Which organisation or individual should be responsible for what?

Step 3: selecting appropriate knowledge intermediary functions

Readers will need to consider carefully how to select appropriate intermediary functions, so that they build on one another to systematically increase social learning. While some of the functions may already be addressed, it will be important (for example) to ensure that any efforts to *matchmake* different types of expertise around an issue are already well supported by efforts to *inform* all the experts of the relevant knowledge. In other words, the functions at the informing end of the spectrum serve as building blocks for those on the collaborating end and it is thus important to ascertain that the former are in place before advancing towards the latter.

Informing

Choose *informing*:

- when it is important to reach as many people as possible;
- where information can be easily understood and acted on; or
- where there is already a latent demand for the information.

Informing is not generally the way to promote direct use of knowledge (such as acting on specific messages in a report or policy brief). However, general dissemination can have effects such as the 'enlightenment' function proposed by Weiss (1979), in which new information can, over time, filter through reflective processes and change the way policy issues are framed (see Box 5.2).

Box 5.2: *Informing* small producers in Peru

In Cajamarca in Peru, Practical Answers (a programme initiated by the international NGO Practical Action) has pioneered innovative information services that have been crucial to the expansion of the dairy industry. Produced by the most technologically advanced Practical Answers office, the Infolactea Portal provides technical information to those involved in the dairy production chain. By consolidating information and facilitating the integration of supply and demand, it has increased the competitiveness of the region's dairy industry and improved outcomes for poor people. For example, the portal helped local producers negotiate the web of government accreditation, ensuring they can sell their products legally. The programme has also produced and distributed training materials, including videos, on topics ranging from pasture management and irrigation to artificial insemination and mastitis. These activities have been facilitated by Practical Answers' local resource centres, which offer live demonstrations of materials and techniques, as well as housing information on machinery and equipment and facilitating links between entrepreneurs and dairy farmers. The potential impact of this knowledge interaction approach remains huge; there is a prospective 'market' of 60,000 regional users, many of whom are yet to be reached.

Source: Mikolajuk (2010)

Is there a specific role for knowledge intermediaries? While knowledge producers are able to use various tools to disseminate what they know, there is a role for specialist communicators who work to understand the needs of specific target audiences and then to package and disseminate what has been produced in ways that retain its objectivity but make it easy for the audience to assimilate it. However, there is a fine line between making complex material digestible for non-experts and a 'misleading selectivity on the part of those presenting or those receiving and interpreting the material' (Owens et al, 2006, p 637). The power dynamics of knowledge intermediaries can be seen even in a function with little social learning, as intermediaries are able to select which types and extracts of the full knowledge base should be used to inform policymakers. This is not necessarily a specific challenge for research or for local knowledge; both may be used 'selectively and strategically' (In't Veld and de Wit, 2000; Kingdon, 2003) or employed to legitimise policy solutions that have been arrived at on overtly political grounds (Juntti et al, 2009). And even if communicated clearly to a targeted audience, findings can be unwelcome if they do not suit predefined agendas or provide answers to preconceived problems. This may be particularly true for issues with international drivers, where the often stark differential in power dynamics may result in a significant bias towards a particular type of knowledge (such as trade policy's emphasis on economic knowledge).

Linking

Choose *linking*:

- when the policy question is clear (such as formal written consultations);
- where robust technical advice is needed in response to specific questions; or
- where it is important to consult with specific groups of people local to a particular problem or issue.

For the decision maker, deciding to engage in *linking* means first ensuring that the terms of reference encourages high-quality analysis of the breadth of available evidence and that the technical language used is appropriate. Seeking out multiple perspectives (even if the final analysis does not agree with some of them) is important for two reasons: to ensure that those with a legitimate voice are well represented in the process; and to draw on the best available knowledge. It is important to be transparent about who is being invited to advise and why, and about any concessions or funding being paid to advisers to facilitate the process.[8]

A *linking* function can enhance the credibility of research (in terms of the expertise gathered), add salience to the end-users (where an intermediary communicates needs clearly and cost-effectively) and build legitimacy with stakeholders and wider audiences by providing transparency to the knowledge generation process (see Box 5.3). However, certain types of *linking* may worsen a delicate balance of interaction or overemphasise the benefits of deliberative processes such as briefings or roundtables in relation to other opportunities for interaction (van Eeten, 1999; Culyer and Lomas, 2006).

> **Box 5.3: *Linking* indigenous knowledge to policy in Ecuador's Protected Areas**
>
> Grupo Faro is an Ecuadorean civil society organisation (CSO) working to move the country away from a development model based on natural resource extraction and an unequal distribution of opportunities. As part of its work on environmental governance, Grupo Faro published the results of a case study that explored the land management approaches of the Cofán people, who live in the low-lying region between the Andes and the Amazon on the borders of Colombia and Ecuador. The Cofán have developed a model of land management based on indigenous knowledge and ancient traditions, informed by Western tools and understanding. Grupo Faro's dissemination of the Cofán's approach is helping Ecuadorean policymakers develop and embed sustainable systems of co-management for other protected areas.
>
> *Source:* Ormaza (2010)

Is there a specific role for knowledge intermediaries? Knowledge intermediaries can help identify which decision makers would benefit from which types of expertise, and facilitate relevant communication. This goes further than simply establishing the demand for knowledge; the intermediary simultaneously assesses who has the expertise and how it would be used most effectively. Intermediaries could also work with decision makers to frame the question so it is answerable and also to ensure that knowledge providers draw on the requisite breadth of knowledge and present their findings in an easily digestible and accessible way. This differs from *informing* in that the *linking* intermediary is beginning to subtly alter the power dynamics between knowledge producer and user, in effect setting themselves up as another provider of expertise – in this case about how to support a balanced exchange of knowledge. Another difference between the *informing* and *linking* intermediary is the need for technical expertise in helping frame the question. While this clearly is of benefit to the knowledge user, it is possible that the intermediary inadvertently brings too much of their personal bias to the framing process.

Matchmaking

Matchmaking is particularly appropriate in the case of strategic or complex policy issues that cross knowledge domains, or where it is important to learn from experiences in other systems or countries (see Box 5.4). This may be particularly relevant for wicked issues such as obesity, climate change, social inclusion and urban regeneration, which cross jurisdictions, organisations, disciplines, functions and generations (Williams, 2002). These cannot be dealt with by a single organisation or a short-term fix, and efforts to address them need to be many-pronged and long in term.

Box 5.4: *Matchmaking* scientists and local communities in Bangladesh

Practical Answers Bangladesh supports a local knowledge node (LKN) initiative, Bengali Gyaner Hat, to meet the burgeoning need for technical information in rural areas. LKNs serve three key functions. First, they provide information and advice on topics ranging from plant disease to seed preservation. This knowledge is communicated in a variety of ways that facilitate community uptake – from video clips, to expert-run workshops and leaflets in local languages. Second, LKNs provide the inputs that sustain community agriculture, such as veterinary medication, fertiliser and packaging materials. Finally, LKNs provide services such as internet access, refrigeration and phones. They also serve as a warehouse for key government forms.

LKNs are staffed by 'infomediaries' – young, local, technically savvy entrepreneurs – and used by the entire community. Farmers obtain information on new seed varieties, acquire the seed and learn how to monitor its moisture content. To promote the two-way exchange of information, their questions are used as a basis for developing new knowledge materials, which are then distributed to all LKNs. NGO staff and agricultural extension agents can use the space for meetings and to share new knowledge – both technical and otherwise. For instance, Practical Answers has raised community awareness on women's land ownership rights, as well as unifying and validating land measurements to avoid dispute. Young people are primary knowledge consumers; Bengali Gyaner Hat offers them content as well as educational support and employment information.

A participatory community appraisal carried out in six communities found that local residents had very favourable opinions of the matchmaking functions undertaken by Practical Answers. Parents appreciate the new educational opportunities for their children. Men enjoy having information that enables them to further their business skills and make better decisions. Women find that knowledge access helps them develop skills and an understanding of their rights, as well as making life better for their families.

Source: Mikolajuk (2010)

If you are outside the policy process, choose *matchmaking*:

- when there is a need to broaden policymakers' horizons; or
- when there is a need to spot potential synergies with other issues and bring a more strategic overview to the table.

If you are inside the policy process, choose *matchmaking*:

- when you need help forging a strategic vision;
- when you need to engage multiple stakeholders around an issue;
- when you are aware of the need to build sustainable relationships and trust, to resolve potential disagreements; or

- when you know that your focus is narrow but are unaware who else could contribute.

Is there a specific role for knowledge intermediaries? Where policy issues are complex, it is often helpful to have independent advice on where to look for wider learning: finding others who have been in similar situations and who have credible lessons to share about what works and what does not can be beneficial. But the role of *matchmakers* is not limited to introductions alone – it will also be important for them to help policymakers identify and synthesise different types of knowledge into a meaningful story, building relationships with knowledge providers. For wicked policy issues, the role of *matchmakers* will be to increase understanding of the system's complexity, helping policymakers weave together the multiple overlapping threads into a coherent picture, so decisions can be taken about the way ahead.

Engaging

Choose *engaging*:

- when there is a need to build a variety of relationships around a predetermined and long-term issue such as a large-scale project or a policy pilot.

Because the issues are long term in nature, there is a need to ensure that relationships are actively managed towards intended outcomes, and this may well be done using contractual arrangements. These relationships will be time-limited and will end when the project or pilot ends. However, it is important to note that power dynamics may play a large part in how relationships evolve over time – particularly if the point of the process is to build capacity. This may be difficult given the often unyielding nature of contracts. Less formal *engagement* may be more flexible in this respect, but it may be more difficult to ensure that key actors remain committed for the lifespan of the issue.

Is there a specific role for knowledge intermediaries? The role of intermediaries here becomes closer to the notion of an 'honest broker of policy alternatives' – who 'engages in decision-making by clarifying and, at times, seeking to expand the scope of choice available to decision-makers' (Pielke, 2007, p 17). Key to the honest broker's role is their explicit attempt to develop alternative courses of action by integrating all types of knowledge with stakeholder concerns.[9] This definition of engagement encompasses *linking* and *matchmaking*, but with longer-term implications for fostering relationships, maintaining flows of knowledge and ensuring that power dynamics remain balanced. Intermediaries may engage one actor on behalf of another, mediating contract negotiations and disagreements and acting as independent adviser to both in order to ensure that the relationship remains productive.

While this may be relatively clear for situations where scientific knowledge needs to be engaged, the role of intermediaries in engaging local or indigenous knowledge is less clear because of the reflexive nature of the interactions between different worldviews. As Michaels (2009) notes, the process of *engaging* local knowledge may be better suited to research projects and programmes with their clearly defined issues and timeframes than to the process of policymaking.

Collaborating

Choose *collaborating*:

- when relationships need to be formalised to ensure continuity.

Collaboration is the key to amplifying all the different voices around an issue (Salas Guzman, 2007), and to building and maintaining a broader base from which to discuss and define lessons that could inform a particular decision (Kamara and Sedoh, 2006).

Is there a specific role for knowledge intermediaries? As well as being that of an 'honest broker', the role of knowledge intermediaries here is to facilitate the collaboration, helping create and host the space and ensuring that it remains neutral, credible, relevant and reliable (see Box 5.5 below). Mediation and facilitation skills may be needed to overcome disagreements and to ensure that the process continues. But simply parachuting in skilled mediators or facilitators will not work; because collaborating intermediaries need to be able to relate to all actors on equal terms, they will have to demonstrate considerable technical expertise and familiarity with the different values and epistemologies of the actors involved, much of which will come from on-the-job experience (Williams, 2002). The risk is that intermediaries will become so enmeshed in the process they will be unable to step back from a neutral facilitation role and instead become an active part of the power dynamics in the collaboration.

Box 5.5: Striving for *collaboration* in Practical Action's Practical Answers

As a knowledge intermediary, part of Practical Answer's remit is to facilitate collaboration among actors at the knowledge–policy interface. It is currently developing a network of village knowledge centres to provide poor people with a front line for their knowledge needs and to serve as community hubs. These centres, which reflect community need and economic reality, can be either freestanding businesses run by local entrepreneurs or housed at schools or community centres staffed by volunteer extension agents. They offer face-to-face information, provide space for events such as talks by agricultural experts and NGO staff and often offer access to both the internet and productive assets, including fertiliser and seed.

Users of Practical Answers' knowledge channels say their new knowledge has enabled them to solve problems by adopting more productive technologies that have reduced costs and

---

improved yields. In Bangladesh, farmers have learned how to manage increasing soil salinity; in Uganda, women have been linked with technology that enables them to dry their spices in in a very humid environment; in the Philippines, farmers are learning techniques that enable them to increase the quality of their coffee. However, there is an unmet need for information on topics such as markets, law and healthcare. Developing a knowledge industry that will enable commercial success in poor communities will take time to realise.

Source: Mikolajuk (2010)

Building adaptive capacity

Choose *building adaptive capacity*:

* when the focus is on supporting organisations, or groups of organisations, to become self-sustaining.

As a concept, *building adaptive capacity* is extremely broad, making it challenging to consider the role of intermediaries. However, it is possible to consider what *adaptive capacity* means and how it varies across individual, institutional and systemic levels (Gavrilovic et al, 2009); doing this brings a level of granularity to the analysis and enables us to understand the nuances of the various power relationships that can be present wherever capacity building is a clear part of an intermediary's function.

For the **individual**, *building adaptive capacity* focuses on enhancing people's skills and competencies through activities such as the provision of formal training initiatives or 'learn-by-doing' approaches, through grant support from donors, NGOs or think-tanks. This may involve training in recognised disciplines; in the business of government; in information and communication technology, information storage and management; or in communicating and relationship building.

Specific activities will depend on the type of actor. For policymakers, the emphasis might be placed on creating and expanding demand for knowledge, locating appropriate intermediaries or methods to communicate this demand to researchers and other knowledge producers. For researchers, activities could build the ability to engage with policymakers and to reframe research outputs accordingly. Advocacy groups may be supported to ensure that all types of knowledge are included and to strengthen their relationships with the decision makers who matter. The Knowledge Management for Development community of practice, for example, provides policymakers, practitioners and academics with individual support that assists them in applying effective principles of knowledge management in a range of institutional contexts.[10] Recent projects have seen the development of a database of frequently asked questions, a knowledge-sharing toolkit and the expansion of a 'practitioners' story guide'. At the individual level, the role of an intermediary is one of *matchmaker:* matching demand and supply for individual skills in the context of the long-term aims of the whole array of actors and the relationships they need to build and maintain in order to implement policies. Box 5.6 outlines how a local NGO supported farmer-led innovation, helping to develop a business by encouraging the innovation itself but also developing the wider policy and fiscal environment to ensure that the business would be sustainable.

Box 5.6: Building adaptive capacity by promoting local innovation

Initiated by a group of Southern and Northern NGOs in 1999, PROLINNOVA is an international learning and advocacy network promoting local innovation in ecologically oriented agriculture and natural resource management. Its focus is on recognising the dynamics of indigenous knowledge, enhancing capacities of farmers (including forest dwellers, pastoralists and fisherfolk) to adjust to change by developing their own site-appropriate systems and institutions of resource management so as to gain food security, sustain their livelihoods and safeguard the environment. PROLINNOVA's thesis is that the essence of sustainability lies in the capacity to adapt. For example, in Ghana, identifying farmers' innovation with a clay-like earth called *siella* led to a collaboration with researchers and other PROLINNOVA Ghana partners to formulate and produce affordable mineral licks for domestic animals, and ultimately to develop a business in producing the licks. As well as fostering social learning about locally important issues and disseminating local innovations, PROLINNOVA's country partners are working on several fronts: piloting decentralised funding mechanisms to promote local innovation and farmer-led participatory research, stimulating national and regional policy dialogue to favour local participatory innovation processes and integrating this approach into formal agricultural research, development and extension institutions.

Source: Wettasinha and Waters-Bayer (2010)

At the **institutional** level, enhancing capacities could focus on particular strategic planning functions, such as the ability to create a communications or influencing programme. For instance, the Overseas Development Institute's Research and Policy in Development (RAPID) programme worked with Transparency International Bangladesh to develop a communications approach that navigated the range of tensions in a challenging political context. Efforts were made to understand and learn from the positive relationships between Transparency International Bangladesh, various government departments and external stakeholders, with outputs identifying short-, medium- and long-term communications steps. Institutional capacity for knowledge translation can also be built by creating or developing operational structures and organisational linkages. Overseas Development Institute's RAPID facilitates the Evidence-based Policy in Development Network (EBPDN), a worldwide community of practice for think tanks, policy research institutes and other similar organisations working in international development. EBPDN partners have noticed changes in relationships with CSOs as well as policymakers; the community's success has led to the establishment of a regional chapter of the network in Latin America (Gavrilovic et al, 2009).

At the **systems** or **enabling environment** level, building capacity for knowledge translation, supply and demand means focusing on the core processes of policymaking to ensure that goal setting, programming, budgeting, business planning, forecasting, consultation and other 'boundary processes' are structured and used in ways that create and maintain effective demand for all types of knowledge. Supporting this process helps develop strong lines of argument about:

- what the policy goals are, whom they are intended to address and why;
- how the goals are expressed as intended outcomes, their distributional effects and intended timeframes for achievement;
- the gap between baseline and intended outcomes; and
- the affordability of different options for plugging that gap.

Is there a specific role for knowledge intermediaries? In a complex policy environment where multiple policy goals overlap, the role of the intermediary is to ensure that the different processes fit together to deliver better outcomes for citizens, that their demands strengthen rather than contradict each other and that organisations and individuals with the requisite skills and experience are in place to manage the processes and deliver the outcomes. At an institutional level, an intermediary needs a deep understanding of local policymaking processes to steward professional relationships and build and strengthen institutional relationships (Michaels, 2009), as well as the expertise and authority to suggest changes to boundary processes such as MTEFs, PRSs, goal-setting and budgeting processes and methods of consultation. Maintaining neutrality will be a constant challenge for an intermediary, since changing processes can alter power dynamics irretrievably and should be done only with great care. However, providing support to fledgling oversight processes (parliamentary budget committees, local management forums) can help embed this neutrality in local and sustainable institutions and processes.

Step 4: interpreting the results and monitoring progress

Interpreting the results of the above analysis will not be a straightforward task, and the answers are unlikely to be clear-cut. Involving a variety of stakeholders will help build a good shared understanding of the needs, likely time and cost challenges inherent in improving knowledge intermediary functions, and potential opportunities to share resources and develop the full range of expertise to address the identified needs. A simple way to begin this interpretive process would be to pin a large diagram of the nested ovals with the six intermediary functions (see

Figure 5.1) on to a wall and facilitate a multi-stakeholder workshop around the following questions:

- Who is currently working within which intermediary function? What are they doing?
- Looking across all organisations, how well do they incorporate the knowledge and views of all stakeholders, including the marginalised? Where are the main gaps? What are the implications of this?
- Who is best placed to act as what sort of intermediary? Where are the gaps and how might they best be filled? Is there a need to seek out a separate intermediary organisation, or is it sufficient to alter what existing stakeholders do?
- How should we collectively monitor progress as we implement knowledge intermediary functions? How do we develop indicators of progress that make sense to each organisation?

For each of the six functions, the precise choice of indicator will depend on the issue at hand and the time and budget available. Table 5.4 suggests some categories within which indicators could be developed; it will be important to ensure that these are not just indicators of a change in 'state' (for example number of reports issued, number of institutions involved). This may mean a different way of thinking about how to assess impact, as the indicators are more about behaviour change than the production of 'outputs'. Demonstrating that social learning is taking place will require careful consideration of how to indicate sustainable behaviour change by all the organisations and individuals involved – emerging process-oriented techniques such as outcome mapping and its variants are likely to be more appropriate than impact assessment based on logical, hierarchical approaches.

Table 5.4: Indicators of progress for each of the six functions

Function	Indicators of progress
What will demonstrate that *informing* is having an impact?	*Availability* of different types of knowledge for different audiences, in reports, websites, newsletters; extent to which television, radio, theatre and other interactive methods are used to transmit knowledge *Credibility* of the knowledge: knowledge-producing organisations ensure that the nature of knowledge being transmitted does not exclude marginalised groups *Methods of communication*: whether the range of techniques used is suitable and sufficient for the various audiences that need to be reached *User surveys*: whether the intended audience is being reached and how their behaviour is being changed as a result of incorporating new knowledge
What will demonstrate that *linking* is having an impact?	*Extent of interaction*: extent to which a range of perspectives are involved in consultation processes, via advisory committees, research or consultancy *Seeing the marginalised as having voices in their own right*: ensuring that the *linking* process does not have a purely technical focus and recognises local/indigenous expertise *Openness of interaction*: extent to which policy processes actively involve stakeholders in consultation and do so transparently
What will demonstrate that *matchmaking* is having an impact?	*Breadth of interaction*: ensuring broad composition of any advisory committees, and that the independence of high-level, strategic advice is embedded in institutional approaches *Active involvement of marginalised voices*: extent to which engagement processes actively seek to complement technical knowledge with other types of knowledge *Openness of interaction*: extent to which policy processes actively involve stakeholders in consultation, including the marginalised

Function	Indicators of progress
What will demonstrate that *engaging* is having an impact?	*Breadth of interaction*: existence of a variety of relationships around a project or programme and formal mechanisms for discussion (including marginalised voices) *Length of interaction*: development of clear plans of action that reflect the nature and types of relationships and the extent to which these plans reflect long-term needs
What will demonstrate that *collaborating* is having an impact?	*Balance in relationships*: how well the relationships between different organisations are balanced and set out in formal and informal agreements; how well they support marginalised communities *Commitment*: institutional and individual commitment to relationships and plans for action
What will demonstrate that *building adaptive capacity* is having an impact?	*At the individual level*: extent and nature of training on issues to do with knowledge, and the way they have been targeted to the needs of specific individuals (including the marginalised) *At the institutional level*: development of strategic planning functions, development of specific organisational structures and linkages that reflect intermediary functions, availability of long-term funding for the organisation or other indicators of its sustainability *At the level of the enabling environment*: extent to which boundary processes of policy making (budgeting, planning, forecasting, strategy, consultation) are structured and used in ways which create and sustain demand for all types knowledge from all types of stakeholder *For knowledge intermediaries*: one potential indicator of the impact of a knowledge intermediary is it is no longer needed, or its function changes completely

Conclusion

Knowledge intermediaries can perform a valuable role in fostering social learning and innovation. They can do this by ensuring that information is made more available, by strengthening relationships and networks of actors or by contributing to collective engagement around an issue and creating self-sustaining and adaptable institutions. They need to take care not to become indispensable, not to allow their own personal biases to materially affect the power dynamics among other actors and – having negotiated this delicate balancing act – to recognise when and how to exit gracefully.

It is not necessary to be badged a knowledge intermediary in order to act like one. As Leeuwis and Aarts note (2011, p 33), 'many forms of "intermediation" are likely to take place without direct involvement of institutionalised intermediaries'. Instead, it may well be possible to change the structures and incentives in existing institutions to allow individuals and small teams to act as knowledge intermediaries *when the situation demands it.* The indicators of impact outlined here will go a long way towards recognising that knowledge intermediary functions are important for all organisations rather than something to be left to think-tanks or NGOs, or done 'off the side of the desk' when the boss is not looking.

Finally, this chapter has presented a practical framework for developing and implementing the six knowledge intermediary functions, intended to be useful to all actors at the knowledge–policy interface. Policymakers considering commissioning research should be able to consider whether they want simply to be *informed* by the research results or whether they would prefer to go one step further and be better *linked* to researchers in future by inviting them on to programme advisory committees. Researchers wanting to set up a community of practice on an issue could consider whether it is enough to use it to *matchmake* the people who join and see what develops from that, or whether more formal processes could be put in place to *engage* the community on a specific issue. Donors funding institutional partnerships could ask whether formal *collaboration* processes such as joint agreements will be enough, or whether and how more effort could be put in over a longer period to foster the social learning necessary to *build adaptive capacity.* No assumption is made that any one function is better than the other, or that any progression through them is necessary. Rather, the strength of this framework lies in the fact that, by looking at all six functions holistically, it is possible to develop a comprehensive and systematic understanding of the powerful contribution knowledge intermediary work can make to policy.

Notes

[1] The phrase was originally developed to analyse the relationships between different academic disciplines, but is often used more broadly. In this chapter we expand the definition to include those who span the boundaries between knowledge and policy.

[2] Broadly, the policy cycle is a set of linked processes of negotiation, decision, implementation and evaluation (Schnell et al, 2005). It can be visualised as a circle of these four steps or as something more complex (Schnell et al, 2005, p 4, for example).

[3] Michaels refers to these as knowledge translation or brokering functions.

[4] As noted previously, fostering knowledge interaction is not without pitfalls in terms of the power dynamics between policy actors; researchers and policymakers may act as boundary spanners within their own organisations, mediating and forging compromises so their preferred paradigm can remain dominant (Radaelli, 1999; Juntti et al, 2009).

[5] Arnstein (1969); Pretty (1994); Kanji and Greenwood (2001), all cited in Ramirez (2008).

[6] Brown (2003); Kurtz and Snowden (2003); Collins and Ison (2006).

[7] 'Wicked issues' were first defined by Rittel and Webber in 1973 for social policy and planning; they are complex problems that cannot be completely defined or bounded and for which there is no single optimal solution, as any intervention gives rise to new issues that may well have not been anticipated. In addition, any action that tries to resolve a wicked issue changes the nature of the issue itself (by altering the relationships between actors) – which means it is impossible to anticipate what the results of intervention are likely to be.

[8] See, for example, the UK's Code of Practice on Scientific Advisory Committees at www.bis.gov.uk/go-science/science-in-government/independent-scientific-advice and related links.

[9] This may include ensuring that internet search strategies are sufficiently wide to overcome the fact that the personalisation of web searches in most browsers affects the type and quantity of information available to each individual, a phenomenon known as 'filter bubbles' (Pariser, 2011).

[10] www.km4dev.org

[11] See www.outcomemapping.ca and related resources.

SIX

Conclusion and policy implications

The central message of this book is that the linkages between knowledge, policy and power are not linear and cannot be understood by using a simple standardised template approach. At the same time, these linkages are not so complex and impenetrable as to render action or analysis impossible. While there is a growing body of literature on the interface between knowledge and policy, this book is the first to draw together the learning and to develop practical recommendations that can be used by academics, policymakers, development practitioners, knowledge intermediaries and donors alike. We show that there are four key dimensions needing attention: the political economy of the knowledge–policy interface, the actors who engage at it, the types of knowledge used and the role of knowledge intermediaries. Each can be analysed rigorously using the simple frameworks we present, which – crucially – offer readers a way of ensuring that power dynamics are taken into account. This is not without its challenges, however, and the book also gives concrete examples of where a greater understanding of power relations can improve the interface between knowledge and policy.

For researchers and students of international development, our synthesis of the literature and the practical messages in the book provide many ideas for further analysis, as well as suggestions about how to better reach decision-making communities (see also Box 6.1). For donors, our analysis shows that a focus on research uptake alone is too narrow: there are three types of knowledge used in policy, each with its own political economy and set of actors. This means thinking more creatively about how and where to engage in generating and using knowledge, fostering local learning and a more networked approach to policymaking processes. For practitioners and policymakers, this book demonstrates that it is possible to take a systematic approach to thinking about work at the knowledge–policy interface that will help target cost-effective action. For the many individuals and organisations that call themselves knowledge intermediaries, we argue that they need to think further than just communicating information to a target audience; instead, they need to consider how they can best contribute to social learning and building adaptive capacity.

Whether the issue is slow burning or whether it is highly politicised and characterised by complexity, conflict and competition, we are optimistic that adopting our approach will make it possible to break down the traditional boundaries between knowledge producers and users. Nobody is a neutral player in this field; policymakers are not transparent facilitators and arbiters of value-free evidence, just as researchers do not provide apolitical information. Indeed, the very decision as to whether or not to get involved in the policy process is always a political choice, and the results will depend on the relative power each actor is able to wield in the system. While this is something think-tank-based researchers are generally aware of, it may be unsettling for those in academia and within government, who need to think carefully about how, where, when and with whom they engage to improve policy. Similarly, non-governmental organisations (NGOs) need to avoid the temptation to approach research as merely a tool to support what they already think and do. Rather, knowledge generation could become an opportunity to explore whether or not existing viewpoints and approaches are valid and to identify possible advocacy initiatives in new, challenging directions.

This concluding chapter highlights the key messages of the book, tailoring the discussion to different audiences – whether it be knowledge producers, users, intermediaries or donors – while connecting with their specific priorities and professional incentive structures. This said, while we realise many people think of themselves as fitting into one of these discrete audiences, the book highlights that, in reality, the lines are often blurred. Readers need to recognise that they can take on a range of roles combining elements of knowledge generation, use and interaction to ensure maximum impact. We believe the framework and tools this book provides will help to equip them with the flexibility and confidence to rise to this challenge.

Box 6.1: Core messages

Our first core message is that systematic mapping of the political context is necessary to improve the success of knowledge–policy interactions. Adopting the position that 'it's all down to political will' is not only inaccurate but also counterproductive to effective action. Chapter Two presented a clear and manageable set of issues for analysis that help identify potential entry and veto points in the policy process. This makes it possible to move beyond simplistic assumptions about the pattern of knowledge–policy interactions in authoritarian versus democratic contexts; it reminds us to consider both formal and informal political dynamics and to determine whether different contexts really have the capacity to absorb change. The framework we advance consists of five key variables that are applicable to a broad range of state types, from consolidated democracies to fragile states, namely; separation of powers; regulation and competitiveness of political participation; informal politics; external forces; and capacity to absorb change.

But political context alone is not enough to explain the dynamics of the knowledge–policy interface. Chapter Three argued that it is also necessary to analyse the role and behaviour of actors. Our key point is that understanding how they behave is not a simple matter of imputing self-interest. Instead, readers need to consider the often messy interplay of actor interests, values/beliefs and credibility and the power relations that underpin these three broad variables. Researchers are only one of many different types of actor.

Chapter Four emphasised that, while research continues to play a dominant role in policymaking, it needs to be complemented by other forms of knowledge; that is, knowledge

---

is not only about 'true, justified belief' but also local conditions and practical experience. Increasing our understanding of how to institutionalise a variety of channels will help us ensure all types of knowledge are given their due in the policymaking process.

In order to do this, Chapter Five presented a framework for appraising and monitoring the role of knowledge intermediaries. Its most important message is that it is not necessary to be badged 'a knowledge intermediary' to act as one. There is no particular requirement for intermediaries to work solely as knowledge producers or as knowledge users, or in the space between the two. Instead individuals, teams or organisations need to consider how they can act as knowledge intermediaries at different times for different issues, working out which functions they may need to perform based on a strategic overview of how they fit together and the power relations they are likely to affect. Intermediaries do more than simply foster participation; by actively meshing different types of knowledge in policy and working with different actors in different contexts, they can make significant contributions to social learning and innovation.

Messages for knowledge producers

Mapping political context

It is simplistic to assume that the knowledge–policy interface operates in particular ways depending on the degree of democratic governance, and that there are rules for how knowledge producers should operate in particular types of state. Our analysis demonstrates that fragile and post-conflict states have their own dynamics in relation to knowledge and policy. However, over and above that, we show there are five issues that have a greater effect on the knowledge–policy interface than state typology alone, meaning that the entry points for knowledge can vary considerably both within and across state types, particularly where there is a degree of decentralised authority. Windows of opportunity for applying knowledge to policy may present themselves in the form of a specific person, point in time or way of framing or approaching an issue. Moreover, the important roles played by veto points and veto players may require building alliances with other actors, possibly seeking out those that are unusual or counterintuitive to have most effect.

This said, for some policy issues, political windows of opportunity may be very narrow or even absent. It may be a matter of biding one's time and continuing to build up a robust evidence base ready to be used should a window open in future. It may be the case, for example, that space for national-level change is largely closed but there are greater options for knowledge uptake and exchange at the decentralised level. Accordingly, knowledge producers need to think intelligently and flexibly about changing political contexts and how best to manoeuvre within them. They need to be aware of how power dynamics are working and interacting on multiple levels simultaneously so it is possible to develop intelligent strategies to actively *integrate* one's knowledge rather than simply relying on targeted dissemination. This means it is important for knowledge producers to remain aware that, in engaging at the knowledge–policy interface, they become political actors, whatever the external context.

Engaging actors and actor networks

When it comes to engaging with other actors at the knowledge–policy interface, our analysis requires knowledge producers to demonstrate greater self-awareness of the political nature of their actions. Evidence does not speak for itself; interests, values, beliefs and registers of credibility will affect how knowledge is framed. Engaging in deliberative processes will give knowledge producers key insights into how to improve the production, communication and interpretation of knowledge, and will also make it clear that they are an integral part of the power dynamics surrounding knowledge and policy.

Different actors use knowledge in different ways, making it important to think carefully about how it will be interpreted and how best to facilitate inputs from key stakeholders. This means knowledge producers will also need to think clearly about who else is in their knowledge network – who is currently deemed to be credible, whether this can be changed and how to leverage different types of expertise so that policy benefits from multiple types of knowledge are appreciated. Further, where values and beliefs are powerful drivers of how knowledge is used, knowledge producers need to consider how to produce information that resonates with actors' values and how this changes their perceptions of costs and benefits of different courses of action. Doing this means understanding the costs and benefits of different actors' engagement and what it means for how information is targeted.

Types of knowledge

Whether you generate research, are responsible for producing practice-informed knowledge or are involved in fostering the use of citizen knowledge in policy, it is entirely possible – and even desirable – to enrich your own knowledge production process by engaging with others. Policymaking is not a straightforward process of problem solving and finding the 'right answer'; instead, it is a dynamic process of understanding what a piece of knowledge means in relation to what needs to be done. This process of establishing meaning is not a neutral one: it will be conditioned by the politics and power dynamics inherent in the policy process and how these are expressed in the definition of 'better outcomes for citizens'. Outcomes are not solely defined by central government, and knowledge producers must be prepared to engage with policy at multiple levels. For example, it is pointless for researchers to disseminate their work only to central government departments if effective policymaking happens at the local level. Local engagement can be political, however, particularly if the greater use of citizen knowledge upends prevailing power dynamics. While knowledge producers should still engage with these processes (rather than standing to the side in the mistaken notion that this makes them neutral), they need to engage with their eyes open.

Facilitating knowledge interaction

It is clear from our framework that any act of producing knowledge is, by definition, an act at the interface between knowledge and policy. This means it is important for knowledge producers to consider carefully whether it is enough just to produce the knowledge or whether they should contribute further to its interpretation and use. It will be up to individuals and organisations to decide how far they want to go along the six-fold knowledge intermediary spectrum (from informing to building adaptive capacity), depending on their organisational mandate and the ultimate goal of their policy, project or programme.

Our framework shows how to do this; it will help knowledge producers work out how far to engage with processes of social learning depending on need, organisational mandate and political context. Our intention in promoting this framework is to begin a more systematic discussion about the roles of intermediaries and the impact they are having. It is clear that there is a great deal of enthusiasm for intermediary functions, but little thought is currently being given to how we assess whether or not they are actually making a difference. Our framework brings a rigour to the discussions that has been lacking in the past, and should help knowledge producers be clear about where their mandate lies and where it ends.

Messages for knowledge users

Mapping political context

A key contribution of this book is to demonstrate that policymakers and other 'knowledge users' can play an active role in improving the knowledge–policy interface using the same framework as knowledge producers, donors and practitioners. This means they can engage more actively with the variety of different actors using a common understanding of the important issues that need to be addressed. Crucially, policymakers cannot use political will as a get-out clause any more; our framework shows how they can systematically analyse the political context within which they operate and analyse how to engage with actors and the different types of knowledge more fruitfully, although we recognise that there are real challenges in getting the incentive structures right for them to do so.

Policymakers and practitioners need to think more systematically about when and from whom they should be actively seeking knowledge they can use to underpin policy decision making. As globalisation gathers apace, even policymakers in autocratic contexts are realising that greater integration brings increasing complexity and the need for increased access to diverse knowledge sources in order to anticipate how best to respond to the evolving context. In Viet Nam, for instance, the global food, fuel and financial crisis underscored the heightened vulnerability of the country to external shocks and served as a wake-up call to legislators that they needed to broaden their knowledge-base beyond the evidence sources provided by the more dominant executive branch (Datta and Jones, 2011).

Another key implication for knowledge users is the importance of continually questioning whether the incentives to use knowledge in a given context are good enough to ensure that policy draws on a sufficiently wide range of knowledge, and to understand what positive steps could be taken to change the processes that effectively filter the knowledge that is ultimately used. Policymakers and other knowledge users should not see themselves as 'passive recipients' of whatever knowledge is available, but should actively build and manage the knowledge base they need for their policy issue, negotiating their particular political context with all its advantages and disadvantages. This will entail thinking through how knowledge can best be integrated at all stages of the policy process and identifying any capacity deficits – perhaps especially at the decentralised level. In such circumstances, knowledge users need to seek out capacity support appropriate to their particular political context[1] and be confident in requesting donors to be responsive rather than supply-driven in their approach to knowledge generation.

Engaging actors and actor networks

Our actor framework recognises that the actions of knowledge users are political – knowledge users are not simply passive recipients of knowledge. This highlights that engaging intelligently with the constellation of actors involved at the knowledge–policy interface means carefully mapping them, seeking to disentangle the role of interests and values from the quality of knowledge they provide. This analysis should not be limited to the usual suspects, such as researchers, NGOs, politicians and lobby groups, but should encompass a broad array of actors, including the media, who play a key role in framing policy knowledge, and legislators, who, although relatively marginalised in many governance structures, are becoming increasingly active and vocal knowledge purveyors. If policymakers and other knowledge users are to become more active managers of their knowledge base, they need to undertake this mapping themselves so as to understand the power dynamics between actors and the implications for how knowledge could be shared more openly and transparently.

Because knowledge is often co-produced, it can be cost-effective for knowledge users to participate actively in networks and various deliberative processes. Relying on a small group of knowledge producers is unlikely to produce all the knowledge needed, and engaging in dialogue and discussion with more actors is likely to tease out far greater understanding. In doing so, however, it is important to be aware of the role of values in shaping knowledge, while recognising that values are not necessarily fixed or constant. Moral values can shape action that goes against narrow individual interests in some circumstances – as the example of white males voting for affirmative action policies demonstrates. Even though some actor groups (such as religious leaders) may play a dominant role in shaping policy dialogues owing to strongly held values, it is important not to assume that this renders transformative action impossible. A deep understanding of the role of values in shaping knowledge–policy interactions may in fact facilitate a path for action. But knowledge users should be rigorous in thinking about how to source credible evidence, being aware of the relationship between values and credibility, and be prepared to work hard to counter narrow definitions of what constitutes credible knowledge.

Types of knowledge

The framework presented in Chapter Four will be a real help to knowledge users who want to improve the breadth of knowledge types used in policy processes. While research is a key part of the knowledge base, we demonstrate that it is misguided to rely on research alone. Readers who are knowledge users will know that this is not an easy task; they have the weight of organisational custom and practice to overcome, as well as some strong vested interests among members of the research community who will not want to lose their privileged position as trusted advisers. We recognise that the incentive structures in place in many organisations will favour research over other forms of knowledge, but our analysis shows that relying on one type of knowledge alone incorporates a bias into the policy process. Knowledge users need to draw on multiple types of knowledge, broadening the channels through which knowledge is sought to build a composite picture of an issue, one that recognises the power dynamics and understands how they affect policy choices.

Ensuring that the richness of available knowledge (research-based, practice-informed and citizen knowledge) is reflected in policy will involve working with a broader range of knowledge producers than in the past – using scientific advisers but also engaging with organisations that are able to articulate the voices of marginalised groups. It will also mean finding resources to build own capacity to use and interpret different types of knowledge, particularly when it is coming from many different sources. In addition, it will be important to work at a more decentralised level, actively using networks that can give the breadth of knowledge that will be needed.

The quality of the processes through which knowledge is sourced and used is as important as the quality of the knowledge itself (see Shaxson, 2005). This means placing as much emphasis on *how* to source, interpret and use knowledge as *what* knowledge to use. There are likely to be four areas where support could be sought: understanding which types of knowledge are needed; developing search strategies or virtual libraries of information; training in appraising the quality of the different types of knowledge; and interpreting biased, uncertain or contradictory information.

Facilitating knowledge interaction

The real strength of the framework for knowledge intermediaries presented in this book is that it can be used inside policymaking organisations; it is not just for academics or think-tanks. Policymakers can use our approach to think systematically about internal processes for sourcing and using knowledge, directing how they engage with knowledge producers. Instead of being passive recipients of whatever knowledge happens to be out there, policymakers can consider themselves a type of knowledge intermediary and use this framework to actively manage their knowledge base in two ways. First, the six-fold framework (from informing to promoting adaptive capacity) allows them to define the types of relationship they want to form with those producing or synthesising knowledge. Second, it helps policy actors play a more active role in sourcing, assembling and interpreting the different types of knowledge for the specific policy context within which they are working.

In playing a more active part, however, knowledge users need to recognise that they affect the power dynamics at the interface between knowledge and policy. In some instances, this may be more obvious: advisory committees that consist only of academic scientists, for example, will clearly favour academic–scientific types of knowledge over those based more on experience, locality or different core belief structures. The 'hidden power' element of this may lead some to believe that science is somehow being used as an instrument of the state, which is likely to damage relationships with those for whom science is not the dominant form of knowledge.

What may be less clear are the ways in which the 'business' dimensions of policymaking (such as strategising, target setting, planning, budgeting) affect how different types of knowledge are incorporated into policy processes and how the different intermediary functions can be used to strengthen them. Budget processes that are not clearly linked to policy priorities, for example, are likely to privilege the needs of those interested in controlling expenditure over those who want to make inclusive policies. It is important for knowledge users to develop a critical awareness of how these 'business-as-usual' processes influence the ways knowledge is used and thus the degree to which they contribute (or not) to wider social learning and innovation.

Messages for knowledge intermediaries

Mapping political context

Because intermediaries are inherently political, the first thing they need to do is understand the political context within which they are working – the possible entry points and why they exist. This is particularly the case where issues are highly politicised, but Chapter Five's analysis shows it is possible to think carefully about how to act in such a way that power dynamics are not inadvertently compromised.

Understanding the different approaches knowledge intermediaries can take will help them devise strategies for different political contexts, helping answer questions such as whether a think-tank should adopt different approaches to providing and interpreting knowledge during different electoral processes? How might an expert advisory process be set up to ensure that policymakers are able to engage fully with all types of knowledge, not just science? How can civil society organisations (CSOs) function most effectively at the knowledge–policy interface? How can intermediary organisations develop strategies that will persuade funding bodies of the impact of their interventions? Our analysis of the six knowledge interaction functions in Chapter Five can help intermediaries develop strategies for action in different political contexts or for a particular policy issue, and decide on the most appropriate way of dealing with any tensions that arise between the immediate need to provide evidence in a timely fashion to feed into policy debates and the more gradual process of building coalitions.

Engaging actors and actor networks

Similarly, being clear about actors' interests, values and beliefs and credibility needs to become a key part of any intermediary's work; our framework demonstrates not only that this is possible but also that there are some specific actions that intermediaries can do to improve the flow of knowledge in policy. As they try to improve the legitimacy and credibility of different types of knowledge, intermediaries often need to work to change actors' perceptions of their own interests through raising awareness of emerging evidence, pointing out unconsidered implications or proposing alternative approaches. In the case of highly politicised issues, it may be impossible to change perceptions that are based strongly on core belief systems. It may be similarly difficult to alter power dynamics where one group of actors and their worldview is very dominant. In these situations, intermediaries can still play a valuable role and be perceived to be relatively neutral by ensuring that all the knowledge that could be used is communicated to all actors so informed choices can be made. Understanding how interests, values and credibility shape behaviour will help intermediaries think intelligently about how to balance the configuration of actors with the processes needed to effectively shape strategies for intermediation via the six different knowledge interaction functions outlined in Chapter Five, from informing and linking through to matchmaking and building adaptive capacity.

Types of knowledge

The framework we present in Chapter Four will help intermediaries clarify the three different types of knowledge in their context, making it easier for them to plan their interventions and to work to ensure that all voices are given sufficient space to be heard (while maintaining necessary rigour of analysis). Any knowledge intermediary will come from a background whose training implicitly predisposes them to a particular type of knowledge – when it comes to knowledge, there is no such thing as complete neutrality. This is particularly the case where issues are highly politicised – where people's values and beliefs shape what they perceive to be relevant to policy. However, it is possible for intermediaries to be sufficiently balanced that they can work effectively to improve the legitimacy, credibility and saliency of all three types of knowledge to all actors. Doing this does not necessarily make the final policy choice any easier, but it does make the process more equitable, open and transparent. Intermediaries can perform a valuable role in helping to understand how knowledge incentive structures shape the knowledge-seeking behaviours of policymakers, whether they engage at national, regional or local levels.

Simply disseminating more knowledge is generally not the issue; there may be systemic blockages in individual skills, organisational capacity and policy processes that bias the broad-based search for knowledge in policy and skew the decisions that are taken subsequently. By identifying these and finding ways to overcome them, intermediaries can help make substantive improvements to how policy is made.

Facilitating knowledge interaction

With the burgeoning enthusiasm for the work of knowledge intermediaries, there are a growing number of frameworks for analysing how they work, although most of these relate to how they foster innovation (Kilelu et al, 2011; Kingiri and Hall, 2011). The framework we propose is general enough to be adapted for different purposes, but specific enough to be functionally useful – to help make strategic decisions about what an intermediary person or organisation ought to be doing and how their impact can be measured. In particular, what we have done is show how important it is to consider how intermediaries contribute to social learning; they do not just broker relationships or translate knowledge. This expands the range of individuals and organisations that could be considered knowledge intermediaries, but also makes it important to look closely at the specifics of what they do and why. It also means that they can be held to account more systematically, and hopefully this rigorous approach will encourage them to raise their game in terms of how they plan what they do and the types of impact they will be able to achieve, as well as helping them identify opportunities for innovative partnering or decentralised activity.

At an individual level, strengthening their role may mean working to build capacity in how to source information, how to apply the principles of knowledge management in appropriate contexts, how to build relationships between partners with historically unequal voices on an issue or how to mediate or resolve conflicts. At an organisational level, it may mean developing skills in strategic planning, communicating and influencing. At the systems level, it may mean looking at how the boundary processes used by partner organisations influence the effective demand for knowledge. Given the complexity of institutional relationships, it will be important to think carefully about the level at which the intermediary will have the most impact; small, targeted local interventions may have more impact than big, strategic programmes of work.

Finally, wherever intermediaries choose to operate, they do need to document their work, assess their impact and share this knowledge widely. Although the role of knowledge intermediaries has been acknowledged for the past decade, there is still a great deal of work to be done to understand their diversity, to recognise where and how they can add the most value to the knowledge–policy interface and to share experiences from around the globe. In the same vein, there is a pressing need to rebuild the traditional policy toolkit, which is not well equipped to deal with issues of complexity, localism, networked relationships, different types of knowledge, power dynamics, belief systems or choice. Standard economic appraisal and evaluation methodologies, expert advisory committees and public consultation processes have their place, but are inadequate for the complex issues of sustainable development. Communities of practice and online forums are contributing to this, but there will always be a need for well-documented analyses and evaluations of what has worked in practice. Indeed, this work on knowledge incentive structures is a challenge not only for developing countries – the developed world also is beginning to question whether policymakers have an effective toolkit for dealing with 'wicked issues', and how this affects their ability to source, assemble and interpret knowledge to deliver better outcomes for citizens.

Messages for donors

Mapping political context

While donors are well aware of the importance of political context for all development work, we argue that a missing piece has been the need for a political economy analysis tailored specifically to analyse the knowledge–policy interface. Our analysis shows it is as important to improve the interface in fragile state contexts as it is in consolidated democracies. Indeed, the former may have open and easily accessible opportunities, but the standard models (such as Drivers of Change and governance assessments) are not sufficient for a full exploration of the links between knowledge and policy. By contrast, our framework synthesises across existing frameworks and explicitly takes into account the role of knowledge, knowledge incentive structures and knowledge–policy interactions in the policy process. Donors are increasing their emphasis on quality of evidence, governance structures and understanding the roles of different actors in complex policymaking processes. A systematic political economy analysis of the knowledge–policy interface will enable them to take a more strategic view of its political context, be aware of power dynamics, identify the veto players and develop strategies to work with them more effectively to ensure that policy processes engage widely and draw on multiple types of knowledge.

Engaging actors and actor networks

An expanded understanding of actors and their motivations should encourage donors to think and act creatively when it comes to defining who the 'experts' are at the knowledge–policy interface. This could entail not only working with a wider array of knowledge producers but also supporting a broader range of governmental and non-governmental actors to improve their capacity to use knowledge. It may also involve thinking more systematically about how to better incentivise openness and sharing of knowledge so as to effectively capture this diversity of voices and perspectives, and in turn how to monitor and evaluate the impacts of such approaches meaningfully. Donors' emphasis on value for money leads to an emphasis on research, but supporting policymaker networks or issue networks could be a more fruitful way of strengthening the knowledge–policy interface.

One avenue that could be especially fruitful in promoting more pluralistic knowledge production and use practices entails resourcing the knowledge-seeking activities of parliamentary select committees so as to help them fulfil their oversight function more effectively. Select committees scrutinise what governments are doing in particular areas in terms of policies, budgets and administration (Hudson, 2006), conducting inquiries and issuing reports. They may look at individual government departments or cross-departmental issues such as public accounts (whole of government spending) or defined areas such as science and technology. Working in public, they can provide good spaces for engagement by CSOs and other groups, and their reports offer parliamentarians opportunities to engage in informed questioning of government. They are potentially very powerful groups in the parliamentary system; their cross–party nature means that, with a focus on the evidence rather than on party loyalties, they can generate a balanced opinion, take time to do thorough analyses and provide a counterweight to any overt politicisation of knowledge elsewhere in government. Training and resourcing select committees to effectively source, assemble and interpret the multiple types of knowledge could exert a powerful influence on governments' knowledge-seeking behaviour.

Types of knowledge

Our framework will help donors take a realistic look at where funding could improve the supply of knowledge. This is not just about funding more research that makes its way into central government departments, but working at a more decentralised level (as the Australian Agency for International Development is doing in Indonesia).

The recent emphasis on research communication and uptake may have come at the expense of understanding how to communicate citizen and practice-informed knowledge; all three are equally important in developing policy and need to be better integrated. However, the focus of support needs to ensure that this is not just a supply push – that knowledge incentive structures inside government departments are realigned so the demand for knowledge is coherent and driven by policy outcomes.

While donors have a long history of supporting the production of all three types of knowledge, this has tended to be done separately, using different budgets and different assessments of effectiveness, owing in part to an approach that has focused on improving the supply of knowledge without commensurate emphasis on how to improve its effective demand by policymakers. We argue that more work needs to be done to improve supply issues across the board: strengthening local research capacity, identifying monitoring and evaluation techniques that make functional contributions to organisational learning and sponsoring activities that encourage the generation of citizen knowledge via elections, CSOs and engagement with local policymaking and implementation. We would also argue that the next frontier for improving the knowledge–policy interface is to take a long, hard look at the tools policymakers have: budgets, expenditure frameworks, strategy processes, business plans and other core processes that have a hidden but very real influence on how the different types of knowledge are sourced, assembled and interpreted for policy. We are only in the early stages of understanding how these can be improved, and considerable effort will be needed, but if donors are serious about improving the use of knowledge in policy, we believe this needs serious attention.

Finally, there is still a need to grapple with the political implications of incorporating different types of knowledge into policy, particularly with the increasing emphasis on aid effectiveness and delivering value for money. While there is a continuing dialogue between the advocates of randomised controlled trials, such as Banerjee and Duflo (2011), and the proponents of mixed methods approaches to impact evaluation (see White, 2008), neither approach explicitly addresses power dynamics and politics in understanding the use of impact evidence in policy. But there is an emerging understanding, encapsulated in work by Monaghan (2011) in the UK, that individual deep core beliefs and values heavily influence how different actors appreciate the same piece of knowledge (whether they view it as relevant or irrelevant to policy), and that this is particularly true where issues are highly politicised and characterised by conflict, competition and controversy. This raises an important question for donors, policymakers, intermediaries and researchers alike: is it possible to use a single set of parameters to define the quality and likely impact of knowledge used in policymaking?

Facilitating knowledge interaction

Clark et al (2010) note that 'improving the ability of global research programs to produce useful knowledge for sustainable development will require greater and more differentiated support for multiple forms of boundary work'. Our analysis echoes this strongly, and our message for donors is that there is an urgent need to invest in capacity-building initiatives to support different types of knowledge intermediary (including those badged knowledge producers and knowledge users) to work in more tailored ways in different political contexts at central and decentralised levels. Our understanding of how knowledge intermediaries function is still young, and a commitment from donors to documenting and critically analysing the work of knowledge intermediaries would be a valuable contribution. Investing in research communication is a good start, but in this book we show there is much more to it than that. We present a framework for working with knowledge intermediaries that demonstrates their potential contribution to social learning and innovation, while allowing donors to make strategic decisions about how to invest in the range of intermediary functions. Our framework clarifies how intermediaries can add value; how they contribute, the incentives that influence their behaviour and potential ways of measuring their impact. As a result of its focus on functions, the framework is relevant to a far wider set of individuals and organisations than those traditionally badged knowledge intermediaries. This means donor organisations can not only suggest the intermediaries framework to recipients of aid funding to improve how they plan, appraise and monitor interventions, but also use it internally to improve how they themselves use knowledge. Indeed, our framework can be used to help donors think critically about how to evaluate the role of intermediaries, contributing to the continually vexed question of how to demonstrate impact. In this regard, we hope that our framework will induce them to move away from short-term quick fixes and seriously consider continuing to invest in knowledge interaction interventions until adaptive capacity has been made sustainable.

Where next?

This book has provided a synthetic discussion of issues surrounding the knowledge–policy interface in the international development context for the first time, and we have worked hard to ensure a balance between the academic and the practical. The process of writing the book has demonstrated that one informs the other; it is not simply a case of translating academic ideas into practice, as experience from practice has also led us to question the concepts set out in some of the literature. As we have emphasised, we are not presenting a fixed template approach; it is up to the reader to work with the frameworks we present, adapt them to their own use and generally improve on them. In doing so, we hope practitioners will continue to help push the boundaries of academic thought, researchers will continue to scrutinise and improve practice, intermediaries will provide intelligent bridges and donors will recognise the breadth of activity that needs support. Equally importantly, we all need to commit to putting these approaches into practice, while systematically documenting and evaluating them to illuminate new and creative lessons. The ultimate aim will be to develop tools that can effectively redress otherwise resistant power imbalances that affect knowledge–policy interactions.

Note

[1] The sort of capacity needed to strengthen policymaking if the political context is one of command–hierarchy will be very different from that needed in an influence–network context.

References

AAPPG (Africa All Party Parliamentary Group) (2008) *Strengthening parliaments in Africa: Improving support*, London: Africa All Party Parliamentary Group.

ACT Development (2008) *A guide to assessing our contribution to change*, Impact project working group, FAKT Consult for Management, Training and Technologies GmbH, Stuttgart: FAKT.

Adolph, B., Herbert-Jones, S., Proctor F.J., Raven, E. and Myers, M. (2010) *Learning lessons on research communication and uptake. A review of DFID's Research and Evidence Division's human development (health and education) and agriculture portfolios and their contribution to the 30% policy*, Part 1 Final Report to DFID, London: Triple Line Consulting Ltd.

Ajzen, I. (1991) 'The theory of planned behavior', *Organizational Behavior and Human Decision Processes*, vol 50, no 2, pp 179-211.

Akabueze, B. (2010) Ministerial Press Briefing by the Hon. Commissioner for Economic Planning and Budget, Bagauda Kalto Press Centre, Alaus Ikeja, 21 April, www.lagosstate.gov.ng/index.php?page=subpage&spid=678&mnu=module&mnusub=ministry&mpid=25.

Alamuti, M. (2002) 'Reforming planning systems towards socio-economic structural change in I.R. Iran: The influence of policy research on a policy document', www.gdnet.org (http://depot.gdnet.org/cms/grp/general/Iran.pdf]).

Albaek, E. (1995) 'Between knowledge and power: utilization of social science in public policymaking', *Policy Sciences*, vol 28, pp 79-100.

Ammons, D.N. and Rivenbark, W.C. (2008) 'Factors influencing the use of performance data to improve municipal services: evidence from the North Carolina benchmarking project', *Public Administration Review*, vol 68, no 2, pp 304-18.

Anderson, I. (2000) 'Northern NGO advocacy: perceptions, reality and the challenge', *Development in Practice*, vol 10, nos 3/4, pp 445-52.

Angell, M. (2000) 'Is academic medicine for sale?', *The New England Journal of Medicine*, vol 342, no 20, pp 1516-18.

Autes, M. (2007) 'The links between knowledge and politics', in B. Delvaux and E. Mangez (eds) *Literature reviews on knowledge and policy*, Knowledge and Policy Project, www.knowandpol.eu.

Banerjee, A. and Duflo, E. (2011) *Poor economics: A radical rethinking of the way to fight global poverty*, New York, NY: Random House.

Barker, M. (2005) *Manufacturing policies: The media's role in policy-making process*, Brisbane: Australian School of Environmental Studies, Griffith University.

Batliwala, S. (2002) 'Grassroots movements as transnational actors: implications for global civil society', *Voluntas: International Journal of Voluntary and International Organisations*, vol 13, no 4, pp 393-409.

Beardon, H. and Newman, K. (2009) *How wide are the ripples? The management and use of information generated from participatory processes in international non-governmental development organisations*, IKM Working Paper 7, Bonn: European Association of Development Research and Training Institutes.

Bebbington, A J., Guggenheim, S., Olson, E. and Woolcock, M. (2006) *The search for empowerment: Social capital as idea and practice at the World Bank*, Sterling, VA: Kumarian Press.

Becker, S., Bryman, A. and Sempik, J. (2006) *Defining quality in social policy research: Views, perceptions and a framework for discussion*, Lavenham: Social Policy Association.

Behrman, J. (2007) *Policy-oriented research impact assessment (PORIA) case study on the International Food Policy Research Institute (IFPRI) and the Mexican Progresa anti-poverty and human resource investment conditional cash transfer program*, Washington, DC: IFPRI.

Beland, D. (2005) 'Ideas and social policy: an institutionalist perspective', *Social Policy and Administration*, vol 39, no 1, pp 1-18.

Benjamin, S. (2000) 'Governance, economic settings and poverty in Bangalore', *Journal of Environment and Urbanisation*, vol 12, no 1, pp 35-57.

Benjamin, S. and Bhuvaneswari, R. (2001) *Democracy, inclusive governance and poverty in Bangalore*, Working Paper 26, Birmingham: International Development Department, School of Public Policy, University of Birmingham.

Bentley, J. (2001) 'Honduran folk entomology', *Current Anthroplogy*, vol 42, no 2, pp 285-301.

Bentley, J.W. and Gonzalo Rodriguez, A. (2001) 'Honduran folk entomology', *Applied Anthropology*, vol 42, no 2, pp 285-300.

Bielak, A., Campbell, A., Pope, S., Schaefer, K. and Shaxson, L. (2008) 'From science communication to knowledge brokering: the shift from "science push" to "policy pull", in D. Cheng, M. Claessens, T. Gascoigne, J. Metcalfe, B. Schiele and S. Shi (eds) *Communicating science in social contexts: New models, new practices*, Dordrecht: Springer.

Bjorkman, M. and Svensson, J. (2009) 'Power to the people: evidence from a randomized field experiment on community monitoring in Uganda', *Quarterly Journal of Economics*, vol 124, no 2, pp 735-69.

Booth, D. (2003) (ed) *Fighting poverty in Africa: Are PRSPs making a difference?*, London: ODI.

Booth, D. and Golooba-Mutebi, F. (2009) *Aiding economic growth in Africa: The political economy of roads reform in Uganda*, Working Paper 307, London: ODI.

Booth, D., Williams, G., Duncan, A., Unsworth, S., Landell-Mills, P. and Cammack, D. (2009) *Political economy analysis*, How To Note, London: DFID.

Box, G. and Draper, N. (1987) *Empirical model-building and response surfaces*, New York, NY: Wiley.

Bozeman, B. (2007) *Public values and public interests: Counterbalancing economic individualism*, Washington, DC: Georgetown University Press.

Brautigam, D.A. and Knack, S. (2004) 'Foreign aid, institutions and governance in sub-Saharan Africa', *Economic Development and Cultural Change*, vol 52, no 2, pp 255-85.

Brehaut, J.D. and Juzwishin, D. (2005) *Bridging the gap: The use of research evidence in policy development*, Edmonton: Alberta Heritage Foundation for Medical Research.

Bremmer, I. (2006) *The J curve: A new way to understand why nations rise and fall*, New York, NY: Simon & Schuster.

Brown, V.A. (2003) 'Knowing: linking the knowledge cultures of sustainability and health', in V.A. Brown et al (eds) *Sustainability and health*, London: Earthscan.

Brown, V.A. (2007) 'Collective decision-making bridging public health, sustainability governance, and environmental management', in C. Soskolne (ed) *Sustaining life on earth: Environmental and human health through global governance*, Lanham, MD: Lexington Books.

Brown, V.A., Harris, J.A. and Russell, J.Y. (2010) (eds) *Tackling wicked problems through the transdisciplinary imagination*, London: Earthscan.

Bryer, D. and Magrath, J. (1999) 'New dimensions of global advocacy', *Nonprofit and Voluntary Sector Quarterly*, vol 28, no 4, pp 168-77.

Buhler W., Morse, S., Beadle, A. and Arthur, E. (2002) *Science, agriculture and research: A compromised participation?*, London: Earthscan.

Burawoy, M. (2005) 'For public sociology', *American Sociological Review*, vol 70, pp 4-28.

Busby, J. (2005) *Bono made Jesse Helms cry: Jubilee 2000, debt relief, and moral action in international politics*, Princeton, NJ: Centre for Globalization and Governance, Princeton University.

Camp, R. (2007) *Politics in Mexico, the democratic consolidation*, Oxford: Oxford University Press.

Campbell, A. and Schofield, N. (2006) *The getting of knowledge: A guide to funding and managing applied research*, Canberra: Land and Water Australia.

Campbell, J.L. (2002) 'Ideas, politics and public policy', *Annual Review of Sociology*, vol 28, pp 21-38, (www.dartmouth.edu/~socy/pdfs/Ideas,%20Politics%20&%20Public%20Policy.pdf).

Carden, F. (2009) *Knowledge to policy: Making the most of development research*, Ottawa: IDRC.

Cash, D.W., Clark, W.C., Alcock, F., Dickson, N.M., Eckley, N., Guston, D.H., Jager, J. and Mitchell, R.B. (2003) 'Knowledge systems for sustainable development', *Proceedings of the National Academy of Sciences*, vol 100, no 14, pp 8086-91.

Chabal, P. and Daloz, J.P. (1999) *Africa works: Disorder as a political instrument*, Oxford: International African Institute in association with James Currey.

Chambers, R. (1994) 'Participatory rural appraisal (PRA): challenges, potentials and paradigm', *World Development*, vol 22, no 7, pp 1437-54.

Chambers, R. (1995) *NGOs and development: The primacy of the personal*, Working Paper 14, Brighton: Institute of Devloment Studies.

Chambers, R. (1997) *Whose reality counts? Putting the first last*, London: Intermediate Technology Publications.

Chambers, R. (2005) *Ideas for development*, London: Earthscan.

Chambers, R. (2008) *Revolutions in development inquiry*, London: Earthscan.

Chapman, J. (1999) *Literature review on NGOs and policy work*, Learning document, Birmingham: University of Birmingham.

Cheema, G. and Maguire, L. (2002) *Democracy, governance and development: A conceptual framework*, Morocco: UNPAN.

Cheema, G. and Rondinelli, D. (1983) (eds) *Decentralizing governance: Emerging concepts and practices*, Washington, DC: Brookings Institution Press.

Chisinga, B. (2007) *The social protection policy in Malawi: Processes, politics and challenges, future agricultures*, Brighton: Institute of Development Studies.

Choi, B., Pang, T., Lin, V., Puska, G., Sherman, M., Goddard, M., Ackland, P., Sainsbury, P., Stachenko, H., Morrison, H. and Clottey, C. (2005) 'Can scientists and policy-makers work together?', *Journal of Epidemiology and Community Health*, vol 59, no 8, pp 632-7.

Clarke, G. and Jennings, M. (2008) (eds) *Development, civil society & faith-based organizations*, London: Palgrave Macmillan.

Clark, W.C., Tomich, T.P., Van Noordwijk, M., Dickson, N.M., Catacutan, D., Guston, D. and McNie, E.C. (2010) *Toward a general theory of boundary work: Insights from the CGIAR's Natural Resource Management Programs* (September 9, 2010). HKS Working Paper No. RWP10-035.

Cleaver, F. and Franks, T. (2008) 'Distilling or diluting? Negotiating the water research–policy interface', *Water Alternatives*, vol 1, no 1, pp 157-77.

Collier, P. (2007) *The bottom billion: Why the poorest countries are failing and what can be done about it*, Oxford: Oxford University Press.

Collier, R. and Collier, D. (1991) *Shaping the political agenda: Critical junctures, the labor movement, and regime dynamics in Latin America*, Princeton, NJ: Princeton University Press.

Collins, K. and Ison, R. (2006) 'Dare we jump off Arnstein's ladder? Social learning as a new policy paradigm', Proceedings of PATH Conference, Edinburgh, 4-7 June.

Collins, K. and Ison, R. (2009) 'Jumping off Arnstein's ladder: Social learning as a new policy paradigm for climate change adaptation'. *Environmental Policy and Governance*, vol 19, pp 358-73.

Cooke, B. and Kothari, U. (2001) (eds) *Participation: The new tyranny?*, London: Zed Books.

Corrales, J. and Penfold-Becerra, M. (2007) 'Venezuela: crowding out the opposition', *Journal of Democracy*, vol 18, no 2, pp 99-113.

Court, J. and Cotterrell, L. (2006) *What political and institutional context issues matter for bridging research and policy?*, Working Paper 269, London: ODI.

Court, J., Hovland, I. and Young, J. (2005) *Bridging research and policy in development: Evidence and the change process*, Rugby: Practical Action Publishing.

CPRC (Chronic Poverty Research Centre) (2008) *The second international chronic poverty report*, Manchester: CPRC.

Cracknell, B. (2001) 'Knowing is all: or is it? Some reflections on why the acquisition of knowledge, focusing particularly on evaluation activities, does not always lead to action', *Public Administration and Development*, vol 21, no 5, pp 371-9.

Culyer, A.J. and Lomas, J. (2006) 'Deliberative processes and evidence-informed decision making in healthcare: do they work and how might we know?', *Evidence & Policy*, vol 2, no 3, pp 357-71.

Datta, A. (2009) 'Obama and USAID: the need for genuine evaluation', in S. Maxwell, C. Stephens, A. Shepherd, N. Jones, C. Harper, A.R. Menocal, A. Datta and J. Brown 'Will the US lead on international development? A collection of opinion pieces to mark the inauguration of President Obama', ODI Blog Post, 20 January., (http://www.odi.org.uk/opinion/details.asp?id=2752&title=united-states-president-obama-us-international-development).

Datta, A. and Jones, N. (2011) *Linkages between researchers and legislators in developing countries: A scoping study*, Working Paper 332, London: ODI.

Datta, A., Jones, N. and Mendizabal, E. (2010) 'Think-tanks and the rise of the knowledge economy', in A. Garcé and G. Uña (eds) *Think-tanks and public policies in Latin America*, Buenos Aires: Fundación Siena and CIPPEC.

Davies, P. (2004) 'Is evidence-based government possible?', UK Cabinet Office presentation to the Fourth Annual Campbell Collaboration Colloquium, Washington, DC, 19 February.

Davies, P. (2005) 'Evidence-based policy at the Cabinet Office', Presentation to ODI Insight to Impact Meeting, London, 17 October.

Dawnay, E. and Shah, H. (2005) *Behavioural economics: Seven principles for policy-makers*, London: New Economics Foundation.

de Guevera, B. (2007) 'Governing via consulting? The role of international think tanks in post-conflict state-building', Paper presented at 48th International Studies Association Annual Convention, Politics, Policy and Responsible Scholarship, Chicago, IL, 28 February-3 March.

deGrassi, A. (2007) 'Linking research and policy: The case of Ghana's rice trade policy', Report to IFPRI, Ghana Strategy Support Program Background Paper No GSSP 0010. Washington DC: International Food Policy Research Institute

Delvaux, B. and Mangez, E. (2008) (eds) 'Towards a sociology of the knowledge-policy relation', www.knowandpol.eu (http://knowandpol.eu/IMG/pdf/literature_sythesis_final_version_english.pdf).

Devas, N. (1999) *Who runs cities? The relationship between urban governance, service delivery and urban poverty*, Theme Paper 4 of Urban Governance, Partnership and Poverty Programme, Birmingham: International Development Department, School of Public Policy, University of Birmingham.

Devas, N. (2000) *Connections between urban governance and poverty: Analysing the Stage 1 City Case Studies*, Birmingham: International Development Department, School of Public Policy, University of Birmingham.

Devas, N. (2002) 'Issues in fiscal decentralisation: Ensuring resources reach the (poor at) the point of service delivery', Paper presented at Workshop on Improving Service Delivery in Developing Countries, Witney, 24-30 November.

DFID (Department for International Development) (2009a) *A strengthened approach for economic appraisals*, How To Note. London: DFID.

DFID (2009b) *Political economy analysis*, How To Note, London: DFID.

Dopson, S. and Fitzgerald, L. (2005) (eds) *Knowledge in action? The diffusion of innovations in health care*, Oxford: Oxford University Press.

Dunning, J (ed) (2000) *Regions, globalization and the knowledge-based economy*, New York, NY: Oxford University Press.

Dür, A. (2008) 'Measuring interest group influence in the EU: a note on methodology', *European Union Politics*, vol 9, no 4, pp 559-76.

Dutraive, V. (2009) 'Economic development and institutions: anatomy of the new new institutional economics', *Revue de la régulation*, vol 6, no 6, (http://regulation. revues.org/index7609.html).

Economist, The (2010) 'Chávez grapples with a 50/50 nation', 23 September, (www. economist.com/node/17093517).

Edelmann, D. (2009) *Analysing and managing the political dynamics of sector reforms: A sourcebook on sector-level political economy approaches*, Working Paper 309, London: ODI.

Edgerton, D. (2009) 'The 'Haldane Principle' and other invented traditions in science policy', Summary of a paper presented at the Wilkins-Bernal-Medawar prize lecture, 2009.

Edwards, M. and Hulme, D. (1992) (eds) *Making a difference: NGOs and development in a changing world*, London: Earthscan.

Edwards, M. and Hulme, D. (1995) (eds) *Non-governmental organizations – performance and accountability: Beyond the magic bullet*, London: Earthscan.

Escobar, A. and Álvarez, S. (1992) *The making of social movements in Latin America: Identity, strategy, and democracy*, Boulder, CO: Westview Press.

Evans, P. and Rauch, J. (1999) 'Bureaucracy and growth: a cross-national analysis of the effects of Weberian state structures on economic growth', *American Sociological Review*, vol 64, no 5, pp 748-65.

Faizi, S. (2002) 'Research, policy and implementation linkages in biodiversity management in Saudi Arabia', www.gdnet.org (http://depot.gdnet.org/cms/ grp/general/Saudi%20Arabia.pdf).

Ferguson, J., Mchombu, K. and Cummings, S. (2008) *Management of knowledge for development: Meta-review and scoping study*, IKM Working Paper 1, Bonn: European Association of Development Research and Training Institutes.

Fewsmith, J. (1996) 'Institutions, informal politics, and political transition in China', *Asian Survey*, vol 36, no 3, pp 230-45.

Fioramonti, L. and Heinrich, V.F. (2007) *How civil society influences policy: A comparative analysis of the CIVICUS Civil Society Index in post-Communist Europe*, Washington, DC: CIVICUS.

Fisher, E. and Holland, J. (2003) 'Social development as knowledge building: research as a sphere of policy influence', *Journal for International Development*, vol 15, no 7, pp 911-24.

Fiszbein, A. and Schady, N. (2008) *Conditional cash transfers: Reducing present and future poverty*, World Bank Policy Research Report, Washington, DC: World Bank.

Fiszbein, A., D. Ringold and S. Srinivasan. (2011) 'Cash transfers, children and the crisis: protecting current and future investments', *Development Policy Review Special Issue: Impacts of Economic Crises on Child Wellbeing*, vol 29, issue 5, pp 585-601, September 2011.

Folbre, N. (2001) *The invisible heart: Economics and family values*, New York, NY: The New Press.

Folke, C., Hahn, T., Olsson, P. and Norberg, J. (2005) 'Adaptive governance of social–ecological systems', *Annual Review of Environment and Resources*, vol 30, pp 441-73.

Foresti, M. (2007) *A comparative study of evaluation policies and practices in development agencies*, Série Notes Méthodologique No 1. Paris: Agence Francaise de Développement.

Foucault, M. (1991) 'On governmentability', in G. Burchell, C. Gordon and P. Miller (eds) *The Foucault effect: Studies in governmentality*, Chicago, IL: University of Chicago Press.

Freeman, R. (2009) '*What is translation?*', *Evidence & Policy*, vol 5, no 4, pp 429-47.

Gamba, M. and Kleiner, B. (2001) 'The old boys' network today', *International Journal of Sociology and Social Policy*, vol 21, nos 8-10, pp 101-7.

Gavelin, K., Wilson, R. and Doubleday, R. (2007) *Democratic technologies?*, Nanotechnology Engagement Group Final Report, London: Involve.

Gaventa, J. (2003) 'Towards participatory local governance: assessing the transformative possibilities', Paper presented at the Conference on Participation: From Tyranny to Transformation, Manchester, 27-28 February.

Gaventa, J. (2006) 'Finding the spaces for change: a power analysis', *IDS Bulletin*, vol 37, no 6, pp 23-33.

Gaventa, J. and Mayo, M. (2008) *Linking the local and the global through citizen-based advocacy? The case of the global campaign for education*, Working Paper 12, Brighton: Institute of Development Studies.

Gavrilovic, M., Chowdhury, N., Hovland, I., Jones, N. and Young, J. (2009) *Knowledge translation in development policy processes: A review of RAPID's capacity development work*, London: ODI.

GCN (Government Communications Network) (2009) *Communications and behaviour change*, London: GCN.

Giannone, D. (2010) 'Political and ideological aspects in the measurement of democracy: the Freedom House case', *Democratization*, vol 17, no 11, pp 68-97.

Gibbons, M., Limoges, C., Nowotny, H., Schwartzmann, S., Scott, P. and Trow, M. (1994) *The new production of knowledge: The dynamics of science and research in contemporary societies*, London: Sage Publications.

Giddens, A. (1984) *The constitution of society. Outline of the theory of structuration*, Cambridge: Polity Press.

Glees, A. (2005) 'Evidence-based policy or policy-based evidence? Hutton and the government's use of secret intelligence', *Parliamentary Affairs*, vol 58, no 1, pp 138-55.

Goetz, A. and Jenkins, R. (2005) *Reinventing accountability: Making democracy work for human development*, Basingstoke: Palgrave Macmillan.

Government Office for Science (2010) *The Government Chief Scientific Advisor's guidelines on the use of scientific and engineering advice in policymaking*, London: Government Office for Science, Department for Business, Industry and Skills.

Gray, I., Fromer, P. and Funicelli, C. (2008) *Examples of adaptive management strategies in urban ecosystems*, San Diego, CA: RECON Environmental Inc.

Greenhalgh, T., Kyriakidou, O. and Peacock, R. (2004) *How to spread good ideas: A systematic review of the literature on diffusion, dissemination and sustainability of innovations in health service delivery and organisation*, Report for National Co-ordinating Centre for NHS Service Delivery and Organisation, Southampton: NCCSDO.

Grindle, M. (2002) *Despite the odds: The contentious politics of education reform*, Princeton, NJ: Princeton University Press.

Grindle, M. and Thomas, J. (1990) 'After the decision: implementing policy reforms in developing countries', *World Development*, vol 18, no 8.

Guijt, I. (2008) 'Seeking surprise: rethinking monitoring and evaluation for collective learning in rural resource management', Unpublished PhD thesis, University of Wageningen.

Haas, P.M. (1992) 'Epistemic communities and international policy coordination', *International Organization*, vol 46, no 1, pp 1-35.

Hagmann, T. and Hoehne, M. (2008) 'Failures of the state failure debate: evidence from the Somali territories', *Journal of International Development*, vol 21, no 1, pp 42-57.

Hall, P. (1993) 'Policy paradigms, social learning, and the state: the case of economic policy-making in Britain', *Comp. Polit.*, vol 25, no 3, pp 275-96.

Hallsworth, M. (2011) '*System stewardship: The future of policymaking?*, Working Paper, London: Institute for Government.

Hammergren, L. (1998) *Political will, constituency building, and public support in rule of law programs*, Washington, DC: Democracy Fellow Center for Democracy and Governance, Bureau for Global Programs, Field Support, and Research, USAID.

Harriss-White, B. (2005) 'Destitution and the poverty of its politics – with special reference to South Asia'. *World Development*, vol 33, no 6, pp 881-91.

Harriss-White, B. (2007) 'Development research and action: four approaches'. *IDS Bulletin*, vol 38, no 2, pp 46-50.

Head, B. (2010) 'Reconsidering evidence-based policy: key issues and challenges', *Policy and Society*, vol 29, no 2, pp 77-94.

Heclo, H. (1978) 'Issue networks and the executive establishment: government growth in an age of improvement', in A. King (ed) *The new American political system*, Washington, DC: American Enterprise Institute.

Herman, E. and Chomsky, N. (2006) *Manufacturing consent: The political economy of the mass media*, New York, NY: Pantheon.

Herring, R.J. (2007) *Whose numbers count? Resolving conflicting evidence on Bt Cotton in India*, Qsquared Working Paper 44, Toronto: University of Toronto.

Hickey, S. (2005) *Capturing the political? The role of political analysis in the multidisciplining development studies*, Global Poverty Research Group Working Paper 6, Manchester: IDPM, (http://economics.ouls.ox.ac.uk/14075/1/gprg-wps-006.pdf).

Hickey, S. and Braunholtz-Speight, T. (2007) *The politics of what works in tackling chronic poverty*, Policy Brief 5, Manchester: Chronic Poverty Research Centre.

Hogwood, B.W. and Gunn, L.A. (1984) *Policy analysis for the real world*, Oxford: Oxford University Press.

Holmes, R. and N. Jones. (2010) *Rethinking social protection using a gender lens*, ODI Working Paper 320, London: Overseas Development Institute.

Holt-Giménez, E. (2006) *Campesino a Campesino: Voices from Latin America's farmer-to-farmer movement for sustainable agriculture*, Oakland, CA: Food First Books.

Hossain, N. (2005) *Elite perceptions of poverty in Bangladesh*, Dhaka: University Press Limited.

Hovland, I. (2005) *Successful communication: A toolkit for researchers and civil society organisations*, London: ODI.

Hudson, A. (2002) 'Advocacy by UK-based development NGOs', *Nonprofit and Voluntary Sector Quarterly*, vol 31, no 3, pp 402-18.

Hudson, A. (2006) *CSOs and parliamentary committees: The UK's International Development Select Committee*, RAPID Background Paper, London: ODI.

Hunter, W. (1997) *Eroding military influence in Brazil: Politicians against soldiers*, Chapel Hill, NC: University of North Carolina Press.

Huntingdon, S. (1991) *The third wave: Democratization in the late 20th century*, Norman, OK: University of Oklahoma Press.

Hyden, G., Court, J. and Mease, K. (2003) *The bureaucracy and governance in 16 countries*, World Governance Survey Discussion Paper 7, London: ODI.

IDA (International Development Association) (2007) *Aid architecture: An overview of the main trends in official development assistance flows*, Washington, DC: IDA.

In't Veld R. and de Wit, A. (2000) 'Clarifications', in R. In't Veld (ed) *Willingly and knowingly: The roles of knowledge about nature and the environment in policy processes*, Utrecht: Lemma Publishers.

Irwin, A. (2001) 'Citizen engagement in science and technology: A commentary on recent UK experience', in M.P. Pimbert and T. Wakeford (eds) *Deliberative democracy and citizen empowerment*, PLA Note 40, London: International Institute for Environment and Development with the Commonwealth Foundation, ActionAid, DFID and Sida.

Ismoilov, S. (2004) *Domestic violence in Uzbekistan: An innovative approach to decrease violence against women*, London: ODI.

Jacobs, A. (2010) 'Creating the Missing Feedback Loop', *IDS Bulletin*, vol 41, no 6, pp 56-64.

Jasanoff, S. (2005) *Designs on nature: Science and democracy in Europe and the United States*, Princeton, NJ: Princeton University Press.

Jochum, V. and Pratten, B. (2009) *Values into action: How organisations translate their values into practice*, London: National Council for Voluntary Organisations.

Johnson, C. and Start, D. (2001) *Rights, claims and capture: Understanding the politics of pro-poor policy*, Working Paper 145, London: ODI.

Jones, H. (2009a) *Policy-making as discourse: A review of recent knowledge-to-policy literature*, Joint IKM Emergent–ODI Working Paper 5, London: IKM Emergent and ODI.

Jones, H. (2009c) *Equity in development: Why it is important and how to achieve it*, Working Paper 31, London: ODI.

Jones, H. (2010) 'Playing the game: Responding to the politics of climate science', ODI Blog Post, February, (http://blogs.odi.org.uk/blogs/main/archive/2010/02/12/politics_science_climate_change.aspx).

Jones, H. (2011) *Taking responsibility for complexity: How implementation can achieve results in the face of complex problems*, Working Paper 330, London: ODI.

Jones, H. and Mendizabal, E. (2010) *Strengthening learning from research and evaluation: Going with the grain*, Report for Independent Advisory Committee on Development Impact, London: ODI.

Jones, N. (2006) *Gender and the political opportunities of democratisation*, New York, NY: Palgrave Macmillan.

Jones, N. and Sumner, A. (2007) *Does mixed methods research matter to understanding childhood well-being?*, Working Paper 40, Bath: ESRC Research Group on Wellbeing in Developing Countries.

Jones, N. and Sumner, A. (2011) *Child poverty, evidence and policy: Mainstreaming children in international development*, Bristol: The Policy Press.

Jones, N. and Young, J. (2007) *Setting the scene: Situating DFID's research funding policy and practice in an international comparative perspective*, London: ODI.

Jones, N., Jones, H. and Walsh, C. (2008) *Political science? Strengthening science–policy dialogue in developing countries*, Working Paper 294, London: ODI.

Jones, N., Romney, D., Jones, H., Walden, D., Mitra, S., Efa, N. and Fish, J. (2009a) *Innovation systems approaches and their use in understanding pro-poor innovation in the renewable natural resources sector*, Conceptual Review for the Impact Evaluation Component of the Research Into Use Programme, London: ODI.

Jones, N. with Bhatta, B., Gill, G., Pantuliano, S., Bahadur Singh, H., Timsina, D., Uppadhaya, S. and Walker, D. (2009b) *Governance and citizenship from below: Views of poor and excluded groups and their vision for a new Nepal*, ODI Working Paper 301, London: ODI.

Jones, N. with EBPDN partners in East Africa and South East Asia (2011) *Involving legislators in evidence-informed policy processes: A neglected part of the democratic governance agenda*, Background Note, London: ODI.

Juntti, M., Russel, D. and Turnpenny, J. (2009) 'Evidence, politics and power in public policy for the environment', *Environmental Science & Policy*, vol 12, pp 207-15.

Kaimowitz, D. (1990) *Making the link: Agricultural research and technology transfer in developing countries*, Boulder, CO: Westview Press.

Kamara, I. and Sedoh, K.T.B. (2006) 'Malaria Competence Network collaborates to roll back malaria', *Knowledge Management for Development Journal*, vol 2, no 3, pp 136-40.

Kauffman, C. and Pape, R. (1999) 'Explaining costly international moral action: Britain's sixty-year campaign against the Atlantic slave trade', *International Organization*, vol 53, no 4, pp 631-68.

Kaufmann, D., Kraay, A. and Mastruzzi, M. (2007) *The Worldwide Governance Indicators Project: Answering the critics*, Washington, DC: World Bank.

Keck, M. and Sikkink, K. (1998) *Activists beyond borders: Advocacy networks in international politics*, Ithaca, NY: Cornell University Press.

Keeley, J. and Scoones, I. (1999) *Understanding environmental policy processes: A review*, IDS Working Paper 89, Brighton: Institute of Development Studies.

Keeley, J. and Scoones, I. (2003) *Understanding environmental policy processes: Cases from Africa*, London: EarthScan.

Kelsall, T. (2008) *Going with the grain of African development*, Africa Power and Politics Programme, London: ODI and DFID.

Kilelu, C.W., Klerkx, L., Leeuwis, C. and Hall, A. (2011) *Beyond knowledge brokerage: An exploratory study of innovation intermediaries in an evolving smallholder agricultural system in Kenya*, Research Into Use Discussion Paper 13, Maastricht: UNU-MERIT (http://www.merit.unu.edu/publications/wppdf/2011/wp2011-022.pdf).

Kingdon, J. (1984) *Agendas, alternatives, and public policies*, New York, NY: Harper Collins.

Kingdon, J. (2003) *Agendas, alternatives, and public policies* (2nd edn), New York, NY: Longman.

Kingiri, A. and Hall, A. (2011) *Dynamics of biosciences regulation and opportunities for biosciences innovation in Africa: Exploring regulatory policy brokering*, UNU-MERIT Working Paper 2011-023, Maastricht: UNU-MERIT.

Kogan, M. (2005) 'Modes of knowledge and patterns of power', *Higher Education*, vol 49, no 1-2, pp 9-30.

KNOTS (2006) *Understanding policy processes: A review of IDS research on the environment*, Brighton: IDS.

Kuhn, T. (1962) *The structure of scientific revolutions*, Chicago, IL: University of Chicago Press.

Kurtz, C. and Snowden, D. (2003) 'The new dynamics of strategy: sense-making in a complex and complicated world', *IBM Systems Journal*, vol 42, no 3, pp 462-83.

Lackey, R. (2006) 'Science, scientists and policy advocacy', *Conservation Biology*, vol 21, no 1, pp 12-17.

Laderchi, C (2001) *Participatory methods in the analysis of poverty: A critical review*, Working Paper 62, Queen Elizabeth House.

Lam A. (2000) 'Tacit knowledge, organizational learning and societal institutions: an integrated framework', *Organization Studies*, vol 21, no 3, pp 487-513.

Landry, P.F. (2008) *Decentralized authoritarianism in China: The Communist Party's control of local elites in the post-Mao era*, Cambridge: Cambridge University Press.

Landry, R., Lamari, M. and Amara, N. (2003) 'The extent and determinants of the utilization of university research in government agencies', *Public Administration Review*, vol 63, no 2, pp 192-205.

Lansing, J. and Miller, J. (2003) *Cooperation in Balinese rice farming*, Santa Fe, NM: Santa Fe Institute.

Lasswell, H. (1951) 'The policy orientation', in D. Lerner and H. Lasswell (eds) *The policy sciences*, Stanford, CA: Stanford University Press.

Lavis, J.N., Robertson, D., Woodside, J., McLeod, C.B. and Abelson, J. (2003) 'How can research organisations more effectively transfer research knowledge to decision makers?', *The Milbank Quarterly*, vol 81, no 2, pp 221-48.

Lavis, J.N., Davies, H.T.O., Gruen, R.L., Walshe, K. and Farquhar, C.M. (2006) 'Working within and beyond the Cochrane Collaboration to make systematic reviews more useful to healthcare managers and policy makers', *Healthcare Policy*, vol 1, no 2, pp 21-33.

Leach, M. and Scoones, I. (2006) *The slow race*, London: Demos.

Leeuwis, C. and Aarts, N. (2011) 'Rethinking communication in innovation processes: creating space for change in complex systems', *Journal of Agricultural Education and Extension*, vol 17, no 1, pp 21-36.

Lessa, L. (2006) 'Discursive struggles within social welfare: restaging teen motherhood', *British Journal of Social Work,* vol 36, no 2, pp 283-98.

Leftwich, A. (2006) *From drivers of change to the politics of development: Refining the analytical framework to understand the politics of the places where we work*, York: Department of Politics, University of York.

Lemieux-Charles, L. and Champagne, F. (2004) *Using knowledge and evidence in healthcare: Multidisciplinary perspectives*, Toronto: University of Toronto Press.

Leonard, M. (2008) 'China's new intelligentsia', *Prospect* 144, 28 March.

Levine, R. and Savedoff, W. (2006) 'The evaluation agenda', in N. Birdsall (ed) *Rescuing the World Bank: A working group report and selected essays*, Washington, DC: Center for Global Development.

Linz, J. and Stepan, A. (1996) *Problems of democratic transition and consolidation*, Baltimore, MD: Johns Hopkins University Press.

Livny, E., Mehendale, A. and Vanags, A. (2006) *Bridging the research and policy gaps in developing and transition countries: Analytical lessons and proposals for action*, Synthesis of findings from the Global Development Network's Bridging Research and Policy Project, (www.ebpdn.org/resource/resource.php?id=691&lang=es).

Lomas, J. (1997) *Improving research dissemination and uptake in the health sector: Beyond the sound of one hand clapping*, Policy Commentary C97-1, McMaster University Centre for Health Economics and Policy Analysis, Hamilton, Ontario.

Lomas, J., Culyer, T., McCutcheon, C., McAuley, L. and Law, S. (2005) *Conceptualizing and combining evidence for health system guidance*, Report for CHSRF, Ottawa: Canadian Health Services Research Foundation.

Long, N. (2001) *Development sociology: Actor perspectives*, London: Routledge.

Luke, A. (2003) 'After the marketplace: evidence, social science and educational research', *Australian Educational Researcher*, vol 30, no 2, pp 87-107.

Lukes, S. (1974) *Power: A radical view*, London: Macmillan.

Lyon, S. (2004) *An anthropological analysis of local politics and patronage in a Pakistani village*, Lampeter: Edwin Mellen Press.

March, J. and Olsen, J. (1989) *Rediscovering institutions*, New York, NY: The Free Press.

Marshall, M.G. and Cole, B. (2009) *Conflict, governance and state fragility: Global report 2009*, Vienna, VA, and Arlington, VA: Center for Systemic Peace and Center for Global Policy.

Marshall, M.G and Jaggers, K. (2009) *Polity IV Project*, Vienna, VA, and Fort Collins, CO: Center for Systemic Peace and Colorado State University.

Marston, G. and Watts, R. (2003) 'Tampering with the evidence: A critical appraisal of evidence-based policy-making', *The Drawing Board: An Australian Review of Public Affairs*, vol 3, no 3, pp 143-63.

Maxwell, S. (1999) *The meaning and measurement of poverty*, Poverty Briefing 3, London: ODI.

McCrae, R.R. (1996) 'Social consequences of experiential openness', *Psychological Bulletin*, vol 120, no 3, pp 23-37.

McGee, R. and Gaventa, J., with Barrett, G., Calland, R., Carlitz, R., Joshi, A. and Acosta, A. (2010) *Review of impact and effectiveness of transparency and accountability initiatives: Synthesis report*, Brighton: IDS.

McKean, M. (2002) 'Nesting institutions for common-pool resource systems', in J. Graham, I. Reeve and D. Brunckhorst (eds) *Proceedings of the 2nd International Symposium on Landscape Futures*, Armidale, 4-6 December 2001, Armidale: University of New England.

McNie, E. (2007) 'Reconciling the supply of scientific information with user demands: An analysis of the problem and review of the literature', *Environmental Science & Policy*, vol 10, pp 17-38.

Mendizabal, E. (2006) *Understanding networks: The functions of research policy networks*, Working Paper 271, London: ODI.

Mendizabal, E. and Sample, K. (2009) *Thinking politics: Think tanks and political parties in Latin America*, London: ODI.

Menkhoff, T., Everrs, H., and Wah, C.Y. (2010) *Governing and managing knowledge in Asia*, Singapore: World Scientific Publishing.

Merton, R.K. (1938) 'Science and the social order', *Philosophy of Science*, vol 5, no 3, pp 321-7.

Michaels, S. (2009) 'Matching knowledge brokering strategies to environmental policy problems and settings', *Environmental Science & Policy*, vol 12, no 7, pp 994-1011.

Mikolajuk, Z. (2010) *Practical Answers case study: Knowledge translation interface*, Report to Practical Action, Rugby: Practical Action.

Millstone, E. and van Zwanenberg, P. (2007) 'Cow disease – painting policy-making into a corner', *Journal of Risk Research*, vol 10, no 5, pp 661-91.

Minear, L. (1987) 'The other missions of NGOs: education and advocacy', *World Development*, vol 15, suppl 1, pp 201-11.

Molle, F. (2008) 'Nirvana concepts, narratives and policy models: insights from the water sector', *Water Alternatives*, vol 1, no 1, pp 131-56.

Mollinga, P. (2008) *For a political sociology of water resources management*, Working Paper 31, Bonn: Centre for Development Research, Department of Political and Cultural Change, University of Bonn.

Molyneux, M. (1985) 'Mobilization without emancipation? Women's interests, the state, and revolution in Nicaragua', *Feminist Studies*, vol 11, no 2, pp 227-54.

Monaghan, M. (2011) *Evidence versus politics: Exploiting research in UK drug policy making?*, Bristol: The Policy Press.

Moore, M. (1995) *Creating public value*, Cambridge, MA: Harvard University Press.

Moore, M. and Teskey, G. (2006) *Capability, accountability, responsiveness: What do these terms mean, individually and collectively?*, Discussion Note for DFID Governance and Conflict Advisors, London: DFID.

Morgan, M. (2008) *'Voice' and the facts and observations of experience*, Working Paper on the Nature of Evidence: How Well do 'Facts' Travel? 31/08, London: Department of Economic History, London School of Economics.

Mosse, D. (2006) 'Anti-social anthropology? Objectivity, objection and the ethnography of public policy and professional communities', *Journal of the Royal Anthropological Institute*, vol 12, no 4, pp 935-56.

Mosse, D., Farrington, J. and Rew, A. (1998) *Development as process: Concepts and methods for working with complexity*, London: Routledge and ODI.

Mouffe, C. (1992) *Dimensions of radical democracy: Pluralism, citizenship, community*, London and New York, NY: Verso.

Moynihan R., Doran, E. and Henry, D. (2008) 'Disease mongering is now part of the global health debate', *PLoS Medicine*, vol 5, no 5, pp 106-14.

Munck, G. and Verkuilen, J. (2002) 'Conceptualizing and measuring democracy: evaluating alternative indices', *Comparative Political Studies*, vol 35, no 1, pp 5-34.

Munro, G. (2010) 'The scientific impotence excuse: discounting belief-threatening scientific abstracts'. *Journal of Applied Social Psychology*, vol 40, no 3, pp 579-600.

Muro, M. and Jeffrey, P. (2006) *Social learning – a useful concept for participatory decision-making processes?*, Cranfield: School of Water Sciences, Cranfield University.

Mushtaque, A., Chowdhury, R., Alam, M. and Ahmed, J. (2006) 'Development knowledge and experience: from Bangladesh to Afghanistan and beyond', *Bulletin of the WHO*, vol 84, no 8, pp 677-81.

Nachiappan, K., Mendizabal, E. and Datta, A. (2010) *Think tanks in East and Southeast Asia: Bringing politics back into the picture*, London: ODI.

Nash, R., Hudson, A. and Lutrell, C. (2006) *Mapping political context: A toolkit for civil society organisations*, London: ODI-RAPID.

Neilson, S. (2001a) *IDRC-supported research and its influence on public policy – knowledge utilization and public policy processes: A literature review*, Ottawa: Evaluation Unit, International Development Research Centre.

Neilson, S. (2001b) *Knowledge utilization and public policy processes: A literature review. IDRC-supported research and its influence on public policy*, Ottawa: Evaluation Unit, IDRC.

Nelson, P. (2003) 'At the nexus of human rights and development: new methods and strategies of global NGOs', *World Development*, vol 31, no 12, pp 2013-26.

New African (2010) 'Zimbabwe: no imminent elections', vol 493, no 44, pp 31-33, March.

Niskanen, W. (1973) *Bureaucracy: Servant or master?*, London: Institute of Economic Affairs.

North, D. (1990) *Institutions, institutional change, and economic performance*, New York, NY: Cambridge University Press.

North, D.C. (1993) *The new institutional economics and development*, Working Paper, St Louis, MO: Washington University.

Nowotny, H., Scott, P. and Gibbons, M. (2003) '"Mode 2" revisited: the new production of knowledge', *Minerva*, vol 441, no 3, pp 179-94.

Nutley, S., Walter, I. and Davies, H.T.O. (2007) *Using evidence: How research can inform public services*, Bristol: The Policy Press.

Nyamugasira, W. (1998) 'NGOs and advocacy: how well are the poor represented?', *Development in Practice*, vol 8, no 3, pp 297-307.

O'Donnell, G. (1996) 'Illusions about consolidation', *Journal of Democracy*, vol 7, no 2, pp 34-51.

OECD (Organisation for Economic Co-operation and Development) (2007) *Principles for good international engagement in fragile states*, Learning and Advisory Process on Difficult Partnerships, Paris: Development Assistance Committee, OECD.

OIOS (Office of Internal Oversight Services) (2008) *Review of results-based management at the UN*, Washington, DC: OIOS.

Ormaza, P. (2010) *Haciendo visible lo invisible: Modelo de gestión territorial desarrollado por Nacionalidad A'I (Cofán) del Ecuador* [Making the invisible visible: a territorial management model developed for the A'I (Cofán) people in Ecuador], Iniciative Ciuidadanizando la Políticaambiental 2010 3, Quito: Grupo Faro.

Ostrom, E. (1990) *Governing the commons: The evolution of institutions for collective action*, Cambridge: Cambridge University Press.

Owens, S., Petts, J. and Bulkeley, H. (2006) 'Boundary work: knowledge, policy and the urban environment', *Environment and Planning C: Government and Policy*, vol 24, no 5, pp 633-43.

Panos (2006) *Getting into the kitchen: Media strategies for research*, London: Panos.

Panos (2008) *Reporting research: Using evidence for effective journalism*, London: Panos.

Pariser, E. (2011) *The filter bubble: What the internet is hiding from you*, Harmondsworth: Penguin Press.

Patton, M. (1998) 'Discovering process use', *Evaluation*, vol 4, no 2, pp 225-33.

Patton, M. (2008) *Utilisation focused evaluation* (4th edn), London: Sage Publications.

Patton, M. (2010) *Developmental evaluation: Applying complexity concepts to enhance innovation and use*, New York, NY: Guilford Publications.

Paudel, N., Ojha, H. and Dhungana, H. (2010) *Research-policy linkages in transitional states: A case of Nepal's forest policy process*, London: Forest Action Nepal with ODI-RAPID.

Pawson, R. (2006) *Evidence-based policy: A realist perspective*, Leeds: University of Leeds.

Pereznieto, P., Harper, C., Clench, B. and Coarasa, J. (2010) *The economic impact of school violence*, Report for Plan International, London: ODI.

Pereznieto, P., Marcus, R., Cullen, E. and Jones, N. (2011a) *A mapping of social protection systems and child-related provisions in the Middle East and North Africa region*, Report commissioned by UNICEF MENA, London: ODI.

Pereznieto, P. with Gbedemah, C., Monjane, P., Roesen, G. and Jones, N. (2011b) *Youth vulnerabilities and adaptation: Exploring the impact of macro-level shocks on youth: 3F crisis and climate change in Ghana, Mozambique and Vietnam*, Report commissioned by DFID, London: ODI.

Perkin, E. and Court, J. (2005) *Networks and policy processes in international development: A literature review*, Working Paper 252, London: ODI.

Petkova, N. (2009) *Integrating public environmental expenditure within multi-year budgetary frameworks*, Environmental Working Paper 7, Paris: OECD.

Pielke, R. (2007) *The honest broker: Making sense of science in policy and politics*, Cambridge: Cambridge University Press.

Pomares, J. and Jones, N. (2009) *Evidence-based policy processes: A systematic review of the knowledge-policy interface across policy areas*, Working Paper 269, London: ODI.

Pollitt, C. (2005) 'Performance information for democracy the missing link?', *Evaluation*, vol 1, no 21, pp 38–55.

Pons, X. and van Zanten, A. (2007) 'Knowledge circulation, regulation and governance', in B. Delvaux and E. Mangez (2008) (eds) *Towards a sociology of the knowledge–policy relation*, www.knowandpol.eu.

Popper, K. (1934) *The logic of scientific discovery*, London: Routledge.

Powell, M. (2006) 'Which knowledge? Whose reality? An overview of knowledge used in the development sector', *Development in Practice*, vol 16, no 6, pp 518–32.

Price, D.K. (1965) *The scientific estate*, New York, NY: Oxford University Press.

Purani, K. and Nair, S. (2006) 'Knowledge community: integrating ICT into social development in developing economies', *AI & Society*, vol 21, no 3, pp 329–45.

Quine, W.V.O. (1951) 'Two dogmas of empiricism', *The Philosophical Review*, vol 60, pp 20–43.

Rached, E. and Craissati, D. (2003) (eds) *Research for development in the Middle East and North Africa*, Ottawa: International Development Research Centre.

Radaelli, C.M. (1999) 'The public policy of the European Union: whither politics of expertise?', *Journal of European Public Policy*, vol 6, no 5, pp 757–74.

Ramalingam, B. (2006) *Tools for knowledge and learning: A guide for development and humanitarian organisations*, London: ODI-RAPID.

Ramalingam, B. and Jones, H. (2008) *Exploring the science of complexity: ideas and implications for development and humanitarian efforts*, London: ODI.

Ramirez, R. (2008) 'A "meditation" on meaningful participation', *The Journal of Community Informatics*, vol 4, no 3, (http://ci-journal.net/index.php/ciej/article/view/390/424).

Rao, V. and Woolcock, M. (1997) 'Integrating quantitative and qualitative approaches in program evaluation', in A. Tashakkori and C. Teddlie (2010) (eds) *Handbook of mixed methods research*, London: Sage Publications.

Rao, V. and Woolcock, M. (2007) 'The disciplinary monopoly in development research at the World Bank', *Global Governance 13*, pp 479-84.

Rath, A. and Barnett, A. (2006) *Innovation systems, concepts, approaches and lessons from RNRRS*, RNRRS: Renewable Natural Resources Research Strategy Synthesis Study 10, London: The Policy Practice.

Ravallion, M. (2005) *Evaluating anti-poverty programs*, Policy Research Working Paper 3625, Washington, DC: World Bank.

Ramazanoglu, C. (2002b) (ed) *Up against Foucault: Explorations of some tensions between Foucault and feminism*, London: Routledge.

Razavi, S. (1997) 'Fitting gender into development institutions', *World Development*, vol 25, no 7, pp 1111-25.

Rich, A. (2004) *Think tanks, public policy and the politics of expertise*, Cambridge: Cambridge University Press.

Riddell, R. (2008) *Measuring impact: The global and Irish Aid programme*, Final report to the Irish Aid Advisory Board, Oxford: Oxford Policy Management.

RIN (Research Information Network) (2009) *Communicating knowledge: How and why UK researchers publish and disseminate their findings*, London: RIN.

Rittel, H. and Webber, M.M. (1973) 'Dilemmas in a general theory of planning', *Policy Sciences*, vol 4, no 2, pp 155-69.

Robinson, W.H. and Gastelum, R. (1998) (eds) *Parliamentary libraries and research services in Central and Eastern Europe: Building more effective legislatures*, The Hague: International Federation of Library Associations and Institutions.

Rodgers, S. (1993) 'Women's space in a men's house: The British House of Commons,' in S. Ardener (ed) *Women and space, ground rules and social maps*, London: Berg.

Rodrik, D., Subramanian, A. and Trebbi, F. (2004) 'Institutions rule: the primacy of institutions over geography and integration in economic development', *Journal of Economic Growth*, vol 9, no 2, pp 131-65.

Röling, N. (1988) *Extension science: Information systems in agricultural development*, Cambridge: Cambridge University Press.

Romney, D., Jones, N., Kibwika, P., Nassuna, M., Okori, P., Efa, N., Legesse, G., Oyewole, D., Ololade, B., Uwaibi, K., Ademeyo, A., Asaba, J. and Chowdhury, N. (2007) *DFID research strategy 2008-2013 – consultation exercise – Africa*, Contract 07 7938, submitted by CABI Africa, ODI, PICO-Uganda and CAPPS, December, Report to DFID (www.dfid.gov.uk/r4d/PDF/Outputs/Consultation/ExecSummaryofAfricaConsultationReportFinal.pdf).

Rosenstock, L. and Lee, L.J. (2002) 'Attacks on science: the risks to evidence-based policy', *American Journal of Public Health*, vol 92, no 1, pp 14-18.

Rudqvist, A. and Woodford-Berger, P. (1996) *Evaluation and participation – some lessons*, Studies in Evaluation 96/1, Stockholm: Sida.

Ruitenbeek, J. and Cartier, C. (2001) *The invisible wand: Adaptive co-management as an emergent strategy in complex bio-economic systems*, Occasional Paper 34, Bogor: Center for International Forestry Research.

Rycroft-Malone, J., Seers, K., Titchen, A., Harvey, G., Kitson, A. and McCormack, B. (2004) 'What counts as evidence in evidence-based practice?', *Journal of Advanced Nursing*, vol 47, no 1, pp 81-90.

Sabatier, P. and Jenkins-Smith, H. (1993) (eds) *Policy change and learning: An advocacy coalition approach*, Boulder, CO: Westview Press.

Sabatier, P.A. and Jenkins-Smith, H.C. (1999) 'The advocacy coalition framework: an assessment', in P. Sabatier (ed) *Theories of the policy process*, Boulder, CO: Westview Press.

Sabharwal, G. and Huong, T. (2005) *Civil society in Vietnam: Moving from the margins to the mainstream*, Global Policy Forum, CIVICUS - World Alliance for Citizen Participation (www.eldis.org/assets/Docs/20050.html).

Saez, L. and Gallagher, J. (2009) 'Authoritarianism and development in the third world', *Brown Journal of World Affairs*, vol 15, no 2, pp 87-102.

Salas Guzman, M. (2007) 'Using ICTs for knowledge sharing and collaboration: an international experience based on Bellanet's work in the South', *Knowledge Management for Development*, vol 3, no 1, pp 68-78.

Sanderson, I. (2004) 'Getting evidence into practice: perspectives on rationality', *Evaluation*, vol 10, no 3, pp 643-77.

Sandison, P. (2005) 'The utilisation of evaluations', in ALNAP Review of Humanitarian Action in 2005, London: ALNAP.

Scartascini. C., Stein, E. and Tommasi, M. (2008) *Veto players, intertemporal interactions and policy adaptability: How do political institutions work?*, Washington, DC: Inter-American Development Bank.

Schaede, U. (1995) 'The "old boy network" and government-business relationships in Japan', *Journal of Japanese Studies*, vol 21, no 2, pp 293-317.

Schmidt, V. and Radaelli, C.M. (2004) 'Policy change and discourse in Europe: conceptual and methodological issues', *West European Politics*, vol 27 no 2, pp 183-210.

Schnell, S., Poulson, P., Condy, A., Tertsunen, M. and Holland J. (2005) *Principles for PSIA process in policy cycles and stakeholder participation*, Joint GTZ and DFI document for the PSIA Network, Department for International Development with the German Agency for Technical Co-operation.

Scholtes, F. (2008) '"Moral knowledge" in development: a concept for the analysis of norms and values in developmental policymaking', Paper presented at the 12th annual conference of EADI, Geneva, 24-28 June.

Scott, A. (2006) 'Communication on environmental research at the Science Policy Interface', Paper presented at the Communicating Interests, Attitudes and Expectations at the Science/Policy Interface (CSPI) Workshop, Brussels, 28-9 November.

Scott, J. (1982) *The upper classes: Property and privilege in Britain*, London: Macmillan.

Scott, M., Rachlow, J.L., Lackey, R.T., Pidgorna, A.B., Aycrigg, J.L., Feldman, G.R., Svancara, L.K., Rupp, D.A., Stanish, D.I. and Steinhorst, R.K (2007) 'Policy advocacy in science: prevalence, perspectives and implications for conservation biologists', *Conservation Biology*, vol 21, no 1, pp 29-35.

Selener, D. (1997) *Participatory action research and social change*, Cornell Participatory Action Research Network, Ithaca, NY: Cornell University.

Shaxson, L. (2005) 'Is your evidence robust enough? Questions for policymakers and practitioners', *Evidence & Policy*, vol 1, no 1, pp 101-11.

Shaxson, L. (2008) 'Who's sitting on Dali's sofa?', in *Evidence-based policy-making*, PMPA/National School for Government Practitioner Exchange Report, London: PMPA.

Shaxson, L. (2009) 'Structuring policy problems for plastics, the environment and human health: reflections from the UK', *Philosophical Transactions of the Royal Society B: Biological Sciences*, vol 364, no 1526, pp 2141-51.

Shaxson, L. (2010) *Reviewing the research landscape for PSA28: Improving the alignment of research council-funded research with policy needs under PSA28*, Report NR0130, London: DEFRA.

Shaxson, L.J. (2011) *Improving the impact of development research through better research communications and uptake*, Report from AusAID-, DFID- and UKCDS-funded workshop, London, 29-30 November.

Siegle, J. (2007) 'Effective aid strategies to support democracy in Africa', Paper presented at the Conference on Africa Beyond Aid conference, Brussels, 24-26 June.

Skrentny, J. (1996) *The ironies of affirmative action*, Chicago, IL: Chicago University Press.

Slater, R. and Farrington, J. (2010) *Appropriate, achievable, acceptable: A practical tool for good targeting*, Social Protection Toolsheet: Targeting Social Transfers, London: ODI.

Snowden, D.J. and Boone, M.E. (2007) 'A leader's framework for decision-making', *Harvard Business Review*, pp 1-9.

Souza, C. (2001) 'Participatory budgeting in Brazilian cities: limits and possibilities in building democratic institutions', *Environment and Urbanization*, vol 13, no 1, pp 159-84.

SPARC (State Project for Accountability, Responsibility and Capacity) (2010) *Research and evidence in policymaking and strategy development*, Guidance Note, London: DFID.

Stacey, R. (1996) *Complexity and creativity in organizations*, San Francisco, CA: Berrett-Koehler Publishers.

Star, S.L. and Griesemer, J.R. (1989) 'Institutional ecology "translations" and boundary objects: amateurs and professionals in Berkeley's Museum of Vertebrate Zoology 1907-39', *Social Studies of Science*, vol 19, no 3, pp 387-420.

Start, D. and Hovland, I. (2004) *Tools for policy impact: A handbook for researchers*, London: ODI-RAPID.

Steinmo, S. (2001) 'The new institutionism', in B. Clark and J. Foweraker (eds) *The encyclopedia of democratic thought*, London: Routledge.

Steinmo, S., Thelen, A. and Longstreth, F. (1992) *Structuring politics: Historical institutionalism in comparative analysis*, Cambridge: Cambridge University Press.

Stiglitz, J. (1999) 'Knowledge as a global public good', *Global Public Goods*, vol 1, no 9, pp 308-26.

Stirling, A. (2008) '"Opening up" and "closing down": power, participation and pluralism in the social appraisal of technology', *Science Technology Human Values*, vol 33, no 2, pp 262-94.

Stone, D. (2004) 'Transfer agents and global networks in the "transnationalization" of policy', *Journal of European Public Policy*, vol 11, no 3, pp 545-66.

Stone, D. (2005) 'Think tanks and policy advice in countries in transition', in T. Hashimoto, S. Hell and S. Nam (2005) *Public policy and research training in Vietnam*, Manila: ADBI.

Struyk, R., Kohagen K. and Miller, M. (2007) 'Were Bosnian policy research organisations more effective in 2006 than in 2003? Did technical assistance play a role?', *Public Administration and Development*, vol 27, no 5, pp 426-38.

Sundet, G. (2010) 'Politics and change in Tanzania', Unpublished mimeo.

Sutcliffe, S. and Court, J. (2006) *A toolkit for progressive policymakers in developing countries*, RAPID Toolkit, London: ODI.

Sutton, R. (1999) *The policy process: An overview*, Working Paper 118, London: ODI.

Tarrow, S. (1995) *Power in movement: Social movements, collective action and politics*, New York, NY: Cambridge University Press.

Tembo, F. (2008) *Study on capacity development support initiatives and patterns: LCDF research and development phase*, Report for Netherlands Development Organisation, London: ODI.

Tembo, F. and Wells, A. (2007) *Multi-donor support to civil society and engaging with 'non-traditional' civil society: A light-touch review of DFID's portfolio*, London: ODI.

Tetroe, J. (2007) *Knowledge translation at the Canadian Institutes of Health Research: A primer*, Technical Brief 18, Ottawa: Canadian Institutes of Health Research.

Thomas, P. (2007) 'Why is performance-based accountability so popular in theory and difficult in practice?', Paper presented at the World Summit on Public Governance: Improving the Performance of the Public Sector, Taipei, 1-3 May.

Tilley, N. and Laycock, G. (2000) 'Joining up research, policy and practice about crime', *Policy Studies*, vol 21, no 3, pp 213-27.

Tornquist, O. (1999) *Politics and development*, London: Sage Publications.

Torres, M. and Anderson, M. (2004) *Fragile situations: Defining difficult environments for poverty reduction*, PRDE Working Paper 1, London: DFID.

Tsebelis, G. (1995) 'Decision making in political systems: Veto players in presidentialism, parliamentarism, multicameralism, and multipartyism', *British Journal of Political Science*, vol 25, no 3, pp 289-326.

Tversky, A. and Kahneman, D. (1981) 'The framing of decisions and the psychology of choice', *Science*, vol 211, no 4481, pp 453-8.

UNDP (United Nations Development Programme) (2008) *Global programme on capacity development for democratic governance: Assessments and measurements*, Oslo: Oslo Governance Centre, UNDP.

Unsworth, S. and Conflict Research Unit (2007) *Framework for strategic governance and corruption analysis: Designing strategic responses towards good governance*, The Hague: Netherlands Institute of International Relations.

van Eeten, M.J.G. (1999) 'Dialogues of the deaf: Defining new agendas for environmental deadlocks', Unpublished PhD thesis, Delft University of Technology.

Victora, C., Habicht, J. and Bryce, J. (2004) 'Evidence-based public health: moving beyond randomised trials', *American Journal of Public Health*, vol 94, no 3, pp 400-5.

WaGoro, W. (2006) 'Problematising the gaze through traducture. Does it matter if you're black or white?', *Athanor*, vol 17, no 10, pp 52-61.

Waldman, L. (2005) *Environment, politics and poverty: Lessons from a review of PRSP stakeholder perspectives*, Brighton: IDS.

Walker, D. and Jones, N. (2010) *Drivers of the chronic poverty policy process*, Research Guides. Manchester: Chronic Poverty Research Centre.

Warner, M. (2001) *Complex problems ... negotiated solutions: The practical applications of chaos and complexity theory to community-based natural resource management*, Working Paper 146, London: ODI.

Waterston, C. (2005) 'Scientists' conceptions of the boundaries between their own research and policy', *Science and Public Policy*, vol 32, no 6, pp 435-44.

Weimer, D. (2005) 'Institutionalizing neutrally competent policy analysis: resources for promoting objectivity and balance in consolidating democracies', *The Policy Studies Journal*, vol 33, no 2, pp 131-46.

Weiss, C. (1977) 'Research for policy's sake: the enlightenment function of social research', *Policy Analysis*, vol 3, no 4, pp 531-45.

Weiss, C. (1979) 'The many meanings of research utilisation', *Public Administration Review*, vol 39, no 5, pp 426-31.

Weiss C. (1987) 'The circuitry of enlightenment: diffusion of social science research to policy makers', *Knowledge: Creation, Diffusion, Utilization*, vol 8, no 2, pp 274-81.

Wettasinha, C. and Waters-Bayer, A. (2010) (eds) *Farmer-led joint research: Experiences of PROLINNOVA partners*, Silang/Leusden: IIRR/PROLINNOVA International Secretariat, ETC EcoCulture.

White, H. (2008) *Of probits and participation: The use of mixed methods in quantitative impact evaluation*,) NONIE Working Paper 7, London: Network of Networks on Impact Evaluation.

Williams, P. (2002) 'The competent boundary spanner', *Public Administration*, vol 80, no 1, pp 103-24.

Wilson, J.Q. (1980) 'The politics of regulation', in J.Q. Wilson (ed) *The politics of regulation*, New York, NY: Basic Books.

Wittgenstein, L. (1953) *The philosophical investigations*, New York, NY: Prentice Hall.

World Bank (1999) *Knowledge for development*, World Development Report 1998/99, Washington, DC: World Bank.

World Bank (2005a) *Fragile states – good practice in country assistance strategies*, Washington, DC: World Bank.

World Bank (2005b) *World Development Report 2006: Equity and Development*, Washington, DC: World Bank.

World Bank (2007) *Building knowledge economies: Advanced strategies for development*, WBI Development Studies, Washington, DC: World Bank.

Yakhlef, A. (2007) 'Knowledge transfer as the transformation of context', *Journal of High-Technology Management Research*, vol 18, no 1, pp 43-57.

Young, J. (2005) 'Research, policy and practice: why developing countries are different', *Journal of International Development*, vol 17, no 6, pp 727-34.

Zhu, X. and Xue, L. (2007) 'Think tanks in transitional China', *Public Administration and Development*, vol 27, no 5, p 454.

Index

Note: Page numbers followed by *n* refer to information in a note. Page numbers followed by *fig* or *tab* refer to information in a figure or a table.